# Birds of
## Puerto Rico and
## the Virgin Islands

T0335333

# BIRDS OF PUERTO RICO AND THE VIRGIN ISLANDS

## FULLY REVISED AND UPDATED THIRD EDITION

## HERBERT A. RAFFAELE, CLIVE PETROVIC, SERGIO A. COLÓN LÓPEZ, LISA D. YNTEMA, AND JOSÉ A. SALGUERO FARIA

Principal Illustrators:
Dale Dyer, Tracy Taylor, and Kristin Williams
Supporting Illustrators:
Cynthie Fisher and Bart Rulon

Princeton University Press

Princeton and Oxford

Published by Princeton University Press
41 William Street, Princeton, New Jersey 08540
6 Oxford Street, Woodstock, Oxfordshire OX20 1TR

press.princeton.edu

Library of Congress Cataloging-in-Publication Data

Names: Raffaele, Herbert A., author.
Title: Birds of Puerto Rico and the Virgin Islands / Herbert A. Raffaele,
   Clive Petrovic, Sergio A. Colón López, Lisa D. Yntema, José A. Salguero Faria.
Other titles: Guide to the birds of Puerto Rico and the Virgin Islands
Description: Third edition. | Princeton: Princeton University Press, 2021.
   | Series: Princeton field guides | Includes bibliographical references
   and index.
Identifiers: LCCN 2020045440 (print) | LCCN 2020045441 (ebook) | ISBN
   9780691211671 (paperback) | ISBN 9780691219257 (ebook)
Subjects: LCSH: Birds—Puerto Rico—Identification. | Birds—United States
   Virgin Islands—Identification.
Classification: LCC QL688.P6 R33 2021 (print) | LCC QL688.P6 (ebook) |
   DDC 598.097295—dc23
LC record available at https://lccn.loc.gov/2020045440
LC ebook record available at https://lccn.loc.gov/2020045441

British Library Cataloging-in-Publication Data is available

Editorial: Robert Kirk and Abigail Johnson
Production Editorial: Ellen Foos
Text Design: D & N Publishing, Wiltshire, UK
Cover Design: Ruthie Rosenstock
Production: Steven Sears
Publicity: Matthew Taylor and Julia Hall
Copyeditor: Laurel Anderton
Cover images: Front: Dale Dyer. Back (top): Kristin Williams;
(middle and bottom): Tracy Taylor (Pedersen)

This book has been composed in Museo Sans

Printed on acid-free paper.

Printed in Italy

10 9 8 7 6 5 4 3 2 1

# CONTENTS

# ARTIST CREDITS

**Tracy Taylor (Pedersen):** Plates 1–4, 12 (Brown Pelican, American White Pelican), 13, 14 (exc. Striated Heron), 15 (exc. Little Egret), 16, 19 (Curlew Sandpiper), 24, 25 (exc. Ruddy Turnstone), 26–27, 28 (exc. Snow Goose), 29–30, 31 (exc. Muscovy Duck), 32, 33 (Black-bellied Whistling-Duck, Fulvous Whistling-Duck, West Indian Whistling-Duck), 35 (Killdeer, Cattle Egret), 40 (exc. Common Nighthawk), 41–43, 44 (Helmeted Guineafowl, Red Junglefowl), 47 (exc. Cedar Waxwing), 48–49, 50 (exc. White-fronted Parrot), 51 (Monk Parakeet, Budgerigar), 52 (exc. Red-masked Parakeet), 54 (Gray Kingbird, Fork-tailed Flycatcher), 55, 56 (exc. Bananaquit), 66–68, 69 (exc. Great-tailed Grackle), 71 (Smooth-billed Ani, Bobolink), 72 (Yellow-crowned Bishop), 73 (Orange-cheeked Waxbill, Northern Red Bishop), 74 (Bobolink, Java Sparrow), 75, 76 (Bobolink, Pin-tailed Whydah), 78 (Northern Jacana, Northern Lapwing, Wood Stork), 79 (White-faced Whistling-Duck), 80 (exc. Tufted Duck), 82 (Short-tailed Swift, White-collared Swift), 83–84, 86 (exc. White-throated Sparrow), 87 (exc. Greater Ani, Painted Bunting).

**Kristin Williams:** Plates 5 (exc. Black-legged Kittiwake), 6–9, 10 (exc. Franklin's Gull), 11 (exc. Franklin's Gull), 12 (Black Skimmer, Double-crested Cormorant), 28 (Snow Goose), 36–39, 44 (Ruddy Quail-Dove, Bridled Quail-Dove, Key West Quail-Dove), 45, 46 (exc. African Collared-Dove), 47 (Cedar Waxwing), 56 (Bananaquit), 70, 71 (Puerto Rican Bullfinch), 72 (exc. Yellow-crowned Bishop), 73 (Red Siskin, Rose-breasted Grosbeak), 74 (Indigo Bunting, Blue Grosbeak, House Sparrow), 76 (Lincoln's Sparrow, Grasshopper Sparrow, Northern Red Bishop, Indigo Bunting, Rose-breasted Grosbeak, Black-faced Grassquit, Yellow-faced Grassquit), 77 (Great Skua, South Polar Skua), 78 (White-winged Tern, Neotropic Cormorant), 79 (Canada Goose, Tundra Swan), 81 (Black Vulture), 87 (Painted Bunting).

**Dale Dyer:** Plates 5 (Black-legged Kittiwake), 10 (Franklin's Gull), 11 (Franklin's Gull), 14 (Striated Heron), 15 (Little Egret), 18 (Western Willet), 31 (Muscovy Duck), 40 (Common Nighthawk), 46 (African Collared-Dove), 50 (White-fronted Parrot), 51 (Turquoise-fronted Parrot, Rosy-faced Lovebird), 52 (Red-masked Parakeet), 53, 54 (Puerto Rican Flycatcher, Puerto Rican Kingbird), 57–65, 69 (Great-tailed Grackle), 71 (Lesser Antillean Bullfinch), 76 (Yellow-crowned Bishop, Blue Grosbeak, Dickcissel, House Sparrow), 77 (Trindade Petrel, Sabine's Gull), 79 (Brant), 80 (Tufted Duck), 81 (exc. Black Vulture), 82 (Violet-green Swallow, Common Swift), 85, 86 (White-throated Sparrow), 87 (Greater Ani).

**Cynthie Fisher:** Plates 17, 18 (exc. Western Willet), 19 (exc. Curlew Sandpiper), 20–23, 25 (Ruddy Turnstone), 35 (Buff-breasted Sandpiper, Upland Sandpiper), 77 (Red Phalarope).

**Bart Rulon:** Plates 33 (exc. Black-bellied Whistling-Duck, Fulvous Whistling-Duck, West Indian Whistling-Duck), 34.

# PREFACE TO THE THIRD EDITION

This third edition represents a substantial redesign from previous versions, with species illustrations and text now on facing pages. This format is far superior for field identification purposes. However, it does place constraints on the text space available for each species account. The trade-off seemed worth it. Many species write-ups and illustrations have also been changed, hopefully for the better. The introduction too had a major rewrite, and the "Places to Bird" section has been entirely updated. We hope these changes will be to the user's satisfaction.

As with the previous editions, many observers throughout the region were extremely generous with their input. Concerning Puerto Rico, particular thanks are extended to José Colón López, Daphne Gemmill, Alcides Morales-Pérez, Adrianne Tossas, and Dr. Joseph Wunderle. In the Virgin Islands important contributions were made by Dr. Nicole Angeli, Dr. Robert Askins, Laurel Brannick, Charlotte Devenish, David Ewert, Robert Norton, Nancy Pascoe, Dr. Renata Platenberg, Vaman Ramlall, Jennifer Valiulis, Dr. Richard Veit, and Susan Zaluski. Their input has been invaluable not only for updating the status of bird species, but also for fine-tuning the manuscript in other ways.

# INTRODUCTION

## AIMS

The primary goal of this guide is to promote an interest in birds among the residents of Puerto Rico and the Virgin Islands. It is only when people appreciate and respect their birdlife that they ever come to protect it. The book also aims to facilitate the enjoyment and study of the region's birds by both novice and professional alike. To that end, it is a self-contained, fully illustrated source for field identification of the birds from Puerto Rico and the Virgin Islands. This edition substantially updates the data on avian distribution and abundance in the region through June 2020.

## SPECIES COVERAGE

The main text contains accounts of 347 bird species known to occur in Puerto Rico and the Virgin Islands with any regularity. These include all naturally occurring species for which there is at least one collected specimen (or an adequate photograph), or three separate sight records by reliable observers. Thirty-five introduced species are among this number. Only those introduced species considered to be established and breeding are presented, with two exceptions—the Budgerigar and Cockatiel. These are so regularly seen that they are important for birders to recognize, and their numbers suggest they have a strong potential to become established at some point. A number of other introduced species observed in the wild, but not believed to be established, have been excluded. This was done to avoid overwhelming users with birds unlikely to be seen. At the same time, nine introduced species have been removed from this edition. These include Northern Bobwhite, Spotted Dove, Yellow-headed Parrot, Nanday (Black-hooded) Parakeet, Red Avadavat, Black-rumped Waxbill, Yellow-fronted Canary, Javan (White-vented) Myna, and Common Hill Myna. All had established wild populations at some point, but these appear to have failed.

One species, the White-necked Crow, has been extirpated from Puerto Rico and thus is not included in this edition. Once common on the island, it was valued as a game bird for its tasty flesh. That, and destruction of its forest habitat were likely the primary causes for its demise. Fortunately, the species survives on Hispaniola.

Those vagrants for which there are insufficient records to support their inclusion in the main section of the book are presented following the species accounts. Such is the case as well for introduced species not known to be established.

## TAXONOMY

The classification of birds and the study of the evolutionary relationship of one species to another have gone on for centuries, if not millennia. Since the first publication of this book, bird classification has changed dramatically with the application of DNA analysis to better understand relationships. Basically, since it is believed that changes in the genetic codes of animals occur very slowly and at a relatively constant rate, differences in genetic codes between species are thought to be the most precise indication of how closely related species are to each other. Prior to DNA becoming a critical tool for this purpose, evolutionary relationships were deduced based primarily on particular anatomical features that were believed to evolve slowly (such as the number of flight feathers in a songbird), along with other factors. The application of genetics to bird classification has substantially altered it in a number of ways, all of which are reflected in the avifauna of Puerto Rico and the Virgin Islands.

From a bird-watcher's perspective, the most obvious change has been what is commonly referred to as the "splitting" of species. Splitting is what happens when birds previously believed to be so similar that they were classified as a single species are, in fact, found to be so different that they are split into several species. As an example, the previous editions of this book present the Stripe-headed Tanager as having a distribution that includes Hispaniola, Jamaica, Cuba, the Bahamas, and Cozumel, an island off Mexico. No longer. Now, what was formerly the Stripe-headed Tanager has been split into four species, the one in Puerto Rico being given new common and scientific names. It is now the Puerto Rican Spindalis (*Spindalis portoricensis*). Furthermore, it is now considered a Puerto Rican "endemic," a bird found in Puerto Rico and no place else in the world—a circumstance that adds significantly to the bird's uniqueness and Puerto Rico's importance as a hotspot for biological diversity. It has been speculated that when genetic characteristics are applied to all the world's birds, the number of species could grow from the present number, on the order of 10,700, to as many as 18,000.

But that is not all. Actually, it is just the tip of the iceberg. As many of us studied in high school, species of birds are grouped into genera, genera are grouped into families, families are grouped into classes, and so on. As a frame of reference, the over 10,700 species of birds are grouped into scarcely over 200 families. Consequently, a bird family is a big deal when compared simply to a bird species. When the Stripe-headed Tanager was split into four species, it was found not to be a tanager after all! This group of four birds was thus placed into a closely related, but entirely new bird family—the Spindalidae, or spindalis tanagers.

Changes in the classification of Puerto Rico's birds did not end with the Puerto Rican Spindalis. The Puerto Rican Tanager was determined to be distinct enough to warrant designation as a family all its own—the Nesospingidae. Few islands anywhere in the world possess a family of birds unique to that one island. Cuba and Hispaniola are the only other Caribbean islands with such a distinction.

Under the present state of bird taxonomy, Puerto Rico has one bird family endemic to the island—the Puerto Rican Tanager—and two bird families shared with other islands but endemic to the West Indies—the spindalis tanagers and the todies. This is quite a shift from but a few decades ago. Puerto Rico's status as a special place for unusual birds has been elevated substantially.

Other splits of note include what was formerly the Black-cowled Oriole into four species, one of which is the endemic Puerto Rican Oriole. Splitting of the Loggerhead Kingbird into three species has created another Puerto Rican endemic—the Puerto Rican Kingbird. Finally, Adelaide's Warbler has been split into three species, and though its common name remains the same, its scientific name (*Setophaga adelaidae*) has changed, and it is now a Puerto Rico/Virgin Islands endemic.

What do all of these changes sum up to? In the 1989 version of this book, Puerto Rico was believed to support 16 endemic bird species and share one bird family, the todies, with other West Indian islands. Now, it supports 19 endemic birds (3 shared with the Virgin Islands) (see "Present Avifaunal Composition"), two endemic West Indian families (the todies and spindalis tanagers), and one endemic family all its own—the Puerto Rican Tanager.

Not only are new species, genera, and even families of birds being described hand over fist, but the relationships among different groups of birds are undergoing major revision as well. Grebes, a family of diving waterbirds, were formerly thought to be closely related to loons, another diving bird. Not so. Turns out that grebes are more closely related to sandgrouse.

In general, this guide follows the taxonomy and common names proposed in the American Ornithological Society's Checklist of North American Birds (1998) and its supplements. There are a few exceptions. These include splitting the Willet into Eastern and Western, splitting the Loggerhead Kingbird into several species including the endemic Puerto Rican Kingbird, and splitting the Lesser Antillean Pewee into three species including the endemic Puerto Rican Pewee. It veers from the taxonomy used by the American

Ornithological Society (AOS) when research by coauthors of *Birds of the West Indies* has suggested otherwise. We hope that at some point the AOS's classification and nomenclature committee will adopt these revisions.

## SPECIES ACCOUNTS

The species accounts have been kept brief in order to fit opposite the bird illustrations. Species are organized by habitat, starting with the most ocean-dependent species and working inland. This approach is intended to make the guide much more user friendly than many other bird guides, which present species in the order in which they are believed to have evolved. While ordering birds based on their evolutionary histories may be useful for experts, it makes comparisons for identification purposes very problematic. In the field, an observer wants to compare an unidentified grebe to other similar-looking waterbirds, not to a sandgrouse. Similarly, in a few instances, individual species have been separated from other members of their bird family and placed among species to which they are most likely to be compared. The Black-legged Kittiwake, for example, has been moved from among the other gulls, all of which are coastal, to the section containing oceanic birds, of which it is one. Likewise, the Smooth-billed Ani has been moved from among the cuckoo family—which contains its relatives, though none of these look like it—to a plate with other large black birds with which it might readily be confused. The land birds, by far the largest group, have also been sorted to facilitate the comparison of species with the greatest similarities. Consequently, you will find plate titles such as "Heavy-billed, Primarily Black Birds" and "Heavy-billed Birds with Red or Orange." Additionally, for the most confusing groups of birds—gulls, shorebirds, and warblers, in particular—species have been presented on multiple plates for better comparison to similar-looking species.

    Endemic species unique to Puerto Rico, Puerto Rico and the Virgin Islands, or the entire West Indies, are color coded for quick recognition. The colors are:

● Found only in Puerto Rico
● Found only in Puerto Rico and the Virgin Islands
● Found only in the West Indies

Importantly, all 49 vagrant species, birds that occur less than once every 10 years, have been placed at the back of the book. This aims to simplify the identification of regularly occurring species. Inserting so many vagrants into the main text would have added unnecessary confusion and complexity to everyday bird identification.

    Descriptions of bird families are included only where they provide useful identification information for a highly distinctive family, usually with a number of species, thus avoiding redundancies in the species accounts.

    Not all islands are birded with equal intensity. The islands of Puerto Rico and St. John are relatively heavily birded. The islands of Anegada and Jost Van Dyke have very little activity. This is not meant as a judgment, but rather as an indication that the status of birds presented in the book reflects what is known today based on relatively limited observations in some places. Over time, these gaps should be filled. Such gaps are particularly noticeable for marine birds, since few birders have the opportunity to travel far offshore.

**Size** is a basic tool in bird identification; thus the body length and weight of each species are listed immediately after its name to offer a sense of the bird's size. In some cases, as for seabirds and raptors, which are often seen soaring, wingspan measurements are also provided. In many cases a range of lengths or weights is displayed, particularly when these measurements vary substantially because of sexual size differences or just basic size variation within the species. Even in cases where only a single length or weight is provided,

11

it should be recognized that this represents an average for the species and that there will be variation from this figure. On each plate every effort has been made to present species in proper size proportion to one another. However, that has proven impossible in some cases, which are noted on the plates.

**Other Common Names** are presented in parentheses and include common names for the bird in Puerto Rico, common names in the Virgin Islands, and other frequently used English names by which the species is known abroad. In cases where a bird was until recently known by another common name—such as the Puerto Rican Kingbird, which was formerly known as the Loggerhead Kingbird—the former name is placed immediately after its new name.

**Behavior** is noted where it provides a useful identification aid. It is placed early in the write-up because behaviors often are of great importance in identification. This may vary from tail wagging to a peculiar feeding behavior such as sallying for insects by flycatchers. Behaviors of particular importance for identification are italicized.

**Description** includes key features to look for when identifying a bird. No attempt is made to describe the species comprehensively, since this is better discerned in the plates. Identification features of special importance are italicized.

**Plumages**, which vary by age, sex, or season, are differentiated. For species that occur in Puerto Rico and the Virgin Islands for only a portion of the year, the plumage most likely to be seen is described first, with the least likely plumage presented last. For example, of the various gull species that occur in the region but do not breed, immature birds occur much more regularly than adults. Consequently, the subadult plumages are described before those of the adult.

12

**Similar Species** highlights the differences between the species being described and any others with which it is likely to be confused. These are placed in parentheses.

**Flight** is described when it is a specific asset to identification.

**Voice** includes any calls, songs, and notes useful for identification.

**Uniqueness** is mentioned if a bird belongs to an endemic species, genus, or family, making it that much more unusual from an evolutionary standpoint.

**Status and Range** contains a number of elements. One includes the terms used to describe the chances of observing the bird. These are the following:

*Very Common:* More than 20 individuals likely in a single day (occurs in very high densities).

*Common:* 5–20 individuals likely in a single day (occurs in high densities). This does not apply to species such as raptors, which, because of large territories, are sighted less frequently.

*Fairly Common:* 1–4 individuals likely in a single day (occurs in moderate densities).

*Uncommon:* Not likely seen on every trip, but expected at least twice per year (occurs in low densities).

*Rare:* Seen less than twice per year, but at least once every 2 years (occurs in very low densities).

*Very rare*: Seen once every 3–10 years.

*Vagrant*: 1–5 records and generally seen no more than once every 10 years.

The following terms are used to represent the overall status of each species:

> *Endemic:* A species that is native to a limited geographic range (island or small
>   group of islands) and occurs nowhere else in the world. Example: Elfin-woods
>   Warbler in Puerto Rico.
> *Permanent resident:* A species that spends its entire life cycle on a particular
>   island or group of islands regardless of any environmental fluctuations from
>   year to year. Example: Antillean Crested Hummingbird.
> *Year-round resident:* A species that spends its entire life cycle on a particular
>   island or island group as long as environmental conditions are adequate, but
>   flies elsewhere when conditions deteriorate. Example: Glossy Ibis.
> *Breeding resident:* A species that breeds on a particular island or group of islands
>   and then migrates elsewhere during the non-breeding season. Example:
>   White-tailed Tropicbird.
> *Non-breeding resident:* A species that breeds elsewhere but occurs on a
>   particular island or group of islands during the non-breeding season.
>   Sometimes referred to as a "visitor" or "visitant." Example: Lesser Yellowlegs.
> *Migrant:* A species that migrates through the region on a seasonal basis and
>   breeds outside the region. Sometimes referred to as a "passage migrant" or
>   "transient." Example: Tennessee Warbler.
> *Visitor or wanderer:* A species that occurs in the region on an irregular basis and
>   does not breed there. Example: Double-crested Cormorant.

13

These categories are based on a skilled observer seeking the bird in the right place at the right time. In some cases, this means visiting a very specific habitat, such as a particular freshwater pond during the migration season. For birds that roost or breed communally (e.g., herons and terns), the status given represents the likelihood of encountering the species under more general field conditions and does not include flocks flying to or from a roost.

Needless to say, some species are substantially more detectable than others. For example, every Snowy Egret in a small swamp can be located easily. However, a single Yellow-breasted Crake in that same swamp would be inordinately more difficult to detect. This would be the case even if crakes were substantially more abundant than egrets. To address this, we have tried to indicate species that are particularly difficult to detect. This is either stated in the text or implied in the description of the bird's habitat, which might be "at sea." The intent, however, is to reflect a bird's true status, thus presuming detection of the bird by an experienced observer using appropriate techniques. We considered a "detectability index," but we felt this would be very subjective, especially because of the increasingly widespread use of tape recordings in the field, a practice that should not be used under most circumstances.

This issue of detectability is particularly important regarding endangered species. The critically endangered Yellow-shouldered Blackbird might be seen during every trip to its roosting or feeding areas in Puerto Rico, thus classifying it as "locally common." This is not to say that the total population size of the species is large.

Misconceptions can be created by some of these terms when applied to small islands. A small island with a small pond may sustain only one pair of Pied-billed Grebes or a single Great Blue Heron. Yet these birds might be observed on every birding trip and are thus "fairly common." Similarly, if that particular pond is full only seasonally, grebes may be present whenever it has water but will be absent when it is dry. It is left to your common sense to determine how circumstances such as these apply to any particular species or island.

Detectability also has to do with being in the right place at the right time. Migrating birds sometimes congregate in numbers at important staging areas. Among the exciting discoveries yet to be made are these special places where unusual birds occur in numbers previously not thought possible.

There are always difficulties in classifying some birds, such as the Broad-winged Hawk, which can regularly be seen at but few localities. In such cases, clarification is attempted in the text. A few species, such as the Golden-winged Warbler, were virtually unknown from the region a few years ago, but there have been a number of recent sightings. In cases similar to the Goldenwing's, where it is more likely the bird was overlooked than that its status changed, an assessment of its status was made accordingly.


## OTHER DEFINITIONS

♀ Female
♂ Male
*Extirpated:* An organism that has been eliminated from a particular area,
    but not from its worldwide range.
*Region:* Puerto Rico and the Virgin Islands.


## RECENT AVIFAUNAL CHANGES

In the 30+ years since the previous edition of this book, the avifauna of Puerto Rico and the Virgin Islands has increased by 73 species. Ten other species—the White-necked Crow plus 9 introduced species—have been lost, for a net gain of 63 species. The vast majority of these "new" species are either very rare migrants or vagrants, many of which were likely undetected previously, primarily because of the scant number of professional and amateur observers in the region. A substantial increase in observers, the locating of birds by using playback recordings, and the documentation of their presence thanks to major advances in photography have all contributed to this dramatic increase in the documentation of rare species. Consequently, for most species, the noted increase in species is almost certainly a reflection of the increase in observers and better technology rather than an actual change in bird distribution patterns. This might not be the case, however, for conspicuous and easily identified species such as the Swallow-tailed Kite. Chances are, that species is now occurring with increased frequency.

That said, there are some notable exceptions that are especially dramatic and exciting. One is the resurgence of the Limpkin, a species considered pretty much extirpated from Puerto Rico a few decades back. It had not been reported for 30 years prior to the previous edition and was included in that book primarily to remind us of its former presence. Today it is alive and well, showing up in all corners of Puerto Rico, a very spectacular freshwater bird now restored to the island's avifauna.

A second extraordinary avifaunal change was the expansion of Adelaide's Warbler to St. John in the Virgin Islands, and a few birds also occurring on St. Thomas. This range expansion is particularly unusual because Adelaide's Warbler had been nearly a single-island endemic. An up-and-down population on Vieques, presently booming, was the only location other than Puerto Rico proper where it occurred. Typically, local endemics are highly sedentary virtually by definition. Were they to wander much, it would not be long before they became multi-island species. Consequently, the expansion of Adelaide's Warbler to Culebra and the Virgin Islands is highly noteworthy. Why has this range expansion occurred at this particular time? That is difficult to say. It is easy to suggest that Adelaide's Warbler, a bird primarily of dry scrubland and thickets, found plenty of unoccupied habitat available in the Virgin Islands and simply took advantage of it. The answer, however, may be more complicated than that since plenty of scrubland and thickets have existed on Culebra and the Virgin Islands for some time. When the previous edition of this guide was written, Adelaide's Warbler was virtually absent from eastern Puerto

Rico, with nothing more than a foothold on Vieques. The availability of adequate habitat did not seem to be constraining its distribution. The changing history of this bird's status and distribution would make for a fascinating study.

The dramatic recovery of the Puerto Rican Parrot is a great success story. On the verge of extinction in 1975, when only 13 wild parrots were known to survive high in the Luquillo Mountains, the species recovered to several hundred birds in two populations prior to the hurricanes of 2017. The storms reduced parrot numbers considerably, but with substantial numbers of captive individuals available, recovery of the bird is decidedly more secure than it was only a few decades ago.

Other notable species whose numbers have increased dramatically over the past decades include the Puerto Rican Nightjar and West Indian Whistling-Duck. The nightjar's continued range expansion likely reflects the regrowth of forests in the lowlands and foothills of Puerto Rico. Reduction in numbers of small Indian mongoose (*Herpestes javanicus*) with the decline of sugarcane likely also benefited this ground-nesting bird. The whistling-duck's success, meanwhile, correlates to the improved condition of freshwater and brackish-water wetlands in Puerto Rico, particularly Cartagena Lagoon, Caño Tiburones, and Humacao Wildlife Refuge. Associated with the improved state of freshwater wetlands has been the natural colonization of Puerto Rico by the White Ibis, a magnificent white wading bird with a long, curved, pink bill, pink legs, and black wingtips. This highly unexpected occurrence has rendered a beautiful addition to the region's avifauna.

The last major natural status change of note is that of the Barn Owl, a nocturnal bird of wide distribution that was previously known from Puerto Rico based on only four records. Recently, not only has this elegant owl been recorded from an ever-increasing number of localities, but it has been found breeding on the island. Considering that among its primary prey are mice and rats, it should be a welcome addition to the avifauna by birders and non-birders alike.

A major development in the British Virgin Islands has been the reintroduction of the American Flamingo on Anegada in 1992 and Necker Island in 2006. Historically, the flamingo was native to Puerto Rico and the Virgin Islands, where a number of localities bear its name. It was extirpated, however, in the late 1800s, likely because of poaching. Prior to these introductions, flamingos had begun to occur in the region with increasing frequency, probably stray birds from Hispaniola, or perhaps Cuba or the Bahamas where the bird is numerous. Both introductions have proven highly successful, with populations on each of the two islands breeding successfully and now numbering in the hundreds. Excellent flyers, flamingos are occurring with increasing frequency and in larger numbers elsewhere in the region. Restoration of the American Flamingo to the Virgin Islands is a dramatic success story.

Similarly, the Scarlet Ibis was introduced on Necker Island in 2010. That too has proven successful, the flock now numbering approximately 50 birds and breeding successfully most years. As with the flamingo, this population of Scarlet Ibises is likely the source of increased sightings elsewhere in the region. Unlike with the American Flamingo, however, the historic evidence of the Scarlet Ibis previously occurring in the region is somewhat dubious; consequently, the bird will be considered more as an attractive exotic species rather than a restored native one.

As appears to be the case with the Scarlet Ibis, a number of other introduced birds have become established in the region and thus are included in this edition. Most of these are members of the parrot family and include the Blue-and-yellow Macaw, White Cockatoo, Cockatiel, Turquoise-fronted Parrot, White-fronted Parrot, Rosy-faced Lovebird, and Red-masked Parakeet. The two introductions not in the parrot family include the Muscovy Duck and Eurasian Collared-Dove. Colonization of the region by any of these birds, however, is not known to be the result of an intentional introduction, but rather the accidental consequence of pet birds escaping or being released. In the case of the Eurasian Collared-Dove, it likely expanded its range to our region following release elsewhere.

While 10 new exotics have now become part of the region's avifauna, 9 others appear to be extirpated. These have been removed from this edition, as mentioned under "Species Coverage."

## PRESENT AVIFAUNAL COMPOSITION

Year-round residents—94 species including 19 Puerto Rico/Virgin Islands
   endemics plus 17 West Indies endemics
Breeding residents (depart after breeding)—14 species
Migrants and winter residents—155 species
Introduced—35 species
Vagrants—49 species
Total species—347

## Puerto Rico/Virgin Islands Endemics—19 Species

Puerto Rican Lizard-Cuckoo—PR only
Puerto Rican Nightjar—PR only
Green Mango—PR only
Puerto Rican Emerald—PR only
Puerto Rican Owl—PR and VI
Puerto Rican Tody—PR only
Puerto Rican Woodpecker—PR only
Puerto Rican Parrot—PR only
Puerto Rican Flycatcher—PR and VI
Puerto Rican Kingbird—PR only
Puerto Rican Pewee—PR only
Puerto Rican Vireo—PR only
Puerto Rican Oriole—PR only
Puerto Rican Tanager—PR only
Puerto Rican Spindalis—PR only
Elfin-woods Warbler—PR only
Adelaide's Warbler—PR and VI
Puerto Rican Bullfinch—PR only
Yellow-shouldered Blackbird—PR only

## West Indies Endemics—17 Species

West Indian Whistling-Duck—PR and VI
Scaly-naped Pigeon—PR and VI (nearly endemic to WI)
White-crowned Pigeon—PR and VI (nearly endemic to WI)
Plain Pigeon—PR
Key West Quail-Dove—PR (nearly endemic to WI)
Bridled Quail-Dove—PR and VI
Zenaida Dove—PR and VI (nearly endemic to WI)
Antillean Mango—PR and VI
Green-throated Carib—PR and VI
Antillean Crested Hummingbird—PR and VI
Pearly-eyed Thrasher—PR and VI
Red-legged Thrush—PR
Antillean Euphonia—PR

Lesser Antillean Bullfinch—VI
Greater Antillean Grackle—PR
Antillean Palm Swift—PR
Vervain Hummingbird—PR

## MIGRATION

Well over half of the native, regularly occurring bird species in Puerto Rico and the Virgin Islands are migratory. Of these, the majority occur most frequently as migrants flying south from their breeding grounds in North America to wintering grounds either in the West Indies or in more southern latitudes in South America. Beginning as early as late August, this migration peaks in September and October and is generally over by early November. Not quite as dominant in the region is the return of birds during northbound migration, which generally peaks in March and April but extends through May. The dominance of the southbound migration reflects different flight paths; many species do not retrace their northward journey but rather follow an entirely different route, one that likely takes advantage of predominant wind patterns, among other things.

A much less frequent pattern involves birds that breed in Puerto Rico and the Virgin Islands and depart during the non-breeding season. Examples are the Sooty Tern, which heads out to sea, and the Antillean Nighthawk, which presumably migrates to South America.

What is referred to as austral migration, the migration northward of birds that breed farther south, is practically non-existent in the region and is reflected only in the very rare occurrence of the Fork-tailed Flycatcher every few years.

An interesting phenomenon, evident among a few birds in our region, might be termed a "migration shadow" because its effect is much like that of the well-known "rain shadow"— wherein clouds, impeded by a mountain or mountain chain, drop their moisture as they rise up and, by the time they are high enough to cross over the barrier, have little moisture left, leaving the leeward side of the mountain dry. Puerto Rico appears to be the "mountain" when it comes to southbound migration of the Scarlet Tanager. October is the primary time for this beautiful bird to occur in Puerto Rico; however, it is nearly unrecorded in the Virgin Islands during this season. What appears to be happening is that most Scarlet Tanagers arriving in Puerto Rico "precipitate out" and remain through the winter, not moving on through the Virgin Islands. As a consequence, the Scarlet Tanager has scarcely been recorded on any of the Virgin Islands in September or October. Contrarily, it is almost exclusively during northbound migration, in March and April, that a few Scarlet Tanagers occur in the Virgin Islands. At this time, their numbers are so few that as they pass on to Puerto Rico they disperse and are scarcely recorded. In sum, the Scarlet Tanager is primarily a southbound migrant in Puerto Rico and a northbound migrant in the Virgin Islands. Other birds that appear to demonstrate this migration shadow effect, though not as dramatically as the Scarlet Tanager, are the Indigo Bunting, Blue Grosbeak, Rose-breasted Grosbeak, Baltimore Oriole, and a single shorebird—the Sanderling. A more profound analysis may well identify other species that demonstrate this phenomenon.

## CAUSES OF AVIFAUNAL INCREASE

Puerto Rico now supports the greatest number of species of breeding land birds of any West Indian island. The island also harbors the second largest total avifauna, surpassed only marginally by Cuba.

An intriguing question is why Puerto Rico and the Virgin Islands (the latter to a much lesser extent) have experienced such a large increase in bird species in the last half century. The explanation appears to be threefold. One reason is accidental introductions. The economic status of the residents of the region has improved substantially over the past few decades, making possible a large expansion in the pet trade, especially of caged birds. As has occurred in various other localities with warm climates, many of these birds escape and establish themselves. That such events explain the high incidence of wild exotics is supported by the fact that 10 of the 11 exotic birds most frequently imported into the United States from 1968 to 1971 (excluding the domestic Canary, which is captively bred) are now, or were, wild in Puerto Rico. With 32 introduced species now established on the island (plus 2 that may be), Puerto Rico far surpasses any other Caribbean island in its number of exotics.

The second reason is the density of birders in the region, particularly Puerto Rico. While no formal analysis has been conducted, it is very likely that Puerto Rico has decidedly more bird-watchers and professional investigators than any other Caribbean island. Furthermore, they are also the best equipped, thus facilitating documentation of vagrant species.

The third and least significant reason is that most of the natural habitat of the region has been substantially altered since European colonization, thus increasing certain habitats such as grassy edges and scrub thickets. Because of their previous scarcity, these habitats supported a limited indigenous avifauna, and their sudden increase apparently provided more niches than could be filled by the original native birds. This probably serves to explain invasions from adjacent islands in the last 100 years by the White-winged Dove, Mourning Dove, Caribbean Elaenia, Lesser Antillean Bullfinch, and Northern Mockingbird (from Puerto Rico to the Virgin Islands), not to mention the profusion of seed-eating exotics.

The potential problems of niche competition, crop damage, and disease transmission by the introduced species should be of concern.

## FIELD HAZARDS

The natural habitats of Puerto Rico and the Virgin Islands are probably among the safest in the world. Nevertheless, there are a few hazards the field observer should be aware of. Some freshwater bodies are infected with a parasitic worm (*Schistosoma*), which causes the disease bilharzia or schistosomiasis. While most waters are uninfected, it is best to avoid contact with the freshwater of swamps, streams, and lakes. Piped drinking water is normally safe at all localities. There are few poisonous organisms, and none are encountered with any regularity. More of a threat are bees and wasps. The introduced spectacled caiman (*Caiman crocodilus*) in Puerto Rico is a potential threat near freshwater canals, lagoons, or rivers, particularly where females are guarding their nests.

There are a few poisonous plants to avoid such as comocladia (carrasco) (*Comocladia glabra*), a bush or small tree with pairs of opposite, spiny leaflets that can cause a burning, itchy rash. There is also the notorious manchineel or poison apple (manzanillo) (*Hippomane mancinella*), a seaside tree with elliptical leaves, rounded at the base, that exude a milky white sap that causes blisters, and a small, apple-like fruit that is toxic.

Typically, the most significant field pests are sand flies and mosquitoes.

# GEOGRAPHY

Puerto Rico, approximately 9,104 km$^2$ (3,515 mi$^2$) in area, presents a combination of topography, geology, and land use history that has created a mosaic of environments. One may travel from the coast up to elevations above 1,000 m (3,280 ft) in less than an hour. Before the arrival of Europeans, Puerto Rico was heavily forested and had few open coastal habitats, even on floodplains of major rivers. Three mountain ranges dominate the landscape and greatly influence local climate and habitats. Tropical rain forests cover these mountains, capped at their highest elevations in a type of dwarf ecosystem called "elfin woods." Here, physiological constraints cause trees to grow slowly, so that they rarely reach more than 7 m (23 ft) in height. In the northeast is the Sierra de Luquillo, whose tall peaks influence the movements of tropical cyclones. Its northeast face receives the highest rainfall in the region, over 6 m (20 ft) per year in some sites. In the southeast, the Sierra de Cayey towers over the scant southern coastal plain. Though a lesser mountain range, it is the source of the largest river (Río Grande de Loíza) as well as the longest river (Río de la Plata) on the island. Almost two-thirds the length of Puerto Rico, the Cordillera Central (Central Mountains) rises above 1,400 m (4,600 ft) at Cerro Punta, dividing the wetter north and drier south. A series of coastal plains are associated with the island's many rivers. These would form a continuous belt were it not for the karst, low-elevation limestone hills referred to as "haystack hills" because of their similarity to agricultural hay mounds. Caves, sinkholes, and underground rivers are karst characteristics. Protected coastal areas are lined by large mangrove forests and freshwater swamps in the east and northeast, associated with the many rivers flowing from the Sierra de Luquillo. In the north and northwest, strong trade winds form sand dunes paralleling the coast. The southwest, semiarid at its extreme tip (Cabo Rojo Lighthouse), is notable for its hypersaline salt flats.

The Virgin Islands are an array of nearly 90 small islands, cays, and rocks lying approximately 70 km (40 mi) east of Puerto Rico. The islands extend from west to east for about 100 km (60 mi). They are separated from the Lesser Antilles by the Anegada Passage, a major channel connecting the Atlantic Ocean and Caribbean Sea. By and large, these islands are volcanic in origin, having risen from beneath the sea. The major exception is Anegada, a limestone slab composed of ancient seafloor sediments. The volcanic origin of most of the Virgin Islands translates into hilly landscapes, sometimes emerging straight from the ocean depths. Sage Mountain, on Tortola, is the highest point in the Virgin Islands at an elevation of 523 m (1,716 ft) above sea level. The rather low elevations and small sizes of the islands result in diminished annual rainfall and a relatively dry climate. Major rivers are absent, and only the largest islands have drainage basins of considerable size where seasonal stormwaters flow. These conditions greatly limit habitat diversity. Cays, small islands, and the lowlands of larger ones sustain dry forest, thickets, and scrub. The higher humidity of hillside valleys supports moist tropical forests. Mangroves, salt flats, and salt ponds occur near shallow bays. Native habitats are almost absent from the larger islands because of deforestation for agricultural purposes or human settlements. Present-day forests are a mix of exotic and native vegetation. Remnants of the native flora are sparse on small cays and islands, and on St. John, most of which is protected as a national park. The islands are divided politically into two jurisdictions. The US Virgin Islands consist of St. Thomas, St. Croix, St. John, and about 50 smaller islets and cays. The British Virgin Islands include the main islands of Tortola, Virgin Gorda, Jost Van Dyke, and Anegada, along with approximately 30 smaller islets and cays.

# BIOGEOGRAPHY

## BARRIERS TO DISPERSAL

Puerto Rico and the Virgin Islands are oceanic islands that formed beneath the sea. They are not known to have been connected to a continental landmass by a land bridge, so the first organisms to inhabit these islands had to arrive by crossing open ocean. The sea is one of the most effective barriers in limiting the movement of terrestrial and freshwater life from one locality to another. Consequently, only a very small number of continental organisms have ever succeeded in reaching this region and becoming established. (Once they arrive, these animals can speciate through local geographic isolation, certainly the main cause of the development of the region's organisms—though not its birds—but this is beyond the scope of this discussion.)

There are several mechanisms by which animals are believed to have reached these islands. Many species are carried on flotsam driven by the currents or blown by the wind. Others are no doubt lifted by the powerful winds of a hurricane or travel within the eye, only to be dropped later some distance from their native land. Very few of these individuals have the good fortune to be deposited near a remote island where there is a niche available in which they can survive. It is hypothesized, however, that this happened when the American Kestrel and the Smooth-billed Ani first reached Mona Island as a result of being carried there by a hurricane that struck the southeast corner of Hispaniola in 1930. Also, the Lesser Antillean Bullfinch may have been transported to the Virgin Islands by Hurricane Donna in 1960.

In addition to the effects of the water barrier, a second factor limiting animal diversity on oceanic islands is the reduced availability of niches. The niche of an animal is the specific set of environmental conditions that the species needs to survive. If the proper conditions for the species are unavailable over a broad spectrum of variables (resource dimensions), the creature is doomed. For example, are foods of the proper size and type present in the habitat? Are they available in adequate amounts? If so, are they obtainable? A seed may have too thick a husk or an insect may be too elusive. Even if present and obtainable, are the foods available year round and do they provide proper nutrition?

Since birds eat either plant or animal foods, the antecedents of these creatures, too, had to have succeeded in crossing a major water barrier. As a result, the food resource spectrum for birds invading islands is generally much smaller than for their counterparts on continents. Not only are food resources less diverse on islands, but the same is true of other important variables such as habitat types, nesting sites, forms of cover, and so on.

The size of the island, its form, and its distance from major landmasses with source organisms all play significant roles in the success of a colonizing species in reaching the island, the diversity of niches that will be present on the island, and the ultimate success of the colonization attempt.

A question that arises in studying the avifauna of this region is why Puerto Rico should support 19 endemic species while the Virgin Islands share only 3 of these and have none of their own. Difficulty of dispersal is not the reason because Puerto Rico and the Virgin Islands, other than St. Croix, were one continuous landmass when sea levels were perhaps 100 m (328 ft) or more lower during the Pleistocene 10,000–20,000 years ago. Therefore, at that time, most of the region's endemics would have inhabited the Virgin Islands. The low number of avian endemics and other forms in the Virgin Islands is almost certainly a consequence of their small size and low maximum elevations, factors that limit habitat diversity. As sea levels rose in recent times and the bank divided into islands, these limited habitat conditions would have led to the extirpation of nearly all the endemics. European colonization during this time doubtless exacerbated the matter. Puerto Rican endemics continue to reach the Virgin Islands at times, despite the present water barrier, as evidenced by the Puerto Rican Lizard-Cuckoo specimen from St. Thomas, but apparently there is not enough suitable habitat for their continued survival.

## DIVERSITY VERSUS UNIQUENESS

As a consequence of the region being oceanic, its fauna is not very diverse. The best illustration of this is the region's native non-aquatic mammalian fauna, the vast majority of which are bats, whose ability to fly gives them an obvious advantage in their capacity to disperse.

What the fauna of the region lacks in diversity it more than makes up for in uniqueness. This inverse relationship of diversity to uniqueness is generally the case for oceanic islands, such as Puerto Rico and most other West Indian islands. This is to say that the farther an island is formed from a continent (assuming islands are of somewhat equal size and elevation), the fewer plant and animal species it will support, but the greater the distinctiveness of those species will be.

This concept can be clarified by comparing various islands. Trinidad and Tobago, two sister islands lying only 32 km (20 mi) from South America, were once connected to that continent by a land bridge. Their combined landmass is little more than half that of Puerto Rico, but their avifauna totals approximately 400 species, about 140 more than occur naturally and with regular frequency in Puerto Rico. However, all the bird species of Trinidad and Tobago, with the sole exception of an endemic guan, are found either in South America proper or elsewhere. Though Puerto Rico's native avifauna (excluding extinctions, introductions, and vagrants) is only 263 species, 19 of these (7%) are endemic to this island (including 3 also occurring in the northern Virgin Islands). Puerto Rico also supports one endemic avian family found nowhere else in the world and shares two other endemic families with other West Indian islands. See the "Taxonomy" section for more details.

At the other extreme, we might look at New Caledonia and the Society Islands in the Pacific Ocean. New Caledonia is separated from the east coast of Australia by approximately 1,126 km (700 mi) of ocean. As a result, and though it is nearly twice the size of Puerto Rico, its avifauna totals a mere 68 species. However, 16 of these (24%) are endemic forms, one being the famous Kagu (*Rhynochetos jubatus*), which is the sole representative of an avian family endemic to the island. The Society Islands, isolated near the center of the Pacific Ocean, support only 17 species of birds, but of these, all except one are not found anywhere else in the world.

## UNIQUENESS: ITS VALUES

The uniqueness of island forms is of particular interest to humankind. The simplicity of island ecosystems, and the distinctive differences between organisms on adjacent islands, provide ideal conditions for the study of the evolutionary process. Indeed, the theory of evolution was crystallized in the mind of Charles Darwin following his study of the finches on the Galápagos Islands off the coast of Ecuador. The same patterns occur in the West Indies.

In addition to providing excellent examples of evolution at work, organisms on islands serve as invaluable tools for understanding portions of the past biological history of the earth. As species on continents evolve, the less adaptable forms are generally replaced. A few relict species such as the crocodile survive, but for the most part scientists must be content with fossil records of this evolutionary process. In unusual circumstances, however, some of these ancient forms may be preserved as "living fossils" through their isolation on islands.

The marsupials of Australia are a vast assemblage of such relict species preserved through isolation on a large island. Early during the evolution of mammals, when pouched forms were much more broadly distributed, Australia and South America drifted away from the great, main landmass with their marsupial populations intact. Placentals evolved and dominated the rest of the world, ultimately crossing into South America by way of a new land connection formed several million years ago, and then drove almost all of its marsupials to extinction. By virtue of isolation, however, the marsupials of Australia survived and remain today as one of science's most precious tools in understanding the evolutionary past.

Puerto Rico and the Greater Antilles, to a lesser extent, play a similar role in the Western Hemisphere. It is known that with the reconnection of North and South America, much of the original fauna of Central America became extinct and was replaced. It is generally believed that some of the fauna of Puerto Rico and the other islands are relict populations of what once existed in Central and even North America. The endemic Puerto Rican Tody is one of the most outstanding living examples of such a relict species. Presently only five species survive of the endemic West Indian family Todidae, all of which are confined to the Greater Antilles. However, new fossil evidence indicates that this family was once fairly widespread, having occurred in the United States and Europe. The period of this family's continental distribution dates to the mid-Oligocene, 30 million years ago.

Evolution is an ongoing process. How fast it proceeds is of great scientific interest. On this front, there are indications that the two exotic finches introduced to Puerto Rico centuries ago, the Orange-cheeked Waxbill and Bronze Mannikin, may be evolving their bill sizes in opposite directions away from those of the intermediately sized native seed eaters, thus reducing competition for food resources. Furthermore, it appears the Bronze Mannikin has lost sexual dimorphism (each sex being different) in bill size, a feature present in its African ancestors. Puerto Rico's introduced avifauna provides fascinating opportunities for evolutionary study.

# CONSERVATION

## THE PROBLEM

As humankind has come to dominate most habitats of the world, new pressures have been placed on wild animals, causing the rate of extinction of vertebrate forms to increase alarmingly in the last few centuries. Of the approximately 10,700 species of birds in the world, about 100 have ceased to exist since the extinction of the Great Auk in 1844. Of particular significance in this region is that the large majority of these were inhabitants of islands. The present number of species threatened with extinction globally is approximately 1,300—nearly one-seventh of the world's avifauna.

Island species are particularly vulnerable for two reasons: limited island size leaves them no peripheral habitat for escape, and in many cases they have evolved in isolation from predators, so they lack mechanisms with which to defend themselves against humans and their beasts.

## PRINCIPAL CAUSES OF EXTINCTION AND ENDANGERMENT

Extinction and endangerment can result from natural causes or may be induced by humans. The latter is by far the most prevalent cause at present. Humankind has prompted the extinction of animals by three principal methods: (1) habitat destruction and human disturbance, (2) overhunting, and (3) introduction of predators and other invasive species that alter habitat. In this region, as in the rest of the world, habitat destruction is the principal cause of endangerment, with invasive pests and overhunting the next most important factors (see table on pp.28–29).

## EARLIEST HUMAN-CAUSED EXTINCTIONS IN THE REGION

Three species of birds are believed to have been driven to extinction by Amerindians or the earliest European colonists prior to the collection of specimens for scientific purposes. One of these, DeBooy's Rail (*Nesotrochis debooyi*), was a flightless ground-dwelling bird of tasty flesh, as evidenced by the accumulations of its bones in the relatively recent midden deposits of the Amerindians. Though unproven, it is quite likely that, as has happened with a number of flightless birds on other islands, the introduced predators and vermin of the settlers such as pigs, dogs, cats, and rats made a quick end of this defenseless bird. The name "carrao," used by many country people to describe a nearly flightless edible bird, is almost certainly referable to the Limpkin, and not DeBooy's Rail as most authors have suggested.

The Puerto Rican Parakeet (*Psittacara maugei*), endemic to Puerto Rico, Mona Island, and perhaps Vieques, expired in the nineteenth century and is now represented by only one preserved specimen. Persecution as an agricultural pest was severe and was likely the primary cause for its extinction, especially if, as with its closest relative, the Hispaniolan Parakeet, flocks exhibited no fear and thus allowed numerous individuals to be killed at once. The parakeet was extirpated from Puerto Rico proper in the 1700s but survived on Mona Island until the late 1890s.

A macaw (*Ara autochthones*), reputedly endemic to St. Croix and Puerto Rico, is known only from bones dug from Amerindian middens; although these appear to be from a species no longer extant, it is probable that Amerindians transported these birds from island to island, so it is doubtful that this macaw was truly endemic to these islands.

## RECENT EXTINCTIONS AND EXTIRPATIONS

Five other bird species have been eliminated relatively recently as breeding residents from the region. One of these was an endemic subspecies—the Culebra race of the Puerto Rican Parrot (*Amazona vittata gracilipes*). The cause of its demise is not known for certain but was probably due to being killed as a crop pest or hunted excessively. The parrot was reported as common on Culebra in 1899, where it was said to cause damage to local crops. Extinction is believed to have occurred prior to 1912.

In the 1700s, the White-necked Crow (*Corvus leucognaphalus*) was abundant, but its numbers and range gradually declined in Puerto Rico through the nineteenth century; by the early part of the twentieth century it appeared to be confined to the Luquillo Mountains. The last sighting in the wild was of two birds high up on El Yunque in 1963. Now extirpated from Puerto Rico, and from St. Croix where it is known only from midden deposits, the species is presently declining on its last remaining island, Hispaniola. The White-necked Crow was reputed to have delicious flesh, but it is questionable whether overhunting was the principal cause of its demise. Certainly the destruction of the native forests in which it lived was partially responsible, as well as it being shot as a crop pest.

The American Flamingo was a widespread resident in Puerto Rico and the Virgin Islands until the late 1800s. Poaching of eggs and young, as well as predation by the introduced mongoose, likely caused its disappearance from the region. Recent efforts in the British Virgin Islands to reestablish breeding populations have proven highly successful.

The two other avian species that were extirpated from the region as breeding residents but still occur very rarely include the Black Rail, young of which were reported to have been taken in the late 1800s; and the Black-bellied Whistling-Duck, which is believed to have bred near Cartagena Lagoon in the early 1900s. Hunting was doubtless a major factor in the demise of the Black-bellied Whistling-Duck. Introduction of the mongoose and other mammalian predators may have been responsible for the elimination of the Black Rail as a breeding bird.

## ENDANGERED AND THREATENED SPECIES

The number of bird species that are endangered or to some degree threatened in this region far outnumbers those already extinct. Twenty-four species fall into this category. In some cases, the threat is to the status of the bird, which may be significantly altered, though the species may not be totally extirpated. For example, the Magnificent Frigatebird is commonly seen over protected bays and islets year round, while Audubon's Shearwater occurs regularly offshore, but there is a danger that the last remaining breeding colonies of these species will soon disappear from the region. The number of regularly active frigatebird rookeries here has dwindled. Audubon's Shearwater is similarly threatened, primarily by rats and increases in recreational boating. While both species might persist as visitors to this region after the destruction of these nesting colonies, they will be dependent on islets belonging to neighboring governments for suitable nesting conditions. Consequently, the frigatebirds and shearwaters would not be self-sustaining within this territory, making them subject to elimination by factors totally outside local control. Two former breeding species, eliminated as such in recent times and now exceedingly rare, include the Black Rail and Black-bellied Whistling-Duck, both discussed earlier. The plights of the frigatebird and shearwater illustrate the continuation of this trend, which is, in their cases, at a dishearteningly advanced stage. Fortunately, greater efforts than ever before are being made to eradicate invasive pest species on some islands in the region.

Of greatest concern are the endemic species and subspecies directly faced with total extinction. The endemic species are discussed in turn under the individual species accounts, while the subspecies are so marked in the table that lists causes of endangerment. The degree of endangerment of each is listed, as well as the cause of endangerment.

Interestingly, all appear to be suffering from human activities, and none, with the exception of the Yellow-shouldered Blackbird, primarily from natural causes.

Since the previous edition of this book, the number of threatened or endangered species has been reduced substantially. This is primarily because greater numbers of bird-watchers throughout the region have increasingly been locating rare birds in localities from which they were not previously known. However, in a few cases, particularly that of the Puerto Rican Nightjar, other factors are at play. The nightjar appears to be benefiting from the dramatic regrowth of secondary forest through Puerto Rico's lowlands, habitat that was all too scarce a half century ago. The recovery of this bird from near extinction, with minimal active human management, has been quite remarkable. Another major positive development was the restoration of Caño Tiburones as a freshwater wetland. Drained for many decades by pumps, this expansive area has been allowed to return to wetland, which has been a boon for many freshwater birds. Some, such as the recently colonizing White Ibis, have adopted Caño Tiburones as their principal breeding area. For others, such as the Purple Gallinule and various waterfowl, it has enabled them to no longer be considered threatened.

## CAUSES OF ENDANGERMENT

### Habitat Destruction and Disturbance

Most of the species in the table are being detrimentally affected by disturbance or destruction of their habitat. The draining and filling of the region's limited freshwater swamps, prior to the previous edition of the book, was having the greatest single negative impact on species habitat. This, coupled with hunting, which during the waterfowl season is concentrated in freshwater and brackish swamps, has had a disastrous effect on breeding ducks as well as many other wetland-dwelling birds. Disturbances to offshore islets vary greatly, from increased boat traffic and poaching of eggs to tourist developments. In any case, several avian species that depend on islets as remote refuges on which to breed are threatened as a result. The destruction of mangroves and their adjacent mudflats has had a detrimental impact on several bird species. For species of higher-elevation forests such as the Elfin-woods Warbler and Sharp-shinned Hawk, the potential impacts of climate change should be of particular concern. Determining how our changing climate is affecting such birds with very narrow habitat requirements will be a challenging endeavor.

25

### Overhunting

Hunting is a traditional pastime practiced for many years in Puerto Rico, often without adequate regulation. As a result, many native breeding game birds have been decimated, and it is often difficult to raise their reduced populations to a less precarious level. The British Virgin Islands have totally eliminated hunting, and the effects are quite noticeable in the unusual tameness of all the local birds. The US Virgin Islands strictly regulate hunting. More recently, Puerto Rico has followed suit, taking a number of seriously declining native game birds such as the Ruddy Duck, White-crowned Pigeon, and Purple Gallinule off the list of huntable species. Unfortunately, striking birds from a hunting list, though a critical first step, does not always suffice as a remedy for recovery of the bird. Effective enforcement is a fundamental element of a sound conservation policy. An additional complication in regulating hunting is that the breeding seasons of many birds in the subtropics are extended and often erratic. For example, there is evidence of the White-cheeked Pintail breeding in the region during every month of the year, and of the Ruddy Duck breeding through the peak of Puerto Rico's hunting season. Consequently, there is no season of the year when hunting can occur without disrupting birds in their nesting cycle. There is no easy way around this problem, yet it is one that must be dealt with.

## Invasive Pests

Since the earliest days of European colonization, various animal species closely associated with these Old World arrivals quickly coinhabited the islands. Unintentional, but among the most detrimental nonetheless, were the Norway rat and black rat. These two pests, long the bane of European civilization—the bubonic plague being transmitted by fleas on these critters—were now to become almost equally so in the New World. Because they colonized so long ago, likely right along with Columbus, their impacts on the region's fauna went undocumented, so that now speculation will have to suffice. How these rats impacted ground-dwelling land birds such as DeBooy's Rail, Black Rail, and Bridled Quail-Dove may never be known, but their impact on colonially nesting seabirds continues to this day and can be devastating.

The domestic cat, likely introduced sometime after the rats and left to roam wild, is right up there with the rats as a notorious threat to native birds, as well as other species. Top-flight predators, feral cats have a sad history of impacting bird populations around the world—island populations, in particular. Keeping cats indoors is the only practical way to stop them from impacting birdlife. And it's far safer for the cats as well.

Other, less renowned pests introduced by Europeans include the domestic pig, which is a notorious rooter and scavenger prone to eat the eggs and young of any ground-dwelling creature. On Mona Island, pigs have been documented to dig up and eat the eggs of every Mona rock iguana nest during seasons when other foods are scarce. The domestic goat, also introduced in the earliest days of colonization, affected the local avifauna in a less direct manner. Though they are herbivores, goats are notorious for nibbling plants down to their bare roots. Over time, they can modify a habitat considerably and, when overpopulated, can turn it into a wasteland. Just what this creature's impact has been in the region can only be guessed, but it does not take much guesswork to speculate that if it were removed from Mona Island, or any of the Virgin Islands, the floral composition of those islands would change substantially and the regeneration of long-absent plants would likely be remarkable. This has been the case with goat removal elsewhere, such as on Guadeloupe Island off the coast of Mexico.

Doubtless the most notorious animal introduction has been the mongoose, brought to the region intentionally between 1877 and 1879 to control the depredations of rats on sugarcane. This aggressive carnivore has likely been the most detrimental wild predator on birds. The mongoose was very probably the major cause of decline of the Puerto Rican Nightjar, Short-eared Owl, Black Rail, Key West Quail-Dove, and Bridled Quail-Dove, all either ground nesters or terrestrial in habit. Fortunately, indications are that all of these except the Black Rail have rebounded since the early 1900s, when most were thought extinct in the region. In fact, the Short-eared Owl is now seen regularly in Puerto Rico, and the Bridled Quail-Dove is fairly common in more heavily wooded portions of the Virgin Islands. Consequently, neither species is presently endangered. Apparently, these birds have reached something of an equilibrium with the mongoose after suffering heavily when that creature was at peak numbers about a century ago. In the case of both of the quail-doves as well as the nightjar, the increase in forest habitat over the past century has also benefited these species.

As if the introduced pests of the past were not challenge enough for the region's birdlife, a number of new threats have become established, particularly in Puerto Rico. Among these are the spectacled caiman, a species of crocodile now well established along much of the coast, particularly near Tortuguero Lagoon. It periodically feeds on waterbirds. The boa constrictor, also known as the red-tailed boa, which grows to 3 m (10 ft) in length and is arboreal, has spread rapidly in western Puerto Rico and should soon span the island. It is also well established on St. Croix. This species too preys on birds, particularly nestlings. The most widespread of the recent introductions, the green iguana, is well established in both Puerto Rico and the US Virgin Islands. Primarily vegetarian, it is already altering the region's plant communities. Significantly, it is reputed to eat bird eggs and, at its present population numbers, has the potential to seriously affect the status of bird populations. Presently, its effects on birdlife remain to be determined. Of little doubt is that the impacts of all these newly established exotic species on the region's birdlife will prove negative.

## Chemicals

Pesticides and other chemicals are not known to have endangered any species in Puerto Rico and the Virgin Islands. The Brown Pelican, which was severely affected by pesticides along the Gulf Coast and the West Coast of the United States, is a breeding resident in the region. The outlawing of DDT, however, has enabled this species to recover throughout its range. The status of breeding insectivorous birds is an indicator of likely impacts.

## Climate Change

To date, only one of our region's endangered species, the Puerto Rican Parrot, has been seriously affected by climate change. That will change. With more extreme weather events in the future—more severe hurricanes, increasingly serious droughts, rising sea levels—it is only a matter of time, and not much time at that, before such events begin to more broadly affect the region's avifauna. Already Hurricane Maria, a category 5 storm that devastated Puerto Rico and St. Croix, is considered the worst natural disaster in the region's history. Such severe storms, now more frequent year after year, are but one demonstration of climate change at work. To believe otherwise, that this hurricane's severity was a coincidence in this day and age, equates with believing the earth was flat in 1492. And though Hurricane Maria did not cause any extinctions, it devastated Puerto Rican Parrot numbers to the point where, were it not for the survival of numerous captive birds, along with intensive management, the species might well have succumbed. Warming temperatures, a primary cause of increased hurricane intensity, are also likely to modify various habitat types, which in turn will affect available food resources, among other things. As mentioned above under "Habitat Destruction and Disturbance," we must be particularly wary of such impacts on habitat-limited species such as the Elfin-woods Warbler and Sharp-shinned Hawk. Regrettably, the threat of climate change to the region, and to the world as a whole, is only destined to become worse. In short order it will become a more serious threat than all others combined.

27

# ENDANGERED SPECIES LIST

This list is customized for Puerto Rico and the Virgin Islands. Consequently, it differs from globally oriented lists such those of the International Union for Conservation of Nature (IUCN) or the US Endangered Species Act. While some species are on those international lists, others are not. This is because their status in Puerto Rico and the Virgin Islands is threatened or endangered, but such is not the case throughout their range.

*Key*
▨—endemic species
▮—endemic subspecies

*Degree of Endangerment*
**A  Critically Endangered:** Species that are practically extinct (or extirpated) from the region. In most cases active steps must be taken to ensure their survival.

B **Endangered:** Species that are so rare or their habitat so restricted that any increase in pressure on them will move them to category A.

C **Threatened:** Species that may be surviving reasonably well but that depend on habitats under pressure by invasive species or human development.

| CRITICALLY ENDANGERED | |
|---|---|
| **SPECIES** | **CAUSES OF ENDANGERMENT** |
| Black-bellied Whistling-Duck | Freshwater wetlands loss, overhunting, invasive pests |
| Black Rail | Freshwater wetlands loss, invasive pests |
| ■ Sharp-shinned Hawk | Forest loss, botfly parasitism, hurricanes |
| ■ Puerto Rican Owl (only Virgin Islands subspecies) | Forest loss |
| ▨ Puerto Rican Parrot | Forest loss, overhunting, invasive pests, hurricanes |
| ▨ Yellow-shouldered Blackbird | Shiny Cowbird parasitism, mangrove loss, scrubland loss, hurricanes |
| **ENDANGERED** | |
| Audubon's Shearwater | Islets loss, invasive pests |
| Masked Booby | Islets loss, invasive pests |
| Magnificent Frigatebird | Islets loss, invasive pests |
| Brown Pelican (Puerto Rico) | Mangrove loss, islets loss |
| West Indian Whistling-Duck | Freshwater wetlands loss, overhunting, invasive pests |
| Snowy Plover | Salt flats associated with mangrove loss, undisturbed sandy beach loss, invasive pests |
| ■ Plain Pigeon | Forest loss, overhunting |
| ▨ Puerto Rican Nightjar | Forest loss, invasive pests |

| THREATENED | |
|---|---|
| **SPECIES** | **HABITAT DESTRUCTION** |
| Red-footed Booby | Islets loss, invasive pests |
| Red-billed Tropicbird | Islets loss, invasive pests |
| Masked Duck | Freshwater wetlands loss, overhunting |
| American Flamingo | Mangrove loss, overhunting, invasive pests |
| Limpkin | Freshwater wetlands loss, overhunting |
| Roseate Tern | Islets loss, invasive pests |
| ■ Broad-winged Hawk | Forest loss |
| White-crowned Pigeon | Mangrove loss, islets loss, overhunting |
| ▨ Elfin-woods Warbler | Forest loss |
| Yellow Warbler (Puerto Rico) | Mangrove loss, Shiny Cowbird parasitism |
| **Total number** | **24** |
| **THREATS** | |
| Loss of islets | 8 |
| Loss of freshwater wetlands | 5 |
| Loss of mangroves | 5 |
| Loss of forests | 7 |
| Overhunting | 7 |
| Invasive pests | 13 |
| Cowbird parasitism | 2 |

# PROPOSED CONSERVATION MEASURES

Since the first printing of this book 38 years ago, conservation in the region has seen some advances and some setbacks. One important positive development is the growth of active conservation groups in both Puerto Rico and the Virgin Islands. While in 1983 there were only a handful of organizations, now there are quite a few. Among these are the following:

Sociedad Ornitológica Puertorriqueña (Puerto Rico Ornithological Society)
Ciudadanos del Karso (Citizens for the Karst)
Para la Naturaleza (Puerto Rico Conservation Trust)
St. Croix Environmental Association
Jost Van Dyke Preservation Society
Virgin Islands Audubon Society
St. Thomas and Hassel Island Preservation Trust
Virgin Islands Conservation Society

Furthermore, several of these focus heavily on specific conservation activities and not just on the enjoyment of nature. The efforts of such groups can potentially play a major role in countering the trend toward continued development, and complement the efforts of governmental agencies responsible for environmental matters.

In Puerto Rico, the most important conservation actions in recent years relate to natural areas. These include creation of the Humacao Wildlife Refuge, the enhancement of Cartagena Lagoon, and the restoration of Caño Tiburones, mentioned above. These major actions are primarily responsible for the recovery of Puerto Rico's previously dwindling populations of native White-cheeked Pintails, West Indian Whistling-Ducks, and Ruddy Ducks—an impressive achievement. Most of Puerto Rico's endangered and threatened birds were formerly wetland species, so the conservation of these three areas is of particular significance.

Other major lands in Puerto Rico set aside for conservation include portions of Vieques, 40% of the former Roosevelt Roads Naval Station, and the islets surrounding Culebra. All of these are of major importance for both Puerto Rico's birdlife and many other natural values.

Importantly, on St. Croix, the Southgate Coastal Reserve was established in 2000, primarily to protect a 10 ha (25 ac) salt pond that is a local hotspot for bird diversity and nesting. Owned and managed by the St. Croix Environmental Association, it has trails and a bird blind, or viewing hide. Reforestation efforts are underway as well.

There are many other elements to the conservation of a region's birdlife besides land protection as described above. However, they will not be discussed here except for one—the only one that matters. And that is the place that birds, and nature in general, occupy in the hearts of the region's inhabitants. It is that simple, or that difficult—depending on how you choose to look at it. The more that people cherish nature, the more they will protect it. Note the word "cherish." This is not about knowledge. It is not about science. It is not about laws. It is not about protected areas. It *is* about people's hearts. Conservation is a *cultural value*. Our challenge is to seek the aspects of our culture that embrace conservation and elevate them to the surface such that conservation becomes an important societal value, and ultimately a behavioral norm. Norms drive our behavior, and it is our behavior that influences everything around us. Ultimately, conservation is not a biological science, as we are widely taught to believe. Conservation is a philosophy of life, a worldview, arguably a religion. Science is a support tool to help us do conservation more wisely. By embracing such an approach, some islands of the Lesser Antilles, St. Lucia in particular, have demonstrated extraordinary conservation successes. There is no reason Puerto Rico and the Virgin Islands, both British and US, cannot do the same.

# DESCRIPTIVE PARTS OF A BIRD

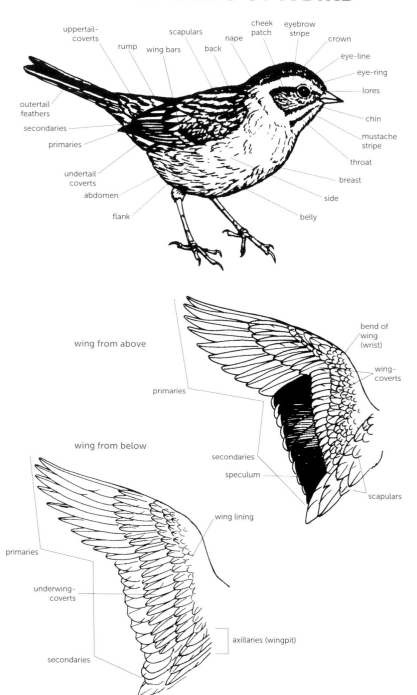

uppertail-coverts
rump
wing bars
scapulars
back
nape
cheek patch
eyebrow stripe
crown
eye-line
eye-ring
lores
outertail feathers
secondaries
primaries
chin
mustache stripe
throat
undertail coverts
abdomen
breast
flank
side
belly

wing from above
primaries
bend of wing (wrist)
wing-coverts
secondaries
speculum
scapulars

wing from below
primaries
wing lining
underwing-coverts
axillaries (wingpit)
secondaries

PLATE 1     OCEAN BIRDS — Shearwaters and Petrels

Generally occur far out at sea. Distinctive flight is gliding on long, narrow, stiff wings low over waves, with periodic shallow flaps. Nest in burrows on remote islets or mountain cliffs that they visit after dark.

**BLACK-CAPPED PETREL** *Pterodroma hasitata* (Petrel antillano, Diablotín) 35–40cm (14–16in); wingspan 96cm (3.2ft); 280g. **BEHAVIOR** Nocturnal at nesting cliffs. At sea, dips in water for food, does not dive. Sometimes forages in flocks. **DESCRIPTION** Upperparts blackish except for *white rump, hindneck, and forehead*. Extent of white variable. (See Great Shearwater.) **FLIGHT** Note black front edge of underwing. Wrist more bent than shearwater's and flight more erratic, often high-arching and wheeling, unlike more direct flight of shearwaters. **VOICE** Calls only at night around nesting colonies. Drawn-out *aaa-aw, eek*, or *ooow, eek*; and yelps like hurt puppy. **STATUS AND RANGE** Very rare off Puerto Rico and Virgin Islands, primarily November–June. Breeds in high mountains of southern Haiti, southern Dominican Republic, and Dominica. May breed in Cuba. These islands comprise entire breeding range. Critically endangered on breeding grounds. **HABITAT** At sea, except when breeding in mountain cliffs.

**GREAT SHEARWATER (GREATER SHEARWATER)** *Ardenna gravis* (Pampero capirotado, Pampero mayor) 48cm (19in); wingspan 105–122cm (3.5–4ft); 850g. One of two large shearwaters in region; noticeable *white bands on hindneck and rump* contrast with black cap and dark grayish-brown upperparts. (Black-capped Petrel looks whiter from a distance due to its white forehand and more conspicuous white collar and rump band; also, its mantle is blacker, heightening the contrast with white markings.) **FLIGHT** Much slower wingbeats than Manx and Audubon's Shearwaters and Black-capped Petrel. **STATUS AND RANGE** Uncommon to rare off Puerto Rico and Virgin Islands, primarily May–July but can occur any month. **HABITAT** At sea (rarely within one mile of land).

**CORY'S SHEARWATER** *Calonectris diomedea* (Pampero ceniciento, Pampero de Cory) 40–53cm (16–21in); wingspan 112–126cm (3.6–4.1ft); 900g. Large, appears featureless at a distance. *Pale yellowish bill* is diagnostic. Brownish back and upper side of wings; grayish head and neck; whitish underside, underwings, and uppertail-coverts, the white on latter variable in extent and sometimes nearly absent. Wings long and broad. (Great Shearwater has a long, thin, black bill; sharply defined black cap; and crisply defined white uppertail-coverts. Also, its flight is more purposeful.) **FLIGHT** Glides effortlessly, holds wings bent at wrist. Flaps minimally. **STATUS AND RANGE** Very rare visitor off Puerto Rico, primarily late May–July but might be expected during any month. **HABITAT** At sea.

**SOOTY SHEARWATER** *Ardenna grisea* (Pampero cenizo) 40–46cm (16–18in); wingspan 94–110cm (3.2–3.6ft); 800g. The only all-dark shearwater in region. Medium-sized, *blackish overall with whitish underwings*. Wings long and narrow. **FLIGHT** Swift and direct, with rapid flapping ascents and long glides usually close to water surface. **STATUS AND RANGE** Very rare visitor off Puerto Rico, primarily late May–July during northward migration but might be expected during any month. **HABITAT** At sea.

Black-capped
Petrel

typical
coloration

atypical
coloration

typical coloration

Great
Shearwater

Cory's
Shearwater

Sooty
Shearwater

**MANX SHEARWATER** *Puffinus puffinus* (Pampero pichoneta, Pampero de Manx) 30–38cm (12–15in); wingspan 76–89cm (2.5–3ft); 400g. Medium-sized. Note its short tail. Blackish above and white below, including wing linings, underside of primaries, and undertail-coverts. Lores are dark. (Audubon's Shearwater is slightly smaller, with browner upperparts; longer tail; shorter, broader, blunter-tipped wings; white spot on lores; dark underside of primaries; sometimes has dark undertail-coverts; lacks white bar behind ear-coverts.) **FLIGHT** Four or five distinctive snappy wingbeats and a rocking glide in light winds or flat seas. **STATUS AND RANGE** Very rare off Puerto Rico. Most likely to occur primarily February–May, though few records to date. **HABITAT** At sea.

**AUDUBON'S SHEARWATER** *Puffinus lherminieri* (Pimleco, Pampero de Audubón) 30cm (12in); wingspan 64–72cm (2–2.3ft); 200g. **BEHAVIOR** Nocturnal at nesting cliffs. **DESCRIPTION** Relatively small; long-tailed, blackish-brown above and white below, white spot on lores, dark undersides of primaries. Undertail-coverts sometimes dark. (Manx Shearwater is slightly larger, with blacker upperparts; shorter tail; longer, narrower, more pointed wings; white bar behind ear-coverts; lacks white spot on lores.) (Sooty and Bridled Terns have forked tails and do not flap and glide like a shearwater.) **VOICE** Mournful, catlike cries at night in flight around nests. **STATUS AND RANGE** The most regularly encountered shearwater in Puerto Rico and Virgin Islands. Locally common in Virgin Islands. Rare in Puerto Rico except around Culebra, Mona, and Desecheo Islands. Breeding sites in Puerto Rico include keys near Culebra. It nests on numerous Virgin Islands with seaward-facing cliffs. Nests in ground burrows, cavities between boulders, or cliff crevices. Endangered as a breeding bird in region. **HABITAT** At sea, particularly in Atlantic Ocean over outer continental shelf, except when breeding on offshore islands.

## Storm-Petrels

34

Small seabirds, little larger than swallows, which occur far out at sea. They swoop and flutter low over the ocean, sometimes pattering the surface with their feet.

**LEACH'S STORM-PETREL** *Hydrobates leucorhous* (Paíño boreal, Pamperito rabo horquillado, Golondrina de mar) 20cm (8in); wingspan 43–48cm (17–19in); 35g. A small, brownish-black seabird with white rump. Has slightly forked tail, pale brown wing band, and *white rump patch appearing divided at close range*. (See Wilson's Storm-Petrel.) **FLIGHT** Feet do not extend beyond tail. Flight more erratic and wingbeats deeper than Wilson's. **STATUS AND RANGE** Decidedly rare migrant and non-breeding resident off Puerto Rico and Virgin Islands, primarily November–June but sometimes occurs in other months. **HABITAT** At sea.

**WILSON'S STORM-PETREL** *Oceanites oceanicus* (Paíño de Wilson, Pamperito rabo cuadrado, Golondrina de mar) 18–19cm (7–7.5in); wingspan 38–42cm (15–16.5in); 34g. **BEHAVIOR** Regularly follows boats, swooping over wake like a swallow and touching sea with its feet. **DESCRIPTION** Small, dark brownish-black seabird with *undivided white rump patch*. (Blacker, wings shorter, broader, and more rounded with less angled wrists than Leach's Storm-Petrel, also more square tail.) **FLIGHT** Feet have yellow toe-webbing and extend beyond tail. Flight fluttery and more direct than Leach's, with briefer glides. **STATUS AND RANGE** Rare off Puerto Rico and Virgin Islands, primarily May and June. Most likely to occur over deep waters of Atlantic Ocean. **HABITAT** At sea.

Manx
Shearwater

Audubon's
Shearwater

Leach's
Storm-Petrel
(not to scale)

Wilson's
Storm-Petrel
(not to scale)

Long-billed, sleek-plumaged seabirds that roost and nest colonially and feed at sea by diving for prey from substantial heights. Their leisurely flapping and gliding flight low over the ocean is characteristic.

**RED-FOOTED BOOBY** *Sula sula* (Boba patirroja, White booby, Tree booby, Red-faced booby) 66–76cm (26–30in); wingspan 1m (3.3ft); 1kg. Smallest of local boobies. **ADULT** Brown phase—Brown, with white hindparts and tail. White phase—All white, with black primaries and secondaries. (Masked Booby has dark tail.) **IMMATURE** Sooty brown; paler below, sometimes slightly darker breast band. **VOICE** Guttural *ga-ga-ga-ga*, of variable length, trails off. Also distinctive squawk. **STATUS AND RANGE** A very locally abundant permanent resident near its nesting grounds in Puerto Rico, but rare to very rare elsewhere. In Puerto Rico it is abundant on the islands of Mona and Monito. It is rare around Desecheo, where a large colony has been extirpated. It periodically comes close to shore at Rincón on Puerto Rico's mainland. It is rare in the Virgin Islands, where it previously nested on cays off St. Thomas, but it is believed not to any longer. Threatened as a breeding bird in region. **HABITAT** At sea except when breeding and roosting on remote islands.

**BROWN BOOBY** *Sula leucogaster* (Boba parda, Boba prieta, Booby, White-bellied booby) 71–76cm (28–30in); wingspan 1.5m (5ft); 1.3kg. **BEHAVIOR** Often rests on buoys or rocky cliffs. **ADULT** *Entirely brown head and upperparts sharply demarcated from white belly and abdomen.* **IMMATURE** Light brown belly and abdomen. (Immature Masked Booby has white hindneck and lacks brown on upper breast.) **VOICE** Hoarse *kak*. **STATUS AND RANGE** Fairly common but local year-round resident offshore around Puerto Rico and widespread in the Virgin Islands. Locally abundant near breeding grounds. The most likely booby seen from shore. **HABITAT** Bays, coastal areas, and at sea. Roosts and breeds on offshore islands.

36

**MASKED BOOBY** *Sula dactylatra* (Boba enmascarada, Blue-faced booby, White booby, Whistling booby) 81–91cm (32–36in); wingspan 1.6–1.7m (5.2–5.5ft); 1.2–2.2kg. **ADULT** Primarily white; *black tail*, primaries, and secondaries. **SUBADULT** Similar to adult, but upperparts brown on head and rump; brown flecks on wing-coverts. (White phase Red-footed Booby has white tail.) **IMMATURE** Head and upperparts brown with white hindneck. Underparts white except throat, undertail, and flight feathers. **STATUS AND RANGE** An extremely local and uncommon year-round resident around its offshore breeding islets. It is resident on Monito and Cayo Alcatraz off Puerto Rico and at Cockroach Cay and Sula Cay in the Virgin Islands. Endangered as a breeding bird in region. **HABITAT** At sea. Roosts and breeds on offshore islands.

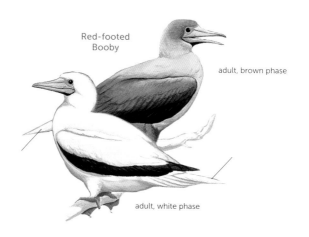

Red-footed
Booby

adult, brown phase

adult, white phase

Brown Booby

adult

adult

Masked Booby

Tropicbirds
Display long, streamer-like central tail feathers. Feed at sea, diving on prey from substantial heights. Nest in cliff crevices, usually on islets.

**WHITE-TAILED TROPICBIRD** *Phaethon lepturus* (Chirre coliblanco, Rabijunco coliblanco, Gaviota caracolera, Trophic, Truphit, White bird, Boatswain bird, Marlinspike, Long-tail) 81cm (31in) (with plumes), 37–40cm (15–16in) (without plumes); wingspan 89–96cm (3–3.2ft); 350g. **ADULT** White overall; *long tail plumes; heavy black stripes on upperwing and outer primaries.* Bill yellow or orange.
**IMMATURE** Barred back; short central tail feathers. Bill yellowish, ringed with black. (Immature differs from immature Red-billed in its coarser black barring on upperparts and lack of black band across hindneck.) **VOICE** Raspy *crick-et.* **STATUS AND RANGE** A locally common breeding resident in Puerto Rico and British Virgin Islands, but uncommon to rare in US Virgin Islands. In Puerto Rico common only at the Guajataca cliffs on the north coast, Caja de Muertos off the south coast, and Mona Island off the west. It is less common around Culebra and Vieques, and infrequent at other coastal locations. It is more widely distributed in British Virgin Islands, including at Steel Point on Tortola's western end. Occurs primarily February–June, but some arrive as early as December or depart as late as August. **HABITAT** At sea except when breeding in sea cliffs.

**RED-BILLED TROPICBIRD** *Phaethon aethereus* (Chirre piquirrojo, Rabijunco piquicolorado, Truphit, Trophic, White bird, Boatswain bird, Marlinspike) 91–107cm (36–42in) (with plumes), 46–51cm (18–20in) (without plumes); wingspan 1–1.1m (3.2–3.5ft); 750g. **ADULT** White overall; black-barred back; *long tail plumes*; red bill.
**IMMATURE** Similar to White-tailed, but back less boldly barred, darker black band across hindneck. **VOICE** Long, harsh, raspy *keé-arrr.* **STATUS AND RANGE** Fairly common and moderately widespread year-round resident in British Virgin Islands. In US Virgin Islands it is uncommon and local on St. Thomas and St. John, and rare on St. Croix. Off Puerto Rico, it is uncommon and very local around Culebra and the Fajardo Cordillera and is rare off Vieques. Threatened as a breeding bird in region. **HABITAT** At sea except when breeding on offshore islands.

38

Frigatebirds
The most accomplished marine aerialists. They cannot dive into or land on the ocean. Thus, they take food from the surface or rob it from other seabirds.

**MAGNIFICENT FRIGATEBIRD** *Fregata magnificens* (Tijereta, Tijerilla, Rabijunco, Man-o-war, Hurricane bird, Weather bird, Scissorstail, Cobbler) 89–114cm (35–45in); wingspan 2.2–2.5m (7–8ft); 1.3kg. **BEHAVIOR** *Floats motionless in air.* Chases other seabirds to rob prey. Does not land on sea surface. **DESCRIPTION** *Long, forked tail; long, slender, pointed wings are sharply bent at wrist.* **ADULT MALE** Black. During courtship, inflatable throat pouch bright red. **ADULT FEMALE** Blackish, with white breast.
**IMMATURE** Blackish; head and breast white. **FLIGHT** Frequently soars motionless. **STATUS AND RANGE** A common year-round resident in Puerto Rico and the Virgin Islands. Colonial roosts on rocky ledges or trees on cays, also on tall trees along the coast of larger islands. Nesting in region is extremely limited because of frigatebird's lack of tolerance for disturbance while incubating. Endangered as a breeding bird in region. **HABITAT** Bays, inshore waters, and offshore cays where it roosts and breeds.

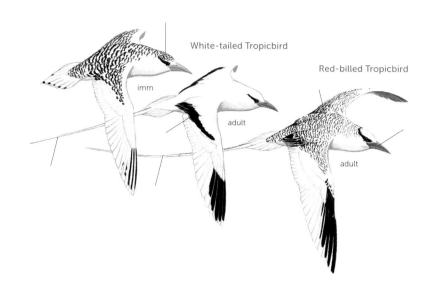

White-tailed Tropicbird

imm

adult

Red-billed Tropicbird

adult

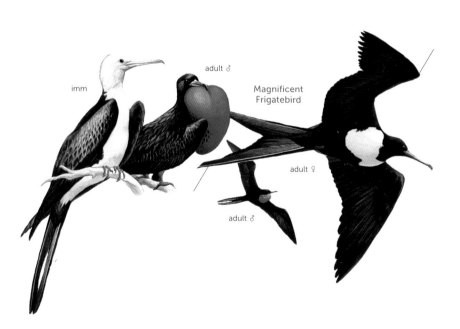

imm

adult ♂

Magnificent
Frigatebird

adult ♀

adult ♂

Gull-like seabirds found over open ocean and rarely seen from land. They are predatory, have hooked bills, and chase other seabirds to rob their prey. Flight is swift and direct like a falcon.

**PARASITIC JAEGER** *Stercorarius parasiticus* (Págalo parásito) 46–67cm (18–26.5in); wingspan 1.1–1.3m (3.5–4ft); male 400g, female 500g. Small jaeger. **ADULT** Light phase—Dark brownish-gray above, whitish below; grayish-brown cap; narrow, dark upper breast band. Dark phase—Dark brown overall. **SUBADULT** Finely barred below; often reddish cast to plumage. Pointed tips to central tail feathers. (Pomarine Jaeger is decidedly larger, with more labored flight and heavily barred sides. Long-tailed Jaegers without long central tail feathers cannot be distinguished reliably.) **FLIGHT** Strong and direct, showing *white patch on primaries*. **STATUS AND RANGE** A generally rare but sometimes uncommon migrant and non-breeding resident off Puerto Rico and the Virgin Islands, June-November. **HABITAT** Well out at sea but occasionally visits bays and estuaries where terns congregate.

**POMARINE JAEGER** *Stercorarius pomarinus* (Págalo pomarino) 65–78cm (25.5–31in); wingspan 1.1–1.4m (3.6–4.5ft); male 650g, female 750g. Heavy-bodied with a noticeably heavy chest; the largest jaeger. Two color phases with intermediate variation. **ADULT** Central tail feathers can be long but are usually twisted to give a spoon-like appearance. Light phase—Blackish cap and broad, dark band across breast. Dark phase—Less frequent; entirely dark, ranging from brown to black. **SUBADULT AND IMMATURE** Usually heavily barred below, especially sides under the wings. Central tail feathers may not extend beyond rest of tail. (Parasitic Jaeger is smaller, has more buoyant flight, lacks heavy barring on sides. Long-tailed is smaller still; adults have very long, pointed tail feathers, no breast band, and graceful tern-like flight.) **FLIGHT** *White patch on primaries.* **STATUS AND RANGE** Irregular in occurrence off Puerto Rico and Virgin Islands, it is generally a rare migrant and non-breeding resident, August-January. **HABITAT** Well out at sea.

40

**LONG-TAILED JAEGER** *Stercorarius longicaudus* (Págalo rabero, Págalo rabilargo) 50–58cm (19.5–23in); central tail feathers 15–23cm (6–10in); wingspan 102–117cm (3.3–3.9ft); 230–444g. **BEHAVIOR** Will follow boats. **DESCRIPTION** The smallest jaeger. **ADULT** Grayish-brown cap; *long central tail feathers*; lacks breast band; back and secondaries gray contrasting with brown primaries. **SUBADULT** Dark phase—Much less frequent; grayish-brown overall; darker cap; tail feathers may not be extended. Light phase—Whitish below with fine barring; grayish-brown above with fine white barring; sometimes head and hindneck pale. Legs blue. Central tail feathers may not be extended. **FLIGHT** Graceful, tern-like. *Small white wing patch.* **STATUS AND RANGE** A very rare migrant off Puerto Rico and likely the Virgin Islands, October–November. **HABITAT** Far out at sea.

**BLACK-LEGGED KITTIWAKE** *Rissa tridactyla* (Gaviota tridáctila) 43cm (17in); wingspan 90cm (3ft); 400g. **FIRST YEAR** White head; black ear-spot, bill, and terminal tail band. **NON-BREEDING ADULT** Yellow bill; white head, black mark behind eye; gray mantle; black wingtips with no white. **BREEDING ADULT** Head entirely white. (First year distinguished from Bonaparte's Gull by black half collar on hindneck and white trailing edge of secondaries.) **FLIGHT** Wings and mantle marked with contrasting *W* from wingtip to wingtip. (See also Plates 9 and 11.) **STATUS AND RANGE** Very rare visitor in Puerto Rico and Virgin Islands, January–March. **HABITAT** Generally far offshore. Sometimes ponds and estuaries.

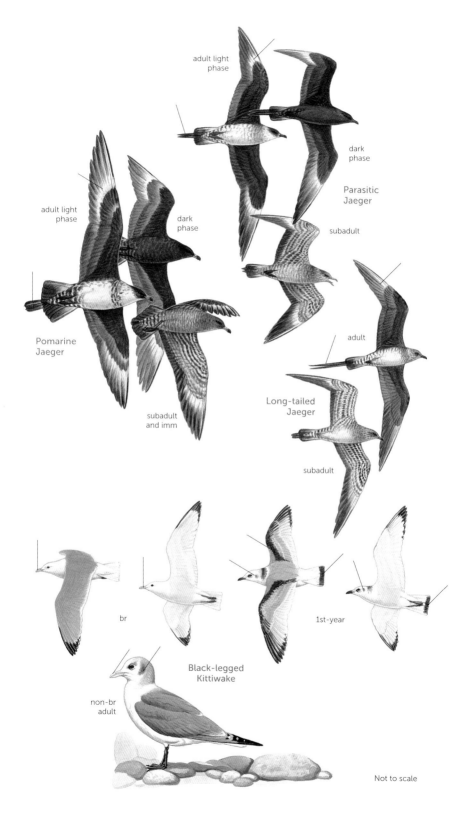

adult light phase

dark phase

Parasitic Jaeger

subadult

adult light phase

dark phase

Pomarine Jaeger

subadult and imm

adult

Long-tailed Jaeger

subadult

br

1st-year

Black-legged Kittiwake

non-br adult

Not to scale

Slim birds, most species occurring in coastal waters. They are usually crested, with forked or notched tails and slender wings. Their flight is graceful, and they conspicuously hover well above the water surface, then dive for prey. They are quite gregarious. Like gulls, they often perch on piers and buoys.

**SOOTY TERN** *Onychoprion fuscatus* (Charrán oscuro, Gaviota oscura, Bubi, Egg bird, Booby, Hurricane bird) 38–43cm (15–17in); wingspan 81cm (32in); 200g. **ADULT** *Blackish above and white below*; tail deeply forked; white outertail feathers; white of forehead extends only to eye. (Bridled Tern has white line from forehead to behind eye, white hindneck, and browner upperparts.) **IMMATURE** Dark brown with whitish spots on mantle and wings; tail less deeply forked. **VOICE** Distinctive, plaintive *wide-a-wake* or *wacky-wack*. **STATUS AND RANGE** Generally, a common but very local breeding resident in Puerto Rico and among Virgin Islands, except off St. Croix, where rare to very rare. Occurs May–August and is rare or absent in other months. **HABITAT** Far offshore, except when breeding on offshore islets or blown near shore by storms.

**BRIDLED TERN** *Onychoprion anaethetus* (Charrán monja, Gaviota monja, Egg bird, Booby) 38cm (15in); wingspan 76cm (30in); 100g. **ADULT** *Grayish-brown above and white below*; *white hindneck*, and *white line above and behind eye*. Tail deeply forked; white outertail feathers. (Sooty Tern is blacker above, lacks white hindneck, and white on forehead does not extend behind eye.) **IMMATURE** Upperparts flecked pale gray. **VOICE** Puppy-like *yep* or whining *yerk*. Also, continuous *ah-ah-ah*. **STATUS AND RANGE** Generally fairly common but local breeding resident in Puerto Rico and among Virgin Islands, though rare off St. Croix. Occurs primarily April–August and is infrequent or absent in other months. **HABITAT** Far offshore except when breeding on offshore islets or when blown near shore by storms.

**BROWN NODDY** *Anous stolidus* (Cervera parda, Lark, Egg bird, Booby blackbird) 38–40cm (15–16in); wingspan 81cm (32in); 200g. **ADULT** *Entirely dark brown except white forecrown* fading to brown on hindneck. **VOICE** Harsh *karrk*. **STATUS AND RANGE** Locally common breeding resident April–August in Puerto Rico and most of Virgin Islands. Occurs rarely through rest of year. It is rare to very rare at any time off St. Croix and Anegada. Away from breeding islets, usually seen only at sea. **HABITAT** Far offshore, except when breeding on rocky offshore islets, or blown near shore by storms. Feeds with other terns in estuaries.

**BLACK NODDY** *Anous minutus* (Cervera negra) 32–35cm (13–14in); wingspan 76cm (2.5ft); 100–145g. Entirely *blackish-brown* with *white crown*. (Very similar to Brown Noddy but smaller and blacker; has longer, thinner bill; more contrasting white cap; noticeably more slender neck; darker underwings; and distinctive voice.) **VOICE** Sharp, dry nasal cackles, chatters, and squeaky notes. Also plaintive, piping, whistled *wheeeaeee*, with rising inflection. **STATUS AND RANGE** Very rare and local in Puerto Rico. At least one pair nested in 1999 on Noroeste Cay off Culebra. Vagrant in Virgin Islands. **HABITAT** Well offshore and around rocky islets.

**ARCTIC TERN** *Sterna paradisaea* (Charrán Ártico, Gaviota Ártica) 35–43cm (14–17in); wingspan 79cm (31in); 85–125g. **NON-BREEDING ADULT** *Blackish line along trailing edge of primaries*; short black bill; short red legs. **BREEDING ADULT** *Bill entirely blood-red*; underparts gray; cheek patch white. **IMMATURE** Incomplete black cap and indistinct shoulder bar; tail shorter than in adults. **FLIGHT** "Neckless" appearance, upperwing uniformly gray. **STATUS AND RANGE** Decidedly rare migrant off Puerto Rico, June–October. Very rare in Virgin Islands. **HABITAT** Generally far out at sea.

Sooty
Tern

adult

imm

Bridled
Tern

adult

Brown
Noddy

adult

imm

Black
Noddy

Arctic
Tern

non-br
adult

imm

br

**FORSTER'S TERN** *Sterna forsteri* (Charrán de Forster, Gaviota de Forster) 35–42cm (14–16.5in); wingspan 79cm (31in); 160g. **NON-BREEDING ADULT** Silvery-white primaries; *large black spot encloses eye*; forked tail extends beyond folded wings. (Non-breeding Roseate, Common, and Arctic terns lack distinctive black eye patch. Black on their heads extends around hindneck. Roseate Tern has much faster wingbeats.) **BREEDING ADULT** *Bill orange with black tip.* **STATUS AND RANGE** Rare migrant and non-breeding resident in Puerto Rico and very rare in Virgin Islands. Likely overlooked because of similarity to other terns. **HABITAT** Calm bays, estuaries, and coastal lagoons.

**COMMON TERN** *Sterna hirundo* (Charrán común, Gaviota común, Gullie, Egg bird) 33–40cm (13–16in); wingspan 76cm (30in); 120g. **BREEDING ADULT** Black cap; red bill with black tip; gray underparts, partly black outer primaries; gray tail with dark gray outer edges does not extend beyond tips of folded wings. **NON-BREEDING ADULT** Bill blackish; shoulder with dark bar; forehead white past eye. **VOICE** Strong *kee-arr-r* with downward inflection. Also a high-pitched *kik*. **STATUS AND RANGE** Its seasonal occurrence among the islands is varied. In Puerto Rico year-round, peaking August to mid-November, when common and numbers can be very high. It remains fairly common in July and December. St. Croix experiences the same peak, with migrants uncommon from late August to mid-November, but it is nearly absent rest of year. The pattern in northern Virgin Islands is opposite, with a June peak followed by October when southbound migrants occur. Birds occur year-round with a small peak in March during northbound migration. **HABITAT** Coastal lagoons and estuaries.

**ROSEATE TERN** *Sterna dougallii* (Palometa, Charrán rosado, Sea gull, David, Davie, Gullie) 35–41cm (14–16in); wingspan 74cm (29in); 110g. *Very long, deeply forked tail;* pale gray mantle and primaries; all white tail extends well beyond wingtips when at rest; outer primaries with white tips and narrow black edges. **BREEDING ADULT** Bill black with red base becoming mainly red by July; white underparts, cap black. **NON-BREEDING ADULT** Bill blackish; indistinct dark shoulder mark; forehead white past eye. **IMMATURE** Dark forehead and crown; bill blackish; back mottled; shoulder with indistinct marks. (Adult Common Tern's mantle and underparts darker gray and primary wing feathers with noticeable blackish on underside. Immature Common Tern has distinct black shoulder mark.) **VOICE** Raspy *krek* and softer, variably harsh two-syllable *tu-íck*, usually with accent on second syllable, but sometimes on the first. The latter differs noticeably from the harsher *kee-arr-r* of Common Tern. **STATUS AND RANGE** Generally a common breeding resident in Virgin Islands, though rare and non-breeding on St. Croix. It is an uncommon breeding resident in Puerto Rico, though a common summer visitor to Vieques, where a few nest on offshore islets. Occurs primarily April–September. Threatened. **HABITAT** Coastal bays, lagoons, and estuaries.

**LEAST TERN** *Sternula antillarum* (Charrancito, Gaviota chica, Gaviota pequeña, Sea swallow, Peterman, Egg bird, Kill-em-polly) 21.5–24cm (8.5–9.5in); wingspan 51cm (20in); 45g. *Smallest* West Indies tern. **BREEDING ADULT** Black crown; *V-shaped white forecrown; pale yellow bill with black tip.* **VOICE** Variable, including a squeaky, high-pitched *o-ik* like a rusty pump; a common *chick*; and a raspy, harsh, drawn-out *waack*. **STATUS AND RANGE** Generally common, but local breeding resident in Puerto Rico and Virgin Islands, primarily May–August. Postbreeding birds head to sea, and very rarely migrants from North America replace them September–March. Least Terns may nest several miles inland, even on rooftops. **HABITAT** Coastal lagoons and estuaries. May go up larger rivers.

**BLACK TERN** *Chlidonias niger* (Fumarel común, Gaviota ceniza) 23–26cm (9–10in); wingspan 61cm (24in); 65g. **NON-BREEDING ADULT** Gray above; forecrown, hindneck, and underparts white except dark patches on sides of breast. Dark patch behind eye. **BREEDING ADULT** Head, breast, and belly black. **IMMATURE** Upperparts washed brownish, sides washed grayish. **FLIGHT** Buoyant and slightly erratic. Often hovers. **VOICE** A sharp, metallic *peek*. **STATUS AND RANGE** Uncommon migrant in Puerto Rico, primarily late August through early October, but occurs in other months. Very rare in Virgin Islands. **HABITAT** Fresh and brackish ponds and estuaries.

Forster's
Tern

br

non-br
adult

br

Common
Tern

non-br
adult

imm

br

non-br
adult

imm

Roseate
Tern

br

Least
Tern

non-br
adult

br

Black
Tern

non-br
adult

br

PLATE 8    COASTAL SEABIRDS — Terns

**CASPIAN TERN** *Hydroprogne caspia* (Charrán caspio, Gaviota caspia) 48–58cm (19–23in); wingspan 1.3m (50in); 660g. *Large tern* with long, *stout, red bill*; black crest; dark gray underside to primaries. **NON-BREEDING ADULT** Crest flecked white. **BREEDING ADULT** Crest black. **IMMATURE** Bill orange-red. (Royal Tern smaller, bill orange-yellow, underside of primaries pale; forehead white in non-breeding plumage.) **STATUS AND RANGE** A rare to very rare visitor to Puerto Rico and very rare on St. Croix. A vagrant on other Virgin Islands. Occurs primarily August–April. **HABITAT** Calm bays, estuaries, and coastal lagoons.

**ROYAL TERN** *Thalasseus maximus* (Charrán real, Gaviota real, Gaby, Sprat bird, Gullie, Egg bird) 46–53cm (18–21in); wingspan 104cm (41in); 470g. Large tern with *orange-yellow bill* and black crest. **BREEDING ADULT** Crown entirely black. **NON-BREEDING ADULT AND IMMATURE** Forehead white. **VOICE** Harsh, high-pitched *kri-i-ik*. **STATUS AND RANGE** Common but local year-round resident in Puerto Rico and Virgin Islands. However, it is uncommon in summer, occurring locally around its few nesting islets. **HABITAT** Bays, harbors, estuaries, coastal lagoons, and reservoirs.

**SANDWICH TERN** *Thalasseus sandvicensis* (Charrán piquiagudo, Gaviota de pico agudo, Cayenne tern, Cabot's tern, Gullie, Egg bird) 41–46cm (16–18in); wingspan 86cm (34in); 200g. Relatively large. **BREEDING ADULT** Appears white; *shaggy black crest; slender black bill tipped yellow.* Sometimes bill patched or entirely dull yellow. **VOICE** Raspy, raucous call notes, *ki-rrit, krrit,* or just *kit.* **NON-BREEDING ADULT** Crown white, flecked black. **STATUS AND RANGE** A common year-round resident in Puerto Rico and Virgin Islands, though less frequent October–March. Numbers increased in recent decades. The yellow-billed Cayenne Tern (*T. s. eurygnathus*), considered by some to be a separate species, has bred off St. Thomas, St. John, and on Anegada. **HABITAT** Bays, estuaries, coastal lagoons, and reservoirs.

46  **GULL-BILLED TERN** *Gelochelidon nilotica* (Charrán piquigordo, Charrán piquicorto, Gullie, Egg bird) 33–38cm (13–15in); wingspan 86cm (34in); 170g. Chunky, gull-like. *Heavy black bill*; broad wings; shallow fork to tail. **BREEDING ADULT** Black crown and hindneck. **NON-BREEDING ADULT** Crown whitish with pale gray flecks; *gray spot behind eye.* **VOICE** Raspy, insect-like two- to three-syllable *za-za-za, kay-wek,* or *kay-ti-did.* **STATUS AND RANGE** Uncommon and local breeding resident in very small numbers on Anegada, April–August. It is an uncommon to rare and local non-breeding resident in other Virgin Islands and Puerto Rico during these same months, but may occur in any month. **HABITAT** Freshwater ponds, estuaries, lagoons, fields.

non-br
adult

Caspian
Tern

br

non-br adult
and imm

Royal
Tern

br

Sandwich
Tern

Cayenne race

non-br adult

br

Gull-billed
Tern

non-br
adult

br

Medium to large birds primarily of coastal waters. More robust than terns, with rounded heads, heavy bills, broad wings, and fan-shaped tails. Usually observed resting on buoys, piers, sandy beaches, or floating in water near the coast. They are quite gregarious.

**GREAT BLACK-BACKED GULL** *Larus marinus* (Gaviota espaldinegra mayor) 69–79cm (27–31in); wingspan 1.5–1.7m (5–5.5ft); male 1.8kg, female 1.5kg. Largest gull in coastal areas. *Very large*, with massive bill. **FIRST YEAR** Mottled grayish-brown; head white with pale flecks on rear and hindneck; bill black; tail with broad black band. **SECOND YEAR** Bill pinkish with large black band near tip; rump white; mantle with black blotches. **NON-BREEDING ADULT** *Black mantle, pink legs*, pale flecks on head, bill yellow with red spot near tip. **BREEDING ADULT** Head white. **STATUS AND RANGE** Uncommon visitor locally in Puerto Rico, October–March. Very rare on St. Croix and vagrant on other Virgin Islands. Numbers are increasing. **HABITAT** Beaches and calm bays. (See also Plate 11.)

**LESSER BLACK-BACKED GULL** *Larus fuscus* (Gaviota sombría, Gaviota espaldinegra menor) 53–63cm (21–25in); wingspan 1.2–1.5m (4–5ft); male 825g, female 700g. Large, with large bill. **FIRST YEAR** Mottled grayish; head brownish in contrast. **SECOND YEAR** Bill pinkish with large black band near tip. Broad black tail band; white rump; brownish-gray wings with no white spots at tip. **NON-BREEDING ADULT** *Dark grayish-black mantle, pale yellow legs*, yellow bill with red spot near tip. **BREEDING ADULT** Head and neck white. (Great Black-backed Gull larger; bill more massive. Winter adult has decidedly less dark feathering on head and hindneck. Adult Herring Gull has paler mantle and pink legs; first- and second-year birds have less pronounced white rump patch.) **STATUS AND RANGE** Uncommon visitor locally in Puerto Rico while very rare in Virgin Islands, primarily St. Croix. Occurs principally October–May. Numbers are increasing. **HABITAT** Beaches, calm bays, and dumps. (See also Plate 11.)

**RING-BILLED GULL** *Larus delawarensis* (Gaviota piquianillada) 46–51cm (18–20in); wingspan 1–1.2m (3.5–4ft); male 550g, female 470g. Fairly large, with medium-sized bill. **FIRST YEAR** Mottled grayish-brown wings; gray back. Broad black tail band; bill pinkish, tipped black. **SECOND YEAR** Upperparts and mantle mostly gray; black primaries with white spot at tip. **NON-BREEDING ADULT** *Bill yellowish with black band; legs yellowish-green.* **BREEDING ADULT** White head and underparts. (Smaller than Herring Gull, more delicate head and bill, yellowish-green or grayish-green legs. Herring Gull lacks bill-ring and has pink legs.) **VOICE** A high-pitched *kee-ow kee-ow, kee-ow.* **STATUS AND RANGE** Irregular in occurrence, but generally an uncommon and local visitor or non-breeding resident in Puerto Rico and uncommon to rare in Virgin Islands. Occurs in all months, but primarily October–June. Numbers increasing. **HABITAT** Coastal harbors, lagoons, and open ground from parking lots to grassy fields. Often urban areas. (See also Plate 11.)

**HERRING GULL** *Larus argentatus* (Gaviota argéntea) 56–66cm (22–26in); wingspan 137–150cm (4.5–5ft); male 1.2kg, female 1kg. Large, with large bill. **FIRST YEAR** Back and wings heavily streaked grayish-brown, bill pinkish at base, tipped black; tail lacks clear band; *legs pink.* **SECOND YEAR** Variable gray on back and wings; outer primaries black; bill pinkish with pale gray band beyond nostril. **THIRD YEAR** Tail white with broad black band; bill yellowish with dark band. **NON-BREEDING ADULT** Heavy yellow bill with red spot near tip of lower mandible; head and underparts white; legs pink. **BREEDING ADULT** Head and underparts white. **STATUS AND RANGE** A rare and local visitor to Puerto Rico and Anegada, November–April. Very rare on other Virgin Islands. Numbers are decreasing. **HABITAT** Coastal areas, harbors, and lagoons. (See also Plate 11.)

48

2nd-year

Great Black-backed
Gull

non-br
adult

2nd-year

Lesser Black-backed
Gull

non-br
adult

non-br adult

Ring-billed
Gull

non-br adult

Herring
Gull

non-br adult

Black-legged Kittiwake
For comparison.
(see also Plates 5 & 11)

non-br adult

**LAUGHING GULL** *Leucophaeus atricilla* (Gaviota gallega, Risueña, Sea gull, Gullie, Booby) 38–43cm (15–17in); wingspan 1–1.1m (39–43in); male 330g, female 290g. **BREEDING ADULT** Black head; dark gray mantle; black wingtips; reddish bill. **NON-BREEDING ADULT** Similar, but diffuse gray mark on rear of white head; bill black. **IMMATURE** Mottled gray-brown; belly whitish. **FIRST YEAR** White rump; gray sides and back; broad black tail band. **SECOND YEAR** Partial hood; spotting on tail; mantle gray. (Adult Black-headed Gull has paler gray mantle; white primaries; red bill and legs; and gray undersides to the primaries. First year has narrower black tail band; black ear-spot; and two-toned bill. Adult Bonaparte's Gull is smaller and has pale gray mantle and white in primaries. Immature has narrow tail band and pale underwing-coverts.) **VOICE** Squawky, variable *caw* and *caw-aw*. Also laugh-like *ka-ka-ka-ka-ka-ka-ka-kaa-kaa-kaaa-kaaa*. **STATUS AND RANGE** A common and widespread resident in Puerto Rico and Virgin Islands, April–September. It is irregular and rare October–March when birds move out to sea. **HABITAT** Calm bays, coastal waters, and islets. (See also Plate 11.)

**BLACK-HEADED GULL** *Chroicocephalus ridibundus* (Gaviota reidora, Gaviota cabecinegra) 39–43cm (15–17in); wingspan 1m (3.3ft); 200–320g. **FIRST YEAR** Black ear-spot; two-toned bill; narrow black tail band; gray undersides to primaries. **NON-BREEDING ADULT** Bill and legs reddish, black-tipped; mantle pale gray; outer primaries white, black-tipped. **BREEDING ADULT** Head dark brown; bill red. (Bonaparte's Gull lacks pale gray undersides to primaries.) **STATUS AND RANGE** A rare and local visitor in Puerto Rico and very rare in Virgin Islands. Occurs primarily November–March, but expected any month. Numbers are slowly increasing. **HABITAT** Coastal harbors and estuaries. (See also Plate 11.)

**BONAPARTE'S GULL** *Chroicocephalus philadelphia* (Gaviota de Bonaparte) 28–36cm (11–14in); wingspan 80–85cm (2.6–2.8ft); 180–225g. **FIRST YEAR** Black ear-spot; thin black bill; narrow black tail band; whitish undersides to primaries. **NON-BREEDING ADULT** Mantle pale gray, tail and outer primaries white; legs red. **BREEDING ADULT** Head black. (Black-headed Gull has gray undersides to primaries.) **STATUS AND RANGE** Decidedly rare visitor locally in Puerto Rico and Virgin Islands, November–January. Occurring more frequently. **HABITAT** Coastal harbors, lagoons, estuaries, and at sea. (See also Plate 11.)

**FRANKLIN'S GULL** *Leucophaeus pipixcan* (Gaviota de Franklin) 37cm (14.5in); wingspan 90cm (3ft); 280g. **FIRST YEAR** Narrow black tail band; white breast and underparts; gray back; *partial blackish hood* and *white forehead*. **NON-BREEDING ADULT** Similar, but only *partial black hood; whitish forehead*. **BREEDING ADULT** Black head; fairly dark gray mantle; *wingtips with black bar bordered with white on both sides*. (First-year and non-breeding adults have more distinctive partial black hood than Laughing Gull, which is larger, with heavier, more curved bill; darker undersides of primaries; and longer legs noticeable when standing.) **STATUS AND RANGE** A very rare visitor to Puerto Rico, November–January. Its occurrence is slowly increasing. **HABITAT** Bays and estuaries. (See also Plate 11.)

immature

Laughing Gull

non-br
adult

non-br
adult

Black-headed
Gull

non-br
adult

Bonaparte's Gull

first year

Franklin's Gull

non-br

PLATE 11    COASTAL SEABIRDS — Gulls Flying

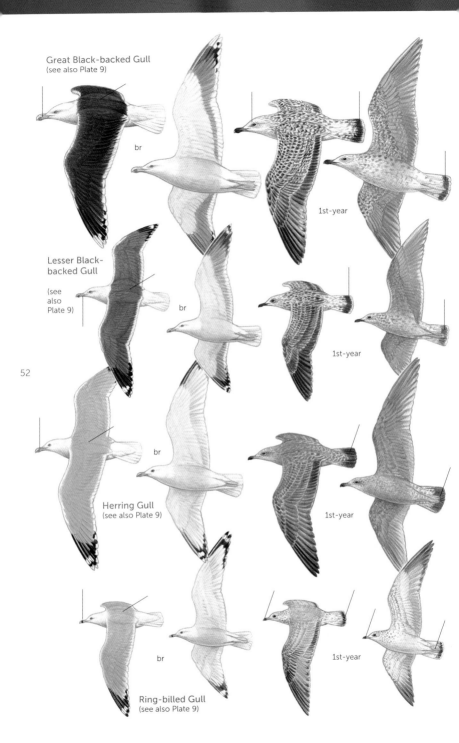

**Great Black-backed Gull**
(see also Plate 9)

br

1st-year

**Lesser Black-backed Gull**

(see also Plate 9)

br

1st-year

52

br

**Herring Gull**
(see also Plate 9)

1st-year

br

1st-year

**Ring-billed Gull**
(see also Plate 9)

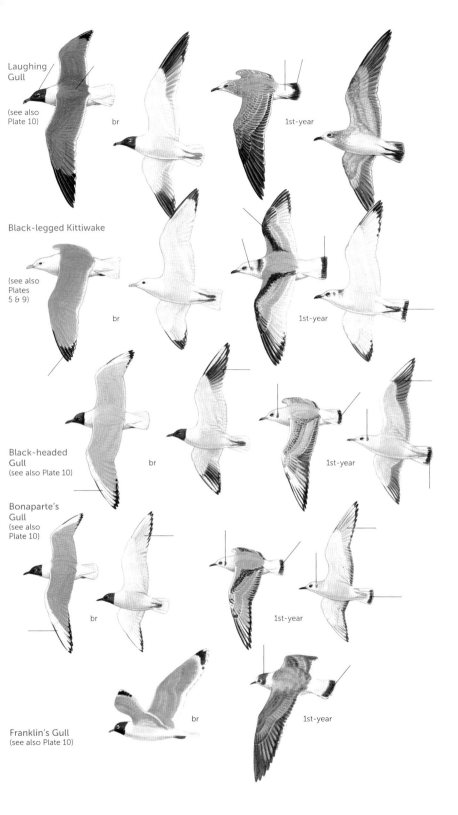

Laughing Gull

(see also Plate 10)

br

1st-year

Black-legged Kittiwake

(see also Plates 5 & 9)

br

1st-year

Black-headed Gull
(see also Plate 10)

br

1st-year

Bonaparte's Gull
(see also Plate 10)

br

1st-year

Franklin's Gull
(see also Plate 10)

br

1st-year

PLATE 12    COASTAL SEABIRDS — Pelicans, Skimmer, and Cormorant

## Skimmers

Large tern-like white and black waterbirds that use their distinctive bill to skim the water surface to feed on small fish.

**BLACK SKIMMER** *Rynchops niger* (Rayador americano) 40–51cm (16–20in); wingspan 1.1–1.3m (3.5–4.2ft); male 350g, female 250g. **BEHAVIOR** Plows water surface with bill, often nocturnal. **DESCRIPTION** Unmistakable *scissor-like black and orange bill* with lower mandible much longer than the upper. **ADULT** Black above, white below. **IMMATURE** Upperparts mottled blackish-brown. **STATUS AND RANGE** A rare but annual migrant off coast of Tortola, a very rare migrant in Puerto Rico and Anegada, and a vagrant elsewhere in Virgin Islands. Occurs primarily April–November. **HABITAT** Calm coastal bays, lagoons, and estuaries. Sometimes occurs well offshore.

## Cormorants

Large, long-necked birds with hooked bills. Those in the region are black with distinctively colored throat patches. They inhabit coastal waters and inland lakes. Cormorants swim with their heads cocked up and their bodies low in the water. They dive expertly in pursuit of fish. All species sit with wings spread to dry their feathers.

**DOUBLE-CRESTED CORMORANT** *Phalacrocorax auritus* (Cormorán crestado) 74–89cm (29–35in); 1.7kg. **BEHAVIOR** *Sits with wings spread*, dives, flocks. **DESCRIPTION** Large, with long neck and *slender, hooked bill*. (Shorter tail than vagrant Neotropic Cormorant, especially noticeable in flight. Also decidedly smaller bulk and thinner bill.) **BREEDING ADULT** Black. Yellowish-orange skin at bill base and chin; small ear-tufts sometimes visible. **NON-BREEDING ADULT** Skin at bill base and chin paler orange; lacks ear-tufts. **IMMATURE** Brown; paler below; skin at bill base and chin pale yellowish-orange. **STATUS AND RANGE** Rare wanderer and non-breeding resident to Puerto Rico and US Virgin Islands, primarily November–April. Very rare in British Virgin Islands, but several recent sightings. Expanding range in region. **HABITAT** Inland and calm coastal waters. Frequents saltwater more than Neotropic Cormorant.

54

## Pelicans

Large waterbirds that use their huge throat pouches to catch fish, often from spectacular dives. The resident Brown Pelican prefers coastal waters. Often in small flocks flying just above wave crests with wingbeats in perfect unison.

**BROWN PELICAN** *Pelecanus occidentalis* (Pelícano pardo, Alcatraz) 107–137cm (4.5–5.5ft); wingspan 2–2.3m (6.8–7.6ft); 3–4kg. **BEHAVIOR** Plunges into sea from substantial height. Congregates in large mangrove roosts. **DESCRIPTION** Large size, *massive bill*, dark coloration. **BREEDING ADULT** Reddish-brown hindneck and back of head, though infrequently the hindneck remains white. **NON-BREEDING ADULT** White hindneck and back of head. **IMMATURE** Overall grayish-brown; paler below. **STATUS AND RANGE** Common year-round resident in Puerto Rico and Virgin Islands. Breeds on offshore islands, building nest in mangroves. In Puerto Rico breeds mostly in cays of La Parguera and Cayo Conejo off Vieques Island. Breeds widely in Virgin Islands. Migrants augment local numbers November–February. Endangered as a breeding bird in region. **HABITAT** Bays, lagoons, other calm coastal waters, inland reservoirs, and larger rivers.

**AMERICAN WHITE PELICAN** *Pelecanus erythrorhynchos* (Pelícano blanco) 125–165cm (4–4.3ft); wingspan 2.4–3m (8–10ft); 5–9kg. Very large size, *massive bill*, white coloration. Black primaries and outer secondaries. **BREEDING ADULT** Bill orange-yellow, knob on upper mandible; hindcrown and hindneck tan. **NON-BREEDING ADULT** Bill orange-yellow; hindcrown and hindneck gray. **IMMATURE** Bill gray. **STATUS AND RANGE** Very rare in Puerto Rico and a vagrant in Virgin Islands. May occur in any month. **HABITAT** Freshwater lakes and coastal bays.

Black Skimmer

adult

Double-crested Cormorant

br

non-br adult

imm

non-br adult

br

imm

Brown Pelican

American White Pelican

non-br adult

 PLATE 13     LONG-LEGGED WETLAND BIRDS (mostly Waders)

## Ibises and Spoonbill

Ibises are fairly large waders with long, decurved bills that forage by probing in muddy fields or shallow wetlands. The unusual bill of the spoonbill has sensors at its tip for detecting prey. Both groups fly with neck outstretched.

**WHITE IBIS** *Eudocimus albus* (Ibis blanco, Coco blanco) 56–71cm (22–28in); wingspan 90cm (3ft); male 1040g, female 760g. **BEHAVIOR** Flocks. **ADULT** White; *long, down-curved, reddish bill*. **IMMATURE** Brown; belly and rump white. **FLIGHT** Outstretched neck, wingtips black. **STATUS AND RANGE** A fairly common but local year-round resident in Puerto Rico, primarily along the north coast. It became established in early 2000s. The White Ibis was later introduced on Necker Island in British Virgin Islands in 2010, where it breeds. The flock numbers approximately 20 birds, some of which may leave periodically. **HABITAT** Freshwater swamps and grassy wetlands, and saltwater lagoons.

**GLOSSY IBIS** *Plegadis falcinellus* (Ibis lustroso, Cigüeña, Coco prieto) 56–64cm (22–25in); wingspan 90cm (3ft); 500–1000g. **BEHAVIOR** Flocks. **ADULT** Very dark, with *long, down-curved bill*. **IMMATURE** Paler. (Immature White Ibis has a white rather than dark abdomen.) **VOICE** Low grunts and high-pitched bleats. **FLIGHT** Outstretched neck. **STATUS AND RANGE** Common year-round resident in Puerto Rico, primarily in southwest and along north coast. Very rare on St. Croix and a vagrant on other Virgin Islands. **HABITAT** Mudflats, marshy savannas, and freshwater ponds and lagoons.

**SCARLET IBIS** *Eudocimus ruber* (Ibis escarlata) 58.5cm (23in); wingspan 90cm (3ft); 1.2kg. **BEHAVIOR:** Flocks. **ADULT** Unmistakable *scarlet plumage*; long, down-curved bill; black wingtips. **NON-BREEDING** Bill pinkish. **BREEDING** Bill blackish. **IMMATURE** White below; brownish above; pale back and rump tinged pinkish-gray. (Immature White Ibis shows no pinkish on rump or back.) Pink birds indicate interbreeding with White Ibis. **STATUS AND RANGE** Introduced on Necker Island in British Virgin Islands in 2010, where it began breeding shortly thereafter. The flock is now approximately 50 birds. Individuals and even small flocks now occur with increasing frequency on other Virgin Islands and Puerto Rico. **HABITAT** Coastal swamps, lagoons, and mangroves.

**ROSEATE SPOONBILL** *Platalea ajaja* (Espátula rosada) 66–81cm (26–32in); wingspan 1.3m (4ft); 1.5kg. **BEHAVIOR** Flocks. Waves bill through water to feed. **ADULT** *Pink coloration*; distinctive *spatula-like bill*. **IMMATURE** White with some pink. **STATUS AND RANGE** Very rare in southwestern Puerto Rico. A vagrant on Anegada in British Virgin Islands. Recent introduction attempts on Necker Island have been unsuccessful. **HABITAT** Shallow saltwater lagoons and edges of mudflats.

## Flamingos

Large pink waders with very long neck and legs. Bill sharply bent downward. Filter small crustaceans and mollusks from shallow lagoons. The tongue is specially adapted for straining water.

**AMERICAN FLAMINGO** *Phoenicopterus ruber* (Flamenco americano, Greater flamingo, Fillymingo) 1.1–1.2m (42–48in); wingspan 1.5m (5ft); 2.5kg. **BEHAVIOR** Flocks. Feeds with head upside down. **ADULT** *Orangish-pink coloration*; long legs and neck; *strangely curved bill*. **IMMATURE** Much paler. **FLIGHT** Head and neck outstretched and drooping; flight feathers black. **VOICE** Goose-like honks. **STATUS AND RANGE** Reintroduced on Anegada (1992) and Necker Island (2006) in British Virgin Islands. Both flocks now number over 300 birds, and breeding is well established. A sizable flock recently began nesting at Josiah's Bay, Tortola. It is an irregular, uncommon, but increasingly frequent visitor to neighboring Virgin Islands. Rare and local visitor in Puerto Rico, but increasing and recently found nesting in small numbers at the eastern tip. Repopulation of the region is well underway. Threatened as a breeding bird in region. **HABITAT** Shallow lagoons and coastal estuaries.

adult

adult

imm

White
Ibis

adult

imm

Glossy Ibis

non-br adult

Scarlet Ibis

imm

adult

imm

adult

American
Flamingo

Roseate
Spoonbill

adult

imm

### Herons, egrets, and bitterns

Most wade in shallow water and hunt by stealth, then spear prey with their long, pointed bills. Bitterns inhabit dense vegetation and often "freeze" with bills pointed upward to avoid detection. All fly with the head drawn back and the neck forming an *S* shape.

**GREAT BLUE HERON** *Ardea herodias* (Garzón cenizo, Garzón azulado, Garzón ceniciento, Blue gaulin, Gray gaulin, Arsnicker, Morgan) 107–132cm (42–52in); wingspan 1.8m (6ft); 2.4kg. *Largest heron* in region. Dark phase—Primarily bluish-gray; large, straight bill; black eyebrow stripe, white ear-coverts. White phase—White overall; yellow bill and legs. (Great Egret is white overall but has black legs.) **VOICE** Deep, throaty croak like large frog, *guarr*. **STATUS AND RANGE** Common migrant and non-breeding resident in Puerto Rico and Virgin Islands, primarily October–April. Uncommon to rare in other months. Rarely breeds. White phase extremely rare in West Indies. **HABITAT** Ponds and lagoons.

**LITTLE BLUE HERON** *Egretta caerulea* (Garza azul, Garza blanca [immature], Garza pinta, Blue gaulin, White gaulin [immature]) 56–71cm (22–28in); wingspan 1m (3.3ft); 340g. Medium size; *bill grayish, tipped black*. **ADULT** Blue-gray overall with a maroon-brown neck. **IMMATURE** Initially white; later mottled with dark feathers. (White immature is distinguished from Snowy Egret by the pale gray base of its bill, lack of yellow on lores, and greenish legs.) **VOICE** Croaking, very throaty *gruuh*. **STATUS AND RANGE** Common year-round resident in Puerto Rico and Virgin Islands. Migrants augment local numbers October–March. **HABITAT** Calm, shallow freshwater and saltwater areas, particularly mangrove shorelines and salt pond edges, infrequent in swift-flowing rivers and streams.

**TRICOLORED HERON** *Egretta tricolor* (Garza pechiblanca, Garza tricolor, Louisiana heron, Gaulin, Switching-neck) 61–71cm (24–28in); wingspan 90cm (3ft); 420g. **ADULT** Gray with *white belly and undertail-coverts*. **IMMATURE** Browner. **STATUS AND RANGE** Common year-round resident in Puerto Rico, uncommon in US Virgin Islands, rare in British. Migrants augment local numbers October–March. **HABITAT** Mangrove swamps and saltwater lagoons, infrequently freshwater wetlands.

**GREEN HERON** *Butorides virescens* (Martinete, Green-backed heron, Least pond gaulin, Little gaulin, Water witch, Poor Joe, Bitlin, Gaulching) 40–48cm (16–19in); wingspan 65cm (2ft); 210g. Small, with short neck, dark coloration, and greenish-yellow to orangish legs. **BREEDING ADULT** Legs bright orange. **IMMATURE** Heavily streaked below. (Striated Heron has pale gray cheeks and sides of neck.) **VOICE** Distinctive, piercing *skyow* when flushed; softer series of *kek*, *kak*, or *que* notes when undisturbed. **STATUS AND RANGE** Common year-round resident throughout Puerto Rico and Virgin Islands. Migrants minimally augment local numbers. **HABITAT** All water bodies at all elevations, from puddles to large lagoons.

**STRIATED HERON** *Butorides striata* (Garcita estriada) 40–48cm (16–19in); 160g. Small, with short neck, greenish-yellow to orangish legs. (Green Heron has deep reddish-brown cheek and sides of neck.) **IMMATURE** Heavily streaked below. **VOICE** *Kek*, *kak*, or *que* notes; piercing *skyow* when disturbed. **STATUS AND RANGE** Recent occurrence in southwestern Puerto Rico, where very rare. Vagrant on St. Thomas and St. John. **HABITAT** Primarily Cartagena Lagoon but also other water bodies.

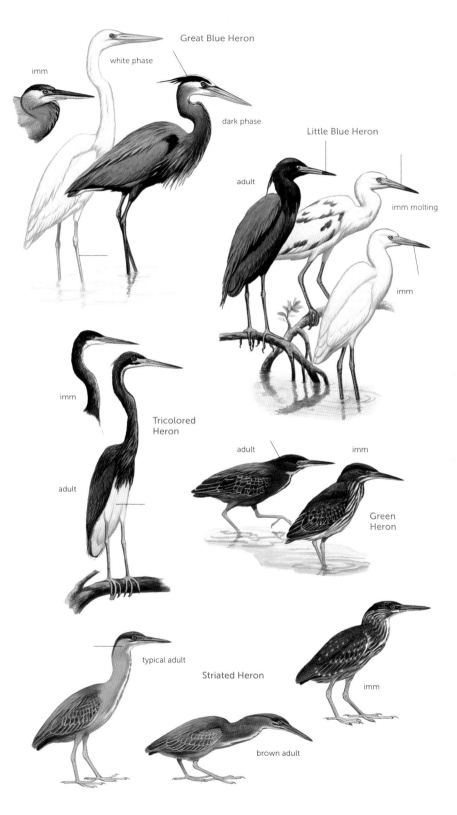

Great Blue Heron

imm

white phase

dark phase

Little Blue Heron

adult

imm molting

imm

Tricolored Heron

imm

adult

adult

imm

Green Heron

typical adult

Striated Heron

brown adult

imm

**LITTLE EGRET** *Egretta garzetta* (Garceta común) 55–65cm (22–25.5in); wingspan 90cm (3ft); 500g. **BEHAVIOR** Usually occurs as single individuals, but may be gregarious with other herons. **ADULT** White overall. Usually *two long head plumes*; bill and legs black, feet yellow. **NON-BREEDING** Gray-green lores. **BREEDING** Reddish lores. (Differs from Snowy Egret primarily by long head plumes, which are less distinctive in breeding and absent in non-breeding Snowy. Little Egret has slightly longer bill. Also, facial skin reddish during breeding and bluish-gray or greenish-gray in non-breeding compared to bright yellow or greenish-yellow in Snowy. Next to Snowy, Little Egret often appears larger, with longer, thinner neck and longer, thicker legs.) A dark morph, which is gray, sometimes with a white chin and throat, does not occur in West Indies. **STATUS AND RANGE** Decidedly rare wanderer or non-breeding resident in Puerto Rico, and very rare in Virgin Islands, where reported from St. John and St. Croix. Recently established breeding populations on Barbados and Antigua may lead to increased sightings in our region. May be present during any month. **HABITAT** Coastal ponds and lagoons.

**SNOWY EGRET** *Egretta thula* (Garza blanca, White gaulin) 51–71cm (20–28in); wingspan 1.1m (3.5ft); 370g. **BEHAVIOR** Gregarious. **ADULT** White overall. *Legs black; feet and lores yellow*; bill thin and black. **IMMATURE** Legs dark in front and greenish-yellow in back. (See Little Egret.) **VOICE** Guttural *guarr*, higher pitched and more raspy than Great Egret. **STATUS AND RANGE** Common year-round resident in Puerto Rico and larger Virgin Islands, while uncommon to rare on the smaller ones. **HABITAT** Freshwater swamps, but also riverbanks and saltwater lagoons.

**GREAT EGRET** *Ardea alba* (Garza real, Garzón blanco, White gaulin, White morgan, Common egret, American egret) 89–107cm (35–42in); wingspan 1.3m (4.3ft); 870g. **BEHAVIOR** Gregarious. **DESCRIPTION** Very large, white overall, with *yellow bill* and *black legs*. (See Cattle Egret.) **VOICE** Hoarse, throaty croak. **STATUS AND RANGE** Common year-round resident in Puerto Rico and larger Virgin Islands, while uncommon to rare on smaller ones. Migrants augment local numbers September–April. **HABITAT** Large freshwater and saltwater swamps, grassy marshes, riverbanks, and shallows behind reefs. Sometimes open areas such as grasslands and golf courses.

**REDDISH EGRET** *Egretta rufescens* (Garza rojiza, Gaulin) 69–81cm (27–32in); wingspan 1.2m (4ft); 450g. **BEHAVIOR** *Dances in water* in pursuit of prey. **ADULT** *Black-tipped bill, pinkish at base; ruffled neck feathers*. Dark phase—Grayish; head and neck reddish-brown. White phase—White overall. (Little Blue Heron at all ages has gray base to bill.) **IMMATURE** Bill entirely dark; neck feathers unruffled. **VOICE** Squawks and croaks. **STATUS AND RANGE** Decidedly rare wanderer to Puerto Rico and very rare in Virgin Islands, October–February. **HABITAT** Shallow, protected coastal waters, also swamp edges.

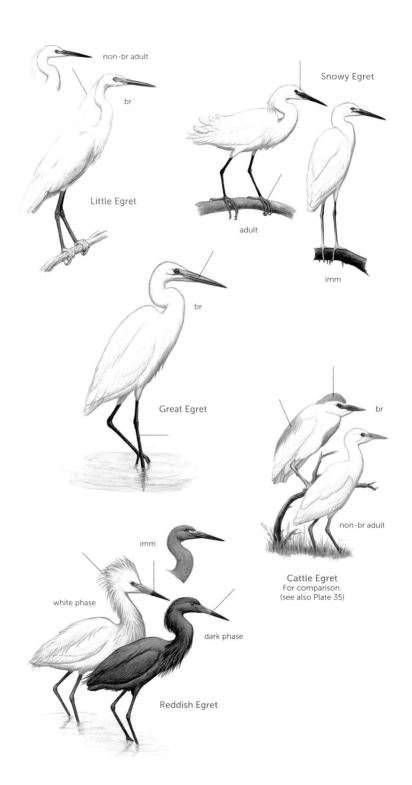

non-br adult

br

Little Egret

Snowy Egret

adult

imm

br

Great Egret

br

non-br adult

Cattle Egret
For comparison.
(see also Plate 35)

imm

white phase

dark phase

Reddish Egret

**AMERICAN BITTERN** *Botaurus lentiginosus* (Yaboa americana, Stake-driver, Shide-poke) 58–61cm (23–24in); wingspan 1.1m (3.5ft); 700g. **BEHAVIOR** Often points bill upward. **DESCRIPTION** Mottled brown overall with *black neck mark*. **FLIGHT** Blackish wingtips. (Immature night-herons darker and lack black on neck and wingtips. Immature Green Heron is smaller, darker, and lacks a black neck mark.) **VOICE** Peculiar pumping sound, *oong-ká-chunk*! **STATUS AND RANGE** Very rare migrant and non-breeding resident in Puerto Rico and larger Virgin Islands, September–April. **HABITAT** Dense vegetation of freshwater swamps.

**LEAST BITTERN** *Ixobrychus exilis* (Martinetito, Bitlin, Gaulin) 28–35cm (11–14in); wingspan 45cm (1.5ft); 90g. Small. Primarily reddish-yellow, with *cream-colored patch on upperwing*. **ADULT MALE** Black crown and back. **ADULT FEMALE** Dark brown crown and back. **IMMATURE** Paler brown crown and back; breast heavily streaked. **VOICE** *Koo-koo-koo-koo*, almost a coo, first syllable often higher, call accelerates slightly. Also, loud, harsh *kack*, sometimes in series. **STATUS AND RANGE** Fairly common year-round resident in Puerto Rico but rare to very rare in Virgin Islands, occurring only on larger islands. **HABITAT** Dense vegetation of freshwater swamps, often with cattails; also mangroves.

**YELLOW-CROWNED NIGHT-HERON** *Nyctanassa violacea* (Yaboa común, Night gaulin, Gray gaulin, Crabcatcher, Crabeater) 56–71cm (22–28in); wingspan 1.1m (3.5ft); 690g. **BEHAVIOR** Primarily nocturnal. **DESCRIPTION** Medium-sized, with chunky appearance. **ADULT** Gray underparts, *black-and-white head markings*. **IMMATURE** Grayish-brown with white flecks. **FLIGHT** Legs and feet extend beyond tail. (See Black-crowned Night-Heron.) **VOICE** Distinctive *quark* heard before sunup and after sundown. **STATUS AND RANGE** Common year-round resident in Puerto Rico and Virgin Islands. Migrants augment local numbers. **HABITAT** Mangrove swamps and, less frequently, freshwater areas, mudflats, and even dry thickets away from water.

62 **BLACK-CROWNED NIGHT-HERON** *Nycticorax nycticorax* (Yaboa real, Night gaulin, Crabcatcher) 58–71cm (23–28in); wingspan 1.1m (3.7ft); 880g. **BEHAVIOR** Nocturnal. **DESCRIPTION** Medium-sized, with chunky appearance. **ADULT** Black crown and back; white face, underparts, and head plumes. **IMMATURE** Brown with white flecks. **FLIGHT** Only feet extend beyond tail. (Browner, with larger white flecks on wings and upperparts, a thinner bill, and shorter legs than immature Yellow-crowned Night-Heron.) **VOICE** Distinctive *quark* heard before sunup and after sundown. **STATUS AND RANGE** A locally common year-round resident in Puerto Rico and large US Virgin Islands, it is rare in the British Virgin Islands. **HABITAT** Freshwater swamps; less frequently brackish lagoons and salt ponds.

**LIMPKIN** *Aramus guarauna* (Carrao) 69cm (27in); wingspan 1.1m (3.5ft); 1kg. **BEHAVIOR** Primarily nocturnal; wades among vegetation in search of snails. **DESCRIPTION** Large, long-legged, long-necked wading bird, brown with white streaks. Long, slightly down-curved bill. **VOICE** Loud, piercing *carrao*, which gives rise to its Spanish name. **STATUS AND RANGE** An uncommon and local resident in Puerto Rico, the species has increased and spread rapidly in recent years to many parts of the island. Threatened as a breeding bird in region. **HABITAT** Herbaceous freshwater wetlands, wooded floodplains, upland forests. Found where apple snails (*Pomacea* sp.), its primary food, occur.

American Bittern

Least Bittern

adult

imm

Yellow-crowned
Night-Heron

imm

adult

imm

adult

imm

adult

imm

adult

Black-crowned
Night-Heron

Limpkin

Shorebirds

A composite of many bird families characterized by relatively long legs and necks, and usually long, thin, pointed bills. Most occur in shallow water or on tidal flats, where they probe for invertebrates. Almost all are highly gregarious and often occur in mixed feeding assemblages. In the region the vast majority are migratory and thus are seen in non-breeding plumage.

**AMERICAN AVOCET** *Recurvirostra americana* (Avoceta) 40–51cm (16–20in); 300g. **BEHAVIOR** Flocks. **DESCRIPTION** Large, *black and white*, with *sharply upturned bill*. **NON-BREEDING** Head and neck gray. **BREEDING** Head and neck cinnamon. **VOICE** High-pitched, melodious *klee*. **STATUS AND RANGE** A decidedly rare non-breeding resident in Puerto Rico, primarily July–January and April. Occurs most frequently in wetlands of southwest coast. A vagrant in Virgin Islands. **HABITAT** Shallow wetland borders, salt ponds, and estuaries.

**HUDSONIAN GODWIT** *Limosa haemastica* (Barga aliblanca) 33–40cm (13–16in); male 220g, female 290g. *Long, slightly upturned bill, pinkish at base; black tail with white base.* **NON-BREEDING** Gray overall, paler below; white eyebrow stripe. **BREEDING** Dark reddish-brown below, heavily barred. Female paler. **FLIGHT ABOVE** White wing stripe and base of tail. **FLIGHT BELOW** Blackish wing linings and white wing stripe. **VOICE** *Ta-wit*, but rarely calls in West Indies. **STATUS AND RANGE** A rare migrant in Puerto Rico and to St. Croix, primarily September–October, sometimes occurring through March. It is very rare on other Virgin Islands. **HABITAT** Grassy freshwater pond edges and mudflats.

**MARBLED GODWIT** *Limosa fedoa* (Barga jaspeada) 40–51cm (16–20in); male 320g, female 420g. Large, with *no white on rump. Long, slightly upturned bill.* **NON-BREEDING** Pale tan underparts. **BREEDING** Reddish-brown underparts barred black. **FLIGHT ABOVE** Cinnamon-colored; blackish primary wing-coverts. **FLIGHT BELOW** Cinnamon-colored wing linings with paler flight feathers. **STATUS AND RANGE** A very rare migrant to Puerto Rico, occurring primarily late August to early April. Vagrant in Virgin Islands. **HABITAT** Mudflats and marshes.

**BLACK-NECKED STILT** *Himantopus mexicanus* (Viuda, Redshank, Soldier, Crackpot soldier, Telltale, Ally-moor, Civil) 34–39cm (13.5–15.5in); 170g. **BEHAVIOR** Flocks. **DESCRIPTION** Large, with *long pink legs, black upperparts, and white underparts.* **FLIGHT** Black wings; white underparts, tail, and lower back, extending as V on back. **VOICE** Loud, raucous *wit, wit, wit, wit, wit*. **STATUS AND RANGE** A year-round resident in Puerto Rico and Virgin Islands, it is generally a common breeding resident March–October, sometimes becoming scarce outside the breeding season. **HABITAT** Mudflats, saltwater and freshwater ponds, and open mangrove swamps.

**AMERICAN OYSTERCATCHER** *Haematopus palliatus* (Ostrero, Caracolero, Whelkcracker) 43–54cm (17–21in); 600g. Large, with *black hood* and *long, heavy bill.* **ADULT** *Orange-red bill; pinkish legs.* **IMMATURE** Dull pinkish bill, dark at tip. Gray legs. **FLIGHT** Broad white wing stripe and uppertail. **VOICE** Emphatic, coarsely whistled *wheep*. **STATUS AND RANGE** Fairly common but local year-round resident in Puerto Rico and Virgin Islands. **HABITAT** Rocky headlands, stony beaches, offshore islands, and cays.

American
Avocet

br

non-br

non-br

br

Marbled
Godwit

Hudsonian
Godwit

br

non-br

non-br

Black-necked
Stilt

adult

American
Oystercatcher

PLATE 18   LONG-LEGGED WETLAND BIRDS (mostly Waders)

**GREATER YELLOWLEGS** *Tringa melanoleuca* (Playero guineilla mayor, Snipe) 33–38cm (13–15in); 170g. **BEHAVIOR** Flocks. **DESCRIPTION** Large, with *orangish-yellow legs*. Long, straight bill often appears slightly upturned and two-toned. (Bill of Lesser Yellowlegs is relatively shorter, and thinner and darker at base.) **FLIGHT** Dark above; white uppertail-coverts. Similar to Lesser Yellowlegs. **VOICE** Loud, raspy, three- or four-note whistle, *cu-cu-cu* or *klee-klee-cu*. **STATUS AND RANGE** A common migrant and non-breeding resident in Puerto Rico, US Virgin Islands, and Anegada; it is uncommon on other British Virgin Islands. Occurs most frequently during southbound migration August–October, less frequently as a non-breeding resident and northbound migrant November–May, and least frequently June–July. **HABITAT** Mudflats and shallows of freshwater and saltwater bodies.

**LESSER YELLOWLEGS** *Tringa flavipes* (Playero guineilla menor, Snipe) 25–28cm (9.75–11in); 80g. **BEHAVIOR** Flocks. **DESCRIPTION** Medium-sized, with *orangish-yellow legs* and thin, straight bill. **FLIGHT** Dark above; white uppertail-coverts. **VOICE** One- or two-note *cu-cu*, softer and more nasal than Greater Yellowlegs. **STATUS AND RANGE** A common migrant and non-breeding resident in Puerto Rico and Virgin Islands. It occurs most frequently during southbound migration August–October, less frequently as a non-breeding resident and northbound migrant November–May, and least frequently June–July. **HABITAT** Mudflats and shallows of both freshwater and saltwater bodies. (See also Plate 23.)

**EASTERN WILLET** *Tringa semipalmata* (Playero aliblanco, Tell-bill-willy, Pilly-willick, Longlegs, Pond bird, Duck snipe, Laughing jackass) 38–40cm (15–16in); 200g. Large. Light gray, with gray legs and thick bill. **BREEDING** Fine black stripes on head, neck, and breast. **NON-BREEDING** More uniformly gray. **FLIGHT** *Black-and-white wing pattern*. **VOICE** Sharp *will willet, will willet*, repeated several times; also sharp whistles. **STATUS AND RANGE** A fairly common but local breeding resident and migrant in Puerto Rico and Virgin Islands, where breeds mid-April to July, but a few may occur year-round. Most likely migrates to South America after breeding. Both willets considered a single species by AOS. **HABITAT** Tidal flats; also borders of saltwater and freshwater bodies.

66

**WESTERN WILLET** *Tringa inornata* (Playero aliblanco, Tell-bill-willy, Pilly-willick, Longlegs, Pond bird, Duck snipe, Laughing jackass) 38–43cm (15–17in); 250g. Very similar to Eastern Willet but slightly larger, with longer neck, legs, and bill. **NON-BREEDING** Pale gray overall, lighter below. **BREEDING** Fine black stripes on head, neck, and breast. **FLIGHT** *Black-and-white wing pattern*. **VOICE** Same as Eastern Willet. **STATUS AND RANGE** Unclear due to similarity to Eastern Willet and recent taxonomic separation from latter. Likely a fairly common to uncommon migrant and non-breeding resident in Puerto Rico and Virgin Islands. May be predominant willet in region October–March. Both willets considered a single species by AOS. **HABITAT** Tidal flats; also borders of saltwater and freshwater bodies.

**RUFF** *Calidris pugnax* (Combatiente) Male 30cm (12in), female 23–28cm (9–11in); 180g. **BEHAVIOR** Feeds sluggishly, often in company of Yellowlegs. **NON-BREEDING** Fairly chunky; erect posture; *whitish around base of bill*; pale gray breast, sometimes scaled; relatively short and slightly drooped bill. Legs often pale, varying from dull yellow to orange, green, or brown. **BREEDING MALE** Extremely variable, but all have elaborate breast and head feathers. **BREEDING FEMALE** Variable. Similar to non-breeding, but darker. **FLIGHT** The U-shaped band around rump is distinctive. **STATUS AND RANGE** A rare to very rare migrant to Puerto Rico and vagrant to larger Virgin Islands including St. Thomas, St. Croix, and Anegada. Occurs primarily late August–October, and May–June. **HABITAT** Mudflats and borders of ponds and lagoons.

Greater
Yellowlegs

Lesser
Yellowlegs

Eastern
Willet

br

non-br

imm

Western
Willet

non-br

non-br

Ruff

br ♂

br ♀

non-br

PLATE 19   MEDIUM-LEGGED WETLAND BIRDS (mostly Waders)

**WHIMBREL** *Numenius phaeopus* (Playero picocorvo, Hudsonian curlew) 38–46cm (15–18in); male 360g, female 400g. **BEHAVIOR** Flocks. **DESCRIPTION** Relatively large, with striped crown and *long, down-curved bill*. **FLIGHT** Underwings barred, without cinnamon color. A vagrant subspecies from Eurasia (*N. p. phaeopus*) displays white rump and lower back. **VOICE** Harsh, rapid whistle, *whip-whip-whip-whip*. **STATUS AND RANGE** An uncommon and local migrant to Puerto Rico, St. Croix, and Anegada, primarily mid-August to mid-October but may remain as a non-breeding resident. Rare to very rare on other Virgin Islands. Occurs in all months, but least frequently June–July. **HABITAT** Edges of coastal lagoons and ponds, mangrove mudflats, swamps, and marshes. Frequents areas with fiddler crabs.

**DUNLIN** *Calidris alpina* (Playero espaldicolorado, Red-backed sandpiper) 20–23cm (8–9in); 55g. **BEHAVIOR** Feeds with slow, deliberate movements. Flocks. **DESCRIPTION** *Heavy bill, distinctively drooping at tip*; short-necked; hunched appearance. **NON-BREEDING** Gray wash on breast, head, and upperparts. **BREEDING** Black belly and reddish back. **FLIGHT** White wing stripe; white rump divided by black bar. **VOICE** Distinctive harsh, nasal *tzeep*. **STATUS AND RANGE** A very rare migrant and non-breeding resident in Puerto Rico and US Virgin Islands. A vagrant in British Virgin Islands. Occurs late August–April. **HABITAT** Borders of still water, particularly mudflats. (See also Plate 23.)

**CURLEW SANDPIPER** *Calidris ferruginea* (Playero zarapito) 18–23cm (7–9in); 60g. *Bill slightly down-curved throughout its length.* **FLIGHT** White rump. (Dunlin has white rump divided by black bar, and bill down-curved only at tip.) **NON-BREEDING ADULT** Upperparts brownish-gray; underparts white. **BREEDING MALE** Reddish-brown. **BREEDING FEMALE** Duller. **FLIGHT** Entirely white rump. **VOICE** A soft *chirrup*. **STATUS AND RANGE** A very rare southbound wanderer in Puerto Rico September–October and much less frequently April–June. A vagrant in Virgin Islands. **HABITAT** Mudflats, marshes, and beaches.

68

**STILT SANDPIPER** *Calidris himantopus* (Playero patilargo) 20–22cm (8–8.5in); 60g. **BEHAVIOR** Flocks. **DESCRIPTION** *Dull greenish legs*; whitish eyebrow stripe. *Long bill, thick at base, slightly drooped at tip.* (Dowitchers have longer, straighter bills.) **NON-BREEDING** Grayish above, whitish below; pale eyebrow stripe. **BREEDING** Reddish-brown ear-patch and heavily barred underparts. **FLIGHT** *White rump*; whitish tail. **VOICE** Very soft, unmusical, and unabrasive *cue*. **STATUS AND RANGE** Generally, a common migrant locally in Puerto Rico and Virgin Islands, primarily late August–early November during southbound migration, less common as a non-breeding resident December–April. May occur in large flocks. Numbers vary year to year, and it occurs in all months. **HABITAT** Mudflats and shallow lagoons. (See also Plate 23.)

Whimbrel

*hudsonicus*

*phaeopus*

non-br

Dunlin

Curlew
Sandpiper

non-br

non-br

br

br

non-br

Stilt
Sandpiper

non-br

PLATE 20    MEDIUM-LEGGED WETLAND BIRDS (mostly Waders)

**SPOTTED SANDPIPER** *Actitis macularius* (Playero coleador) 18–20cm (7–8in); 40g. **BEHAVIOR** Distinctive *teetering walk*. **NON-BREEDING** White underparts; *dark mark on side of neck; orangish base of bill*. **BREEDING** *Dark spots on underparts; orange bill with black tip*. **FLIGHT** *Shallow, rapid wingbeats*; white wing stripe. **VOICE** Whistled *we-weet*. **STATUS AND RANGE** Generally a common migrant and non-breeding resident in Puerto Rico and Virgin Islands August–May, less common during other months. **HABITAT** Water edges of mangroves, coastlines, and streams. (See also Plate 23.)

**SOLITARY SANDPIPER** *Tringa solitaria* (Playero solitario) 19–23cm (7.5–9in); 50g. **BEHAVIOR** *Bobs body frequently*; often solitary. **DESCRIPTION** *White eye-ring*, dark upperparts, black barring on outertail feathers; dark greenish legs; black mark down center of rump with white on either side. **FLIGHT** *Wingbeats deep; flight erratic*. Dark above; bars on white-edged tail; underwings dark. **VOICE** Series of emphatic whistles, *weet-weet-weet*, when alarmed. Also a soft *pip* or *weet* when undisturbed. **STATUS AND RANGE** Varies yearly but generally a common southbound migrant September–October in Puerto Rico, St. Croix, and St. John; uncommon on St. Thomas and Anegada; and rare in remaining Virgin Islands. It is less frequent northbound March–April, while some occur as a non-breeding resident November–February. **HABITAT** Freshwater edges. (See also Plate 23.)

**WILSON'S SNIPE** *Gallinago delicata* (Becasina, Common snipe) 27–29cm (10.5–11.5in); 100g. *Long bill; striped head* and back, reddish-brown tail. (Similar to dowitchers, but has more prominently striped head and back, lacks white rump patch.) **FLIGHT** Zigzag flight while uttering call note. **VOICE** Guttural squawk when flushed. **STATUS AND RANGE** Of irregular occurrence, but generally an uncommon migrant and non-breeding resident in Puerto Rico and Virgin Islands, primarily October–April. **HABITAT** Grassy freshwater edges and flooded agricultural fields. (See also Plate 23.)

**SHORT-BILLED DOWITCHER** *Limnodromus griseus* (Agujeta piquicorta, Chorlo pico corto) 26–30cm (10–12in); 100g. **BEHAVIOR** Flocks. *Feeds with vertical bill thrusts* (sewing machine–like). **DESCRIPTION** *Very long, straight bill*. **NON-BREEDING** Gray above, whitish below, pale gray breast with fine spots, white eyebrow stripe. **BREEDING** Variable. Pale reddish-brown head and breast blending to white on belly. Breast finely barred, flanks moderately barred. (See Long-billed Dowitcher.) **FLIGHT** *White rump patch extends well up back*. (Wilson's Snipe more prominently striped on head and back; lacks white rump patch.) **VOICE** In flight, soft, rapid whistle, *tu-tu-tu*, harsher when alarmed. Similar to Lesser Yellowlegs. **STATUS AND RANGE** Fairly common but local migrant and non-breeding resident in Puerto Rico and Virgin Islands, primarily August–April and rarely May–July. **HABITAT** Tidal mudflats. (See also Plate 23.)

**LONG-BILLED DOWITCHER** *Limnodromus scolopaceus* (Agujeta piquilarga, Chorlo pico largo) 28–32cm (11–12.5in); 100g. **BEHAVIOR** Flocks. *Feeds with vertical bill thrusts* (sewing machine–like). **DESCRIPTION** *Very long, straight bill*. **NON-BREEDING** Gray above, paler below, with white eyebrow stripe. **BREEDING** Reddish breast, belly, and abdomen. Breast finely barred, flanks moderately barred. (Very similar to Short-billed Dowitcher; best distinguished by call. In non-breeding Long-billed the gray of breast is darker, unspotted, and extends lower onto belly. In breeding Long-billed the reddish underparts extend to lower belly, whereas Short-billed has white belly.) **FLIGHT** *White rump patch extends well up back*. **VOICE** Thin, high-pitched *keek*, singly or in series. When flushed issues a rapid twitter. **STATUS AND RANGE** Status uncertain because of similarity with more frequent Short-billed. Apparently a rare migrant and very rare non-breeding resident in Puerto Rico, and likely of same status in Virgin Islands, though reports are few. **HABITAT** Primarily shallow fresh and brackish water, also tidal mudflats.

Spotted Sandpiper

br

non-br

non-br

non-br

Solitary
Sandpiper

non-br

Wilson's
Snipe

non-br

non-br

br

Short-billed
Dowitcher

non-br

non-br

br

Long-billed
Dowitcher

**SEMIPALMATED SANDPIPER** *Calidris pusilla* (Playero gracioso, Peep) 14–16.5cm (5.5–6.5in); 26g. **BEHAVIOR** Flocks. **DESCRIPTION** Small, with black legs. Medium-length black bill slightly longer and more drooped at tip in female than in male. The principal small sandpiper to know well. **NON-BREEDING** Grayish-brown above; whitish below. **BREEDING** Finely barred upper breast; reddish-brown tints on upperparts. **FLIGHT** Fine white wing stripe; white rump divided by black bar. **VOICE** Soft chatter; also fairly deep, hoarse *cherk*. **STATUS AND RANGE** The most abundant shorebird in the region, it is a very common southbound migrant in Puerto Rico and Virgin Islands August–October and less frequent northbound April–May. Generally, an uncommon non-breeding resident November–March. It occurs in every month. May occur in large flocks. **HABITAT** Mudflats; still water edges from puddles to salt ponds and sandy beaches. (See also Plate 23.)

**WESTERN SANDPIPER** *Calidris mauri* (Playero occidental, Peep) 15–18cm (5.75–7in); 27g. **BEHAVIOR** Often in mixed flocks with Semipalmated Sandpiper. Look for Western in slightly deeper water. **DESCRIPTION** Bill relatively long, heavy at base, narrower and drooping at tip. (Bill characters overlap with very similar Semipalmated Sandpiper. Best distinguished by voice.) **NON-BREEDING** Grayish-brown above; whitish below. **BREEDING** Reddish-brown crown, ear-patch, and scapulars. **VOICE** *Kreep*, coarser and more scratchy than Semipalmated Sandpiper. **STATUS AND RANGE** A fairly common migrant and non-breeding resident in Puerto Rico and rare in Virgin Islands August–March, most frequently during southbound migration August–October. May occur in large flocks. Overlooked because of similarity to other sandpipers. **HABITAT** Primarily mudflats.

**LEAST SANDPIPER** *Calidris minutilla* (Playero menudo, Peep) 12.5–16.5cm (5–6.5in); 21g. **BEHAVIOR** Flocks. **DESCRIPTION** Tiny. Brown with streaked breast. *Yellowish-green legs* distinguish it from all other small sandpipers. Thin bill has slightly drooping tip. **NON-BREEDING** Brown above and on breast; white belly and abdomen. **BREEDING** Plumage more mottled with reddish-brown tints. **FLIGHT** Dark above; very faint wing stripe. **VOICE** Thin, soft whistle, *wi-wi-wit*. Also whinny-like trill dropping in pitch and volume, *tr-tr-tr-tr* ... **STATUS AND RANGE** Generally a common migrant in Puerto Rico and Virgin Islands August–October and April–May; an uncommon to rare non-breeding resident November–March. A few in June–July. **HABITAT** Mudflats and still water borders. (See also Plate 23.)

**WHITE-RUMPED SANDPIPER** *Calidris fuscicollis* (Playero rabadilla blanca, Peep) 18–20cm (7–8in); 44g. **BEHAVIOR** Flocks. **DESCRIPTION** White rump. When standing, wings extend beyond tail. Easily overlooked. (Larger than Semipalmated and Western; darker gray in non-breeding plumage and darker brown in breeding plumage; breast more heavily streaked.) **NON-BREEDING** Brownish-gray above and on upper breast, appearing hooded. **BREEDING** Browner; reddish-brown tints on crown, upper back, and ear-patch. **FLIGHT** *White rump*. Fine white wing stripe. **VOICE** Mouse-like squeak, *peet*, or *jeet*. Also thin, high-pitched trill. **STATUS AND RANGE** Irregular, but generally an uncommon southbound migrant to Puerto Rico and Virgin Islands August–November and rare northbound migrant March–May. Generally arrives later and leaves later than other sandpipers. **HABITAT** Wet grassy fields, mudflats, and borders of still water. (See also Plate 23.)

**BAIRD'S SANDPIPER** *Calidris bairdii* (Playero de Baird) 18–19cm (7–7.5in); 38g. **BEHAVIOR** Picks food rather than probes; tends to feed on drier ground than similar sandpipers; occurs singly or in small groups. **DESCRIPTION** Long wings extending noticeably beyond tail give streamlined appearance. (Larger than Semipalmated and Western, and wings extend beyond tail. Browner than White-rumped Sandpiper, but best separated in flight; white on rump of Baird's divided by dark central stripe.) **NON-BREEDING** Brownish-gray above and on breast. **BREEDING** Browner, with faint reddish-brown tints. **VOICE** Frequently a musical, rolling trill in flight. **STATUS AND RANGE** A very rare migrant in Puerto Rico, and rare to very rare on St. Croix and Anegada in Virgin Islands. Occurs primarily August–October. Status poorly known because of similarity to other sandpipers. Likely more frequent than records indicate. **HABITAT** Damp grasslands and edges of inland wetlands. Often some distance from water.

Semipalmated
Sandpiper

non-br

Western
Sandpiper

br

non-br

Least
Sandpiper

non-br

non-br

non-br

White-rumped
Sandpiper

br ♂

non-br

Baird's
Sandpiper

br

non-br

**SANDERLING** *Calidris alba* (Playero arenero) 18–22cm (7–8.5in); 50g.
**BEHAVIOR** Flocks; typically advances and retreats with waves at tide line. **NON-BREEDING** The lightest-colored sandpiper; *white underparts and light gray upperparts.* Often has *black mark on bend of wing.* **BREEDING** Reddish-brown head and breast. **FLIGHT** White wing stripe; pale gray upperparts. **VOICE** Distinctive *whit.* **STATUS AND RANGE** Irregular, but generally a fairly common migrant and non-breeding resident in Puerto Rico September–April. A few occur May–August. It is uncommon in Virgin Islands. **HABITAT** Sandy beaches. (See also Plate 23.)

**RED KNOT** *Calidris canutus* (Playero gordo) 25–28cm (9.75–11in); 140g.
**BEHAVIOR** Flocks. **DESCRIPTION** Medium-sized, with chunky build, usually *greenish legs*, and *relatively short bill.* **NON-BREEDING** Gray above; white below. **BREEDING** Orangish-red face and underparts. **FLIGHT** Barred above; pale gray rump; white wing stripe; pale gray wing linings. **STATUS AND RANGE** Generally an uncommon southbound migrant in Puerto Rico September–October, less frequent northbound March–April. Rarer still as non-breeding resident November–February. It is rare on St. Croix and very rare on other Virgin Islands with ample mudflats. Sometimes occurs in numbers. **HABITAT** Sandy and rocky beaches, sandy tidal flats, mangrove lagoon edges. (See also Plate 23.)

**PECTORAL SANDPIPER** *Calidris melanotos* (Playero manchado, Playero pectoral, Grassbird) 20–24cm (8–9.5in); 100g. **BEHAVIOR** Flocks. **DESCRIPTION** Yellowish-green bill and legs; *sharp demarcation between heavily streaked breast and white belly.* **NON-BREEDING** Gray-brown upperparts, head, and breast. **BREEDING MALE** More mottled; breast heavily streaked with black. **FLIGHT** Fine white wing stripe; white rump divided by black bar. **VOICE** Low, harsh *krip.* **STATUS AND RANGE** Irregular, but some years locally common in Puerto Rico during southbound migration August–early November. Rare during northbound migration March–April. It is fairly common to uncommon on St. Croix and generally uncommon to rare on other Virgin Islands, primarily during southbound migration. Infrequently, great flocks occur. **HABITAT** Wet meadows, golf courses, and grassy areas after rains; also mudflats and mangrove lagoon edges. (See also Plate 23.)

**WILSON'S PHALAROPE** *Phalaropus tricolor* (Falaropo tricolor, Falaropo de Wilson) 23cm (9in); 50g. **BEHAVIOR** Spins on water surface to feed. **DESCRIPTION** Thin, straight black bill. **NON-BREEDING** White breast; *thin dark gray mark through eye.* **BREEDING MALE** *Reddish-tan wash on neck.* **BREEDING FEMALE** *Dark reddish-brown band from shoulder blending to black behind eye.* **FLIGHT** White rump; dark upperparts. **STATUS AND RANGE** A rare and local migrant and less frequently non-breeding resident August–May in Puerto Rico, where it occurs primarily on wetlands in the southwest. Very rare in Virgin Islands, where recorded primarily on St. Croix. **HABITAT** Shallow ponds and lagoons. (See also Plate 23.)

**RED-NECKED PHALAROPE** *Phalaropus lobatus* (Falaropo picofino) 18cm (7in); 35g. **BEHAVIOR** Spins on water surface to feed. **DESCRIPTION** Thin, straight black bill. **NON-BREEDING ADULT** Black cap; white forehead and breast; *broad black bar through eye and ear-coverts.* (Non-breeding Wilson's Phalarope has thin gray eye-stripe and longer bill.) **BREEDING FEMALE** Black cap, dark back streaked white or pale gray, *pale reddish-brown neck band*, golden wing-coverts. **BREEDING MALE** Duller than female. (Non-breeding Wilson's Phalarope has a thin gray eye-stripe rather than a broad black bar; it has a long bill and lacks white stripes on back.) **FLIGHT** White wing stripe; white stripes on back. **STATUS AND RANGE** A very rare and local migrant and non-breeding resident in Puerto Rico October–February. A vagrant in Virgin Islands. **HABITAT** Usually out at sea; sometimes ponds and lagoons. (See also Plate 23.)

non-br

br

Sanderling

non-br

non-br

Red Knot

non-br

br

Pectoral
Sandpiper

br

non-br

non-br

non-br

Red-necked
Phalarope

Wilson's Phalarope

br ♀

br ♀

non-br

non-br

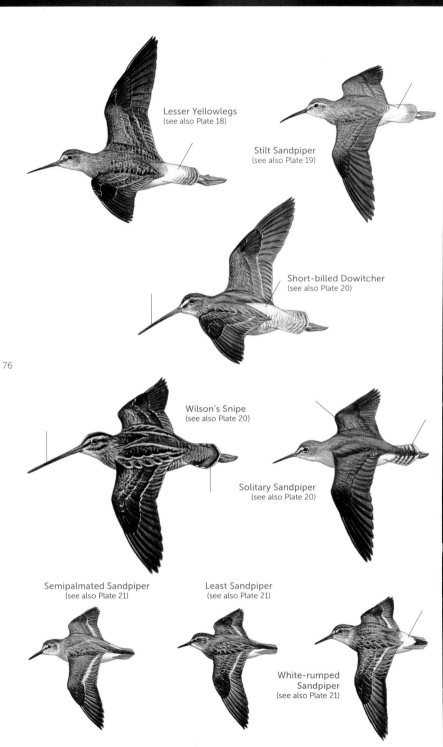

Lesser Yellowlegs
(see also Plate 18)

Stilt Sandpiper
(see also Plate 19)

Short-billed Dowitcher
(see also Plate 20)

76

Wilson's Snipe
(see also Plate 20)

Solitary Sandpiper
(see also Plate 20)

Semipalmated Sandpiper
(see also Plate 21)

Least Sandpiper
(see also Plate 21)

White-rumped
Sandpiper
(see also Plate 21)

Dunlin
(see also Plate 19)

Spotted
Sandpiper
(see also
Plate 20)

Sanderling
(see also Plate 22)

Pectoral Sandpiper
(see also Plate 22)

Red Knot
(see also Plate 22)

Red-necked Phalarope
(see also Plate 22)

Wilson's Phalarope
(see also Plate 22)

PLATE 24   MEDIUM-LEGGED WETLAND BIRDS – Short billed

## Plovers

Chunky birds with relatively shorter bills, legs, and necks than the similar-appearing sandpipers. All species in region, except Killdeer, frequent water edges, where they pick prey from mud or sand surfaces. All in region have neck or breast markings and all have a distinctive broadening bill tip, which sandpipers lack. Ruddy Turnstone, a sandpiper, is placed here due to its relatively short bill.

**SEMIPALMATED PLOVER** *Charadrius semipalmatus* (Chorlito acollarado, Playero acollarado) 18.5cm (7.25in); 50g. **BEHAVIOR** Flocks. **DESCRIPTION** *Brown upperparts*; dark breast band; *stubby bill; orange legs.* Sometimes breast band shows only as bars on either side of breast. (Piping Plover much paler above; Wilson's larger, with much larger bill and pinkish legs.) **NON-BREEDING** Bill dark and may lack orange at base. **BREEDING** Base of bill orange. **VOICE** Plaintive *weet.* Also, a plaintive *tee-weet.* **STATUS AND RANGE** A common migrant and non-breeding resident in Puerto Rico and larger Virgin Islands including Anegada, and uncommon on smaller ones. Occurs primarily August–May, but occurs year round. Most frequent September–October. **HABITAT** Mudflats of salt ponds and bays; also rocky and sandy beaches.

**WILSON'S PLOVER** *Charadrius wilsonia* (Chorlito marítimo, Playero marítimo, Sand bird, Little ploward, Nit, Thick-billed plover) 18–20cm (7–8in); 60g. Broad breast band; *long, thick, black bill.* **ADULT MALE** Breast band black. **ADULT FEMALE AND IMMATURE** Breast band brown. (Semipalmated Plover smaller, with orange legs and smaller bill.) **VOICE** Emphatic, raspy whistles, or a quick *ki-ki-ki.* **STATUS AND RANGE** A common breeding resident in Puerto Rico and Virgin Islands April–August. Numbers appear to decline outside breeding season, but this may be because of increased nocturnal foraging to avoid predators. **HABITAT** Salt pond borders and undisturbed sandy beaches.

78

**PIPING PLOVER** *Charadrius melodus* (Chorlito melódico, Playero melódico) 18cm (7in); 60g. *Pale gray upperparts*; short stubby bill; *orange legs.* **NON-BREEDING** Bill black; breast band may be partial or absent. **BREEDING** Base of bill orange; breast band may be partial or complete. **FLIGHT** White uppertail-coverts and black spot near tip of tail. **VOICE** Thin, whistled peep and *peé-lo,* second syllable lower. **STATUS AND RANGE** Rare migrant and non-breeding resident in Puerto Rico and Anegada, primarily late August–March. Very rare on other Virgin Islands. Endangered in US. **HABITAT** Dredged spoils and sandy water edges.

**SNOWY PLOVER** *Charadrius nivosus* (Chorlito blanco, Playero blanco) 14–15cm (5.5–5.75in); 40g. Tiny. *Pale coloration,* with slender black bill, dark neck marks, and *blackish or dark legs.* **BREEDING** Black ear-patch. **IMMATURE** Lacks black markings. **VOICE** Weak rising whistle, like calling someone's attention, *ku-weeet,* with accent on second syllable. **STATUS AND RANGE** Uncommon and local year-round resident on Anegada in Virgin Islands. Rare and very local year-round resident in Puerto Rico, primarily at Cabo Rojo salt ponds. Some individuals disperse along sandy beaches in Puerto Rico during winter months. Very rare on other Virgin Islands. Endangered as a breeding bird in region. **HABITAT** Sandy beaches and lagoon borders with extensive salt flats.

Semipalmated Plover

br

non-br

♀

♂

Wilson's Plover

Piping Plover

br

non-br

Snowy Plover

br

non-br

PLATE 25   MEDIUM-LEGGED WETLAND BIRDS — Short billed

**BLACK-BELLIED PLOVER** *Pluvialis squatarola* (Chorlito cabezón, Playero cabezón, Gray plover) 26–34cm (10–13.5in); 220g. **BEHAVIOR** Flocks. **DESCRIPTION** Large, stocky, with short bill. **NON-BREEDING** Light mottled gray; indistinct contrast between gray crown and whitish eyebrow stripe. **BREEDING** Black underparts. **FLIGHT ABOVE** White uppertail-coverts, white tail with dark bars and distinct white wing stripe. **FLIGHT BELOW** Black wingpits. (See American Golden-Plover.) **VOICE** Plaintive *klee* or *klee-a-lee*. **STATUS AND RANGE** Generally common migrant and non-breeding resident in Puerto Rico and Virgin Islands August–May, but occurs in all months. **HABITAT** Tidal mudflats, sandy beaches, and other coastal water edges.

**AMERICAN GOLDEN-PLOVER** *Pluvialis dominica* (Chorlito dorado, Playero dorado, Lesser golden-plover) 26cm (10in); 150g. **BEHAVIOR** Flocks, prefers uplands. **DESCRIPTION** Fairly large and stocky, with short bill. **NON-BREEDING** Mottled gray; contrast between dark crown and whitish eyebrow stripe. **BREEDING** Black underparts; broad white patch edging breast; golden cast on mottled upperparts. (Black-bellied Plover is larger, has larger bill, and is grayer in non-breeding plumage. In breeding plumage has light crown and hindneck, and white rather than dark undertail-coverts.) **FLIGHT ABOVE** Dark tail and uppertail-coverts; lacks white wing stripe. **FLIGHT BELOW** Lacks black wingpits. **VOICE** A single loud whistle, and a soft warbled *chee-dle-wur*, sometimes given as a loud whistle. **STATUS AND RANGE** Uncommon in Puerto Rico and rare in Virgin Islands as southbound migrant August–November. In Virgin Islands occurs most regularly on St. Croix and Anegada. Very rare northbound March–April. Less frequent in other months. **HABITAT** Wet fields, plowed agricultural lands, and golf courses; less frequent on tidal flats.

**RUDDY TURNSTONE** *Arenaria interpres* (Playero turco) 21–23cm (8–9in); 120g. **BEHAVIOR** Flocks. **NON-BREEDING** *Dark breast markings; orange legs.* **BREEDING** *Unusual black-and-white facial markings; reddish-orange back.* **FLIGHT** Distinctive white pattern on upperwings, back, and tail. **VOICE** Loud, nasal *cuck-cuck-cuck*, increasing in volume. **STATUS AND RANGE** A common migrant and non-breeding resident in Puerto Rico and Virgin Islands in all months except June and July, when uncommon. **HABITAT** Mudflats, pond edges, sandy and rocky coasts. Sometimes on docks, and even in restaurants (Anegada).

Killdeer
For comparison.
(see also Plate 35)

adult

non-br

non-br

non-br

br

Black-bellied Plover

non-br

non-br

non-br

br

American
Golden-Plover

br

Ruddy
Turnstone

non-br

non-br

## Rails

Chicken-like marsh-dwelling birds. They are secretive and much more frequently heard than seen. Rails are primarily terrestrial and rarely flush, preferring to run for cover. Flight is labored, with legs dangling conspicuously.

**CLAPPER RAIL** *Rallus crepitans* (Pollo de mangle, Marsh hen, Mangrove hen) 32–41cm (12.5–16in); male 320g, female 270g. **BEHAVIOR** Most active dawn and dusk. Stalks among mangroves, difficult to locate. **DESCRIPTION** Gray, chicken-like, with *long, slender bill*. Upperparts mottled gray and black; cheek gray; breast grayish with variable amounts of tan on throat and belly. **VOICE** Loud, grating cackle, *kek-kek-kek-kek* ... , slowing at end. **STATUS AND RANGE** Common permanent resident in Puerto Rico and locally so in Virgin Islands. **HABITAT** Salt ponds, salt marshes, and mangroves.

**SORA** *Porzana carolina* (Gallito sora, Sora rail, Sora crake) 22cm (8.5in); 75g. Difficult to locate. **DESCRIPTION** Small, brownish-gray, with *stubby yellow bill*. **ADULT** Blackish face, throat, and breast. **IMMATURE** Black absent. **VOICE** Clear, descending whinny and plaintive, rising whistle, *ker-wee*. **STATUS AND RANGE** An uncommon and local migrant and non-breeding resident in Puerto Rico, and on St. Croix and Anegada in Virgin Islands. Rare or absent on other Virgin Islands. Occurs October–April. **HABITAT** Wet grassy marshes, dense vegetation of freshwater swamps; sometimes saltwater ponds and mangroves.

**BLACK RAIL** *Laterallus jamaicensis* (Gallito negro) 14cm (5.5in); 35g. Very difficult to locate. **BEHAVIOR** Nocturnal. **DESCRIPTION** *Tiny*, with *short black bill; white spots on back*, dark reddish-brown hindneck. (Downy young gallinules, coots, and rails are black but lack these markings.) **VOICE** Whistled *ki-ki-kurr*, last note lower. **STATUS AND RANGE** A very rare and local migrant and non-breeding resident in Puerto Rico October–March. Reportedly formerly bred, but likely extirpated by introduction of mongoose. Critically endangered as a breeding bird in region. **HABITAT** Wet grassy marsh edges, saline and fresh.

**YELLOW-BREASTED CRAKE** *Hapalocrex flaviventer* (Gallito amarillo) 14cm (5.5in); 25g. Very difficult to locate. **BEHAVIOR** Most active at dusk and dawn. **DESCRIPTION** *Tiny. Pale yellowish-brown*, with blackish crown and *white eyebrow stripe*. **VOICE** Medium-pitched *tuck* and high-pitched, whistled *peep*. **STATUS AND RANGE** Uncommon and local permanent resident in Puerto Rico, where it occurs primarily at Caño Tiburone and Cartagena Lagoon. **HABITAT** Freshwater swamps and canals with borders of short grass or other aquatic vegetation.

## Kingfishers

Distinctive group with large heads, crests, and long, pointed bills. Hover well above the water and then dive for fish.

**BELTED KINGFISHER** *Megaceryle alcyon* (Martín pescador, Pájaro del rey, Kingfisherman) 28–36cm (11–14in); 150g. **BEHAVIOR** *Hovers before diving.* **DESCRIPTION** *Large bill; conspicuous crest.* **MALE** Blue breast band. **FEMALE** One blue and one orange breast band. **VOICE** *Loud, harsh rattle.* **STATUS AND RANGE** Fairly common migrant and non-breeding resident in Puerto Rico and Virgin Islands September–April. However, may occur in any month. **HABITAT** Calm bodies of water, both saline and fresh.

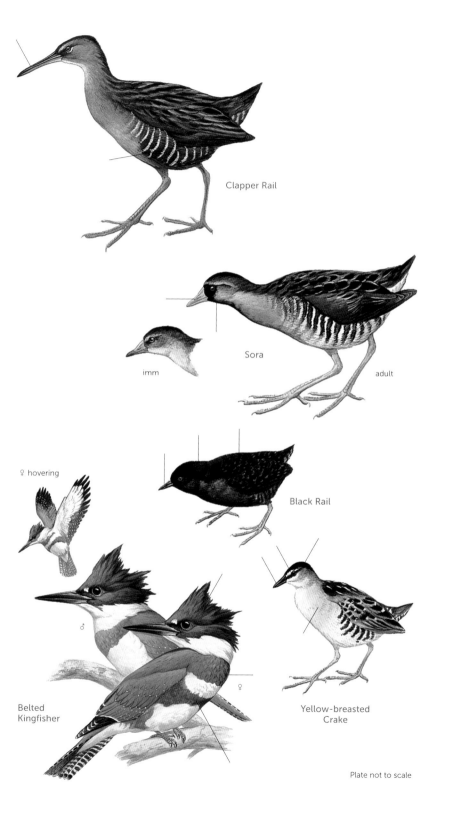

Clapper Rail

Sora

imm

adult

♀ hovering

Black Rail

Belted
Kingfisher

♂

♀

Yellow-breasted
Crake

Plate not to scale

PLATE 27     DUCKS/DUCK-LIKE WATERBIRDS — Coot, Gallinules, and Grebes

## Coots and Gallinules

Larger than rails and more aquatic, coots are most at home in water. Resemble ducks, but have a distinctive bill with a frontal shield and, when swimming, characteristically jerk their heads.

**AMERICAN COOT (CARIBBEAN COOT)** *Fulica americana* (Gallinazo americano, Water fowl, Mud hen) 38–40cm (15–16in); male 720g, female 550g. **BEHAVIOR** Swims with bobbing head; dives; flocks. **DESCRIPTION** Duck-like. **ADULT** Grayish-black overall, *white bill* and undertail-coverts. In some birds (Caribbean subspecies) white frontal shield extends onto crown. **IMMATURE** Paler. Caribbean Coot (resident) now a subspecies of American Coot (migratory). **VOICE** A variety of croaks and cackles. **STATUS AND RANGE** A common migrant September–April, and less so as a year-round resident in Puerto Rico and larger Virgin Islands. It is uncommon to very rare on smaller Virgin Islands. **HABITAT** Open freshwater with much submergent vegetation, including golf course ponds; also brackish ponds.

**PURPLE GALLINULE** *Porphyrio martinica* (Gallareta azúl, Gallareta inglesa) 33cm (13in); 240g. **BEHAVIOR** Wades among dense swamp vegetation. **ADULT** *Bluish-purple plumage; yellow legs*; bluish-white frontal shield. **IMMATURE** Golden-brown, bluish wings. (Immature lacks flank stripe of Common Gallinule and is tanner, with bluish wings.) **VOICE** High-pitched, melodious *klee-klee*. **STATUS AND RANGE** An uncommon and local year-round resident in Puerto Rico, where it occurs in numbers at Cartagena Lagoon. It is a rare migrant and non-breeding resident on St. Croix primarily February–April, and very rare or vagrant elsewhere in Virgin Islands. **HABITAT** Freshwater bodies with dense vegetation.

**COMMON GALLINULE (COMMON MOORHEN)** *Gallinula galeata* (Gallareta común, Water fowl) 34cm (13.5in); 300g. **BEHAVIOR** Swims with bobbing head. **DESCRIPTION** Duck-like. **ADULT** *Red bill tipped yellow, red frontal shield; white line down flank.* **IMMATURE** Gray and brown; bill lacks red. **VOICE** Piercing, laugh-like cackle, slowing at end: *ki-ki-ki-ki-ka, kaa, kaaa.* **STATUS AND RANGE** A common year-round resident in Puerto Rico and Virgin Islands. **HABITAT** Most wetlands, rivers, ponds, and canals with water plants, including mangroves.

## Grebes

Can gradually sink out of sight, or submerge until only the head remains above the surface.

**LEAST GREBE** *Tachybaptus dominicus* (Tigua, Diver, Helldiver, Diving dapper) 23–26cm (9–10in); 120g. **BEHAVIOR** Excellent diver. **DESCRIPTION** *Small; blackish coloration*, with *thin bill* and yellow-orange eye. White wing patch not always visible. **VOICE** Rising, reed-like *week.* **STATUS AND RANGE** Uncommon and local year-round resident in Puerto Rico and larger Virgin Islands. Occurrence fluctuates with availability of freshwater ponds. **HABITAT** Primarily freshwater cattail swamps and small ponds with plant cover. In arid areas occurs in temporary ponds formed after torrential rains.

**PIED-BILLED GREBE** *Podilymbus podiceps* (Zaramago, Diver, Helldiver, Diving dapper) 30–38cm (12–15in); 440g. **BEHAVIOR** Excellent diver. **DESCRIPTION** Grayish-brown, duck-like, with *conical bill.* **BREEDING ADULT** *Black throat; bill with black band.* **NON-BREEDING ADULT** White throat; bill lacks black band. **IMMATURE** Head mottled brown and white. **VOICE** Harsh cackle breaking into distinctive *kowp, kowp, kowp,* slowing at end. **STATUS AND RANGE** A common year-round resident in Puerto Rico and US Virgin Islands; uncommon and local in British Virgin Islands. **HABITAT** Primarily freshwater, but also brackish and hypersaline lagoons.

adult

imm

adult

N American
race

American Coot

Caribbean
race

adult

imm

Purple Gallinule

Common
Gallinule

adult

non-br
adult

Least Grebe

br

non-br
adult

Pied-billed Grebe

imm

br

PLATE 28   DUCKS/DUCK-LIKE WATERBIRDS — Whistling-Ducks and Goose

Medium to very large waterbirds with webbed feet and flattened beaks. Most feed in water or along borders. Largely migratory.

**SNOW GOOSE** *Anser caerulescens* (BLUE GOOSE [dark form])(Ganso blanco) 58–71cm (23–28in); wingspan 1.4m (4.6ft); 2.5kg. **BEHAVIOR** Often grazes; flocks. **ADULT** Two color phases. White phase—*White overall* with *black primaries*; pink bill and legs. Dark phase—Bluish-gray body with white head and upper neck; pink bill and legs. **STATUS AND RANGE** Very rare wanderer to Puerto Rico, where reported primarily from Caño Tiburones. No recent records from Virgin Islands. Expected to occur October–March. Only the white form reported from the region. Numbers are increasing gradually in West Indies. **HABITAT** Borders of freshwater ponds and swamps, flooded uplands, croplands.

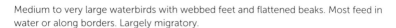 **WEST INDIAN WHISTLING-DUCK** *Dendrocygna arborea* (Chirirría caribeña, Yaguaza, Chirirría antillana, Pato nocturno, Whistler, West Indian tree duck) 48–56cm (19–22in); 1.2kg. **BEHAVIOR** Flocks, primarily nocturnal, surface feeder, often grazes. **DESCRIPTION** Deep brown plumage with *white abdomen with black markings*; erect stance. **FLIGHT** Dark overall; black-and-white abdomen; gray upperwing-coverts. Head and feet droop; feet extend beyond tail. **VOICE** Shrill whistle, *chiriría*. **STATUS AND RANGE** Uncommon and local year-round resident in Puerto Rico and a vagrant in Virgin Islands. This duck was formerly a common breeding resident in the region. Endangered. It is endemic to the West Indies. Endangered as a breeding bird in region. **HABITAT** Mangroves, savannas, wooded swamps, lagoons. Said to roost, feed, and nest in trees in the hills. (See also Plate 33.)

**FULVOUS WHISTLING-DUCK** *Dendrocygna bicolor* (Chirirría bicolor, Chirirría amarillenta, Pato silbón, Chirirría dominicana, Yaguaza dominicana, Fulvous tree duck) 46–51cm (18–20in); 700g. **BEHAVIOR** Flocks, surface feeder, sometimes grazes. **DESCRIPTION** Pale yellowish-brown plumage with *thin white side stripe*, white uppertail-coverts, erect stance. **FLIGHT** Pale yellowish-brown; white stripe at wing base; white rump; dark wings; reddish-brown upperwing-coverts. Head and feet droop; feet extend beyond tail. **VOICE** Squealing whistle, *puteow*. **STATUS AND RANGE** A rare and irregular wanderer in Puerto Rico and a vagrant in Virgin Islands. Formerly more abundant in Puerto Rico during the 1970s; its numbers have declined. **HABITAT** Freshwater with emergent plants. It is more of a swamp-dwelling bird than the other whistling-ducks and unlike them is more active during daylight. (See also Plate 33.)

**BLACK-BELLIED WHISTLING-DUCK** *Dendrocygna autumnalis* (Chirirría pinta, Black-bellied tree duck) 46–53cm (18–21in); 850g. **BEHAVIOR** Fairly nocturnal, surface feeder, sometimes grazes, flocks. **DESCRIPTION** *White wing patch; black belly; reddish bill and legs*. **FLIGHT** Large white upperwing patch; black belly; reddish bill and legs. Head and feet droop; feet trail beyond tail. **VOICE** Shrill, chattering whistle. **STATUS AND RANGE** A very rare wanderer to Puerto Rico and a vagrant in Virgin Islands. Formerly more common in Puerto Rico, where it reportedly bred. Its range is expanding in the West Indies. Sometimes occurs in numbers. Critically endangered as a breeding bird in region. **HABITAT** Freshwater and brackish lagoons. (See also Plate 33.)

dark phase

white phase

imm

imm

Snow Goose

West Indian
Whistling-Duck

Fulvous
Whistling-Duck

Black-bellied
Whistling-Duck

**BLUE-WINGED TEAL** *Spatula discors* (Pato zarcel, Pato de la Florida) 38–40cm (15–16in); 300–400g. **BEHAVIOR** Surface feeder. **DESCRIPTION** Small, with blue forewing. **FEMALE AND NON-BREEDING MALE** Mottled brown; speculum green; very similar to female and non-breeding male Green-winged Teal, but Blue-winged has *light spot on lores* and a darker belly, lacks pale patch beneath tail, and has yellow legs. **BREEDING MALE** *White face crescent.* (Female and non-breeding male Green-winged Teal lack white spot on lores, have paler belly, and have a pale patch beneath tail.) **FLIGHT** Small, with *blue forewing*; green speculum. **STATUS AND RANGE** Numbers vary year to year, but generally fairly common locally in Puerto Rico and most Virgin Islands. Occurs primarily October–April, but found year round. **HABITAT** Shallow wetlands from freshwater lakes to hypersaline salt ponds. (See also Plate 33.)

**CINNAMON TEAL** *Spatula cyanoptera* (Pato canela, Pato colorado) 38–40cm (15–16in); 400g. **BEHAVIOR** Surface feeder. **DESCRIPTION** Small. Fairly large bill. **FEMALE AND NON-BREEDING MALE** Mottled brown; speculum green. (Very similar female and non-breeding male Blue-winged Teal have light spot on lores, dark line through eye, and smaller bill; lack reddish tint to plumage, most notably on face.) **BREEDING MALE** Cinnamon-colored head and underparts. **FLIGHT** *Blue forewing*; green speculum. **STATUS AND RANGE** Decidedly rare migrant and non-breeding resident in Puerto Rico, and very rare on St. Croix. A vagrant elsewhere in Virgin Islands. Occurs October–March. **HABITAT** Shallow wetlands from freshwater lakes to hypersaline ponds. (See also Plate 33.)

**GREEN-WINGED TEAL** *Anas crecca* (Pato aliverde) 33–39cm (13–15.5in); 300–400g. **BEHAVIOR** Surface feeder. **DESCRIPTION** Small; green speculum; lacks blue in forewing. **FEMALE AND NON-BREEDING MALE** Mottled brown; dark lores; whitish belly; pale patch beneath tail; dark legs. (See Blue-winged Teal.) **BREEDING MALE** Green eye-patch and speculum; reddish-brown head; white vertical bar in front of wing. Vagrant European race lacks vertical bar; has horizontal white stripe on wing edge. **FLIGHT** Small; green speculum; lacks blue in forewing. **STATUS AND RANGE** Uncommon and local migrant and non-breeding resident in Puerto Rico and rare in Virgin Islands, where it occurs most frequently on St. Croix and Anegada. It occurs primarily October–March. **HABITAT** Primarily shallow freshwater, but sometimes brackish and saline ponds. (See also Plate 33.)

**GADWALL** *Mareca strepera* (Pato gris) 46–57cm (18–22.5in); 800–1,000g. **BEHAVIOR** Surface feeder. **DESCRIPTION** *White speculum.* **MALE** Mottled gray overall; rump black; head dark brown. **FEMALE** Mottled brown; whitish belly; bill slightly orange with dark gray ridge. (Female Mallard has whitish tail and blue speculum. Female American Wigeon has light blue bill and green speculum.) **FLIGHT** *White speculum set off by black to front and sides.* **STATUS AND RANGE** A very rare migrant and non-breeding resident in Puerto Rico, October–March. Vagrant in Virgin Islands. Numbers are increasing. **HABITAT** Shallow freshwater wetlands. (See also Plate 34.)

88

br ♂

♀ & non-br ♂

Blue-winged
Teal

♀ & non-br ♂

br ♂

♀ & non-br ♂

Cinnamon
Teal

br ♂

br ♂

♀ & non-br ♂

Green-winged
Teal

♀ & non-br ♂

br ♂

N American race

adult ♂

Eurasian race

♂

♀

Gadwall

♀

♂

PLATE 30    DUCKS/DUCK-LIKE WATERBIRDS — Dabbling Ducks

**NORTHERN PINTAIL** *Anas acuta* (Pato pescuecilargo) male 69–74cm (27–29in), female 54–56cm (21–22in); male 1,040g, female 990g. **BEHAVIOR** Surface feeder. **FEMALE AND NON-BREEDING MALE** Mottled brown; *pointed tail; long, slender neck*; gray bill. **BREEDING MALE** Brown head; white breast and neck stripe; long, pointed tail. **FLIGHT** Long, slender neck; *pointed tail*. **FEMALE AND NON-BREEDING MALE** White border on trailing edge of brown speculum; gray underwing contrasts with white belly. **BREEDING MALE** Greenish speculum, pale tan inner border; white trailing edge. **STATUS AND RANGE** An uncommon migrant and non-breeding resident in Puerto Rico. It is rare in Virgin Islands. Occurs September–April. It is one of first migratory ducks to arrive in region, occurring as early as September. **HABITAT** Shallow wetlands, where it prefers freshwater but is also found in salt ponds. (See also Plate 34.)

**WHITE-CHEEKED PINTAIL** *Anas bahamensis* (Pato quijada colorada, Brass wing, Brass wing teal, Summer duck, Whitehead, Whitethroat, White-jaw, Bahama pintail) 38–48cm (15–19in); 550g. **BEHAVIOR** Surface feeder, flocks. **DESCRIPTION** Note the *red bill mark* and *white cheek*. Speculum green, edged tan. **FLIGHT** Red bill mark, white cheek; green speculum edged tan. **STATUS AND RANGE** Locally common year-round resident in Puerto Rico and Virgin Islands. It is the most common duck in the Virgin Islands. Threatened. **HABITAT** Shallow wetlands from freshwater lakes to hypersaline ponds and mangrove swamps with standing shallow water. (See also Plate 34.)

**AMERICAN WIGEON** *Mareca americana* (Pato cabeciblanco, Baldpate) 46–56cm (18–22in); 500–1,300g. **BEHAVIOR** Surface feeder, flocks. **MALE** Note the *white crown, light blue bill*, green eye-patch. **FEMALE** Brownish; gray head; light blue bill. **FLIGHT** *White patch on forewing*; green speculum; white belly. **STATUS AND RANGE** An uncommon migrant and less frequent non-breeding resident in Puerto Rico and Virgin Islands, principally October–April. **HABITAT** Shallow wetlands from freshwater lakes to hypersaline salt ponds. (See also Plate 34.)

90

**MALLARD** *Anas platyrhynchos* (Pato cabeciverde, Pato inglés) 51–71cm (20–28in); 750–1,500g. **BEHAVIOR** Surface feeder. **DESCRIPTION** Large, with *blue speculum edged white*. **NON-BREEDING MALE AND IMMATURE** Mottled brown overall, olive bill. **ADULT FEMALE** Bill orange with black markings. **BREEDING MALE** *Rounded green head, yellow bill, maroon breast*. **FLIGHT** Blue speculum with white borders. **STATUS AND RANGE** Very rare migrant and non-breeding resident October–April in Puerto Rico and St. Croix. Often difficult to determine whether sightings are of Mallards released locally. **HABITAT** Shallow wetlands from freshwater lakes to hypersaline ponds. (See also Plate 33.)

♀ & non-br ♂

Northern Pintail

br ♂

br ♂

♀ & non-br ♂

White-cheeked
Pintail

♀ & non-br ♂

♂

American
Wigeon

♀

♀

♂

adult ♀

br ♂

Mallard

adult ♀

adult ♂

non-br ♂

PLATE 31    DUCKS/DUCK-LIKE WATERBIRDS — Dabbling and Diving Ducks

**MUSCOVY DUCK** *Cairina moschata* (Pato criollo) Male 86cm (34in), female 64cm (25in); 3–5kg. **BEHAVIOR** Surface feeder. **DESCRIPTION** A very large duck, variable in coloration. Wild state—Black overall with green cast and *large white wing patch*. Domesticated varieties—*Varying amounts of white in plumage*, some entirely white; *bare face patch often red*. **STATUS AND RANGE** Introduced widely, where escaped birds now feral or semiferal. Uncommon and local in Puerto Rico, and on Tortola and Beef Island in the British Virgin Islands. There are unconfirmed reports of feral ducks from other islands. **HABITAT** Ponds, often near farms or towns.

**NORTHERN SHOVELER** *Spatula clypeata* (Pato cuchareta, Spoonbill, Shovel-mouth) 43–53cm (17–21in); 620g. **BEHAVIOR** Surface feeder, flocks. **DESCRIPTION** Note the *unusually large bill*. **MALE** Green head, white breast, *reddish-brown sides and belly*. **FEMALE** Mottled brown. **FLIGHT** Large bill; green speculum; *blue patch on forewing*. **STATUS AND RANGE** An uncommon migrant and non-breeding resident in Puerto Rico, St. Croix, and Anegada. Rare and local elsewhere in Virgin Islands. Occurs primarily October–May. **HABITAT** Shallow wetlands, both fresh and brackish. (See also Plate 33.)

**WOOD DUCK** *Aix sponsa* (Pato joyuyo, Arcoiris) 43–51cm (17–20in); 650g. **BEHAVIOR** Surface feeder. **DESCRIPTION** Crest. **MALE** *Unusual facial pattern*. **FEMALE** *Asymmetrical eye-ring*. **FLIGHT** Long, squared tail; large head; bill tilted down. **VOICE** Male—Thin but emphatic *zweeeet!* increasing in intensity. Female—Squawking *oo-eeek*, very unlike a duck. **STATUS AND RANGE** Irregular in occurrence but generally a rare to very rare wanderer to Puerto Rico. Most likely to occur October–April. **HABITAT** Canals, lagoons, and impoundments. (See also Plate 33.)

**RING-NECKED DUCK** *Aythya collaris* (Pato acollarado, Pato del medio, Black duck) 40–46cm (16–18in); 700g. **BEHAVIOR** Dives, flocks. **MALE** *White bill-ring, black back*, and *white vertical bar in front of wing*. **FEMALE** Pale bill-ring and *eye-ring*, sometimes a *trailing white streak between cheek and crown*. **FLIGHT** Dark upperwing-coverts contrast with *pale gray secondaries*. Sharp demarcation between dark breast and pale belly. **STATUS AND RANGE** An irregular but generally uncommon migrant and non-breeding resident in Puerto Rico October–March. It is uncommon to rare on St. Croix and Anegada, and generally rare on the other larger Virgin Islands. This duck sometimes occurs in numbers. **HABITAT** Open freshwater; sometimes brackish lagoons. (See also Plate 34.)

92

**LESSER SCAUP** *Aythya affinis* (Pato pechiblanco menor, Pato turco, Black duck, Black-head) 38–46cm (15–18in); 500–1,000g. **BEHAVIOR** Dives, flocks. **MALE** Dark head, breast, and tail; whitish back and flanks. **FEMALE** Brown; *large white mark behind bill*. **FLIGHT** White secondaries and black primaries. Sharp demarcation between dark breast and pale belly. **STATUS AND RANGE** An uncommon and local migrant and non-breeding resident in Puerto Rico. Rare in Virgin Islands, where it occurs most frequently on St. Croix and Anegada. Occurs primarily November–March. **HABITAT** Open water of bays, lagoons, ponds, and lakes. (See also Plate 34.)

wild form

Muscovy Duck

domestic variety

♀

♂

Northern Shoveler

♀

♂

Wood Duck

♀

♂

♀

♂

Ring-necked Duck

♂

♀

Lesser Scaup

♀

♂

♂

♀

**RUDDY DUCK** *Oxyura jamaicensis* (Pato chorizo, Rubber duck, Diving teal, Red diver) 35–43cm (14–17in); 550g. **BEHAVIOR** *Tail often erect*, dives, flocks. **MALE** *Reddish-brown coloration; white cheek patch; blue bill.* **FEMALE AND IMMATURE** Mostly brown; *single brown stripe below eye.* (Female Masked Duck has two dark facial stripes.) **FLIGHT** Chunky body; long tail; dark upperwings. **STATUS AND RANGE** Locally common year-round resident in Puerto Rico; uncommon and local year-round resident in Virgin Islands, though sometimes locally common on St. Croix, particularly at Southgate Pond, and on Tortola at Josiah's Bay Pond. Often occurs in numbers. Migrants augment local populations October–March. **HABITAT** Deep, open freshwater bodies; also brackish lagoons. (See also Plate 34.)

**MASKED DUCK** *Nomonyx dominicus* (Pato dominico, Pato enmascarado, Quail duck, Squat duck) 30–36cm (12–14in); 370g. Difficult to locate. **BEHAVIOR** Erect tail, dives. **DESCRIPTION** White wing patch in all plumages. **BREEDING MALE** Reddish-brown coloration, black face, blue bill. **NON-BREEDING MALE, FEMALE, AND IMMATURE** Two brown facial stripes. **FLIGHT** Chunky body; white wing patch; long tail. **STATUS AND RANGE** Uncommon and local year-round resident in Puerto Rico. Very rare in Virgin Islands, primarily on St. Croix. Occurrence varies with availability of freshwater ponds. Threatened as a breeding bird in region. **HABITAT** Dense vegetation of freshwater swamps, ponds, and lagoons. (See also Plate 34.)

**HOODED MERGANSER** *Lophodytes cucullatus* (Mergansa encapuchada, Mergansa de caperuza) 40–48cm (16–19in); 600g. **BEHAVIOR** Dives. **DESCRIPTION** *Crest; slender, hooked bill.* **MALE** Large white patch on crest. **FEMALE** Dark plumage and bill; *bill dull orange near base.* (Larger but similar female Red-breasted Merganser has darker face, bill, and back.) **FLIGHT** Crest; dark upperparts; small white patch on secondaries. **MALE** Pale forewing. **STATUS AND RANGE** Very rare migrant and non-breeding resident in Puerto Rico and St. Croix, primarily November–February. Vagrant elsewhere in Virgin Islands. **HABITAT** Inland ponds, lagoons. (See also Plate 34.)

94

**RED-BREASTED MERGANSER** *Mergus serrator* (Mergansa pechirroja) 51–64cm (20–25in); 1kg. **BEHAVIOR** Dives. **DESCRIPTION** *Crest; long, slender, hooked bill.* **MALE** Green head, white collar, dark breast. **FEMALE** Reddish-brown head and bill; whitish chin, foreneck, and breast; gray back. (Differs from Hooded Merganser by lighter face and back; reddish bill.) **FLIGHT MALE** White secondaries and forewing, crossed by two bars. **FEMALE** White secondaries, crossed by one bar. **STATUS AND RANGE** A decidedly rare migrant and non-breeding resident in Puerto Rico and a vagrant on St. John. Occurs primarily November–March. **HABITAT** Open bays, ocean near shore, inland lagoons. (See also Plate 34.)

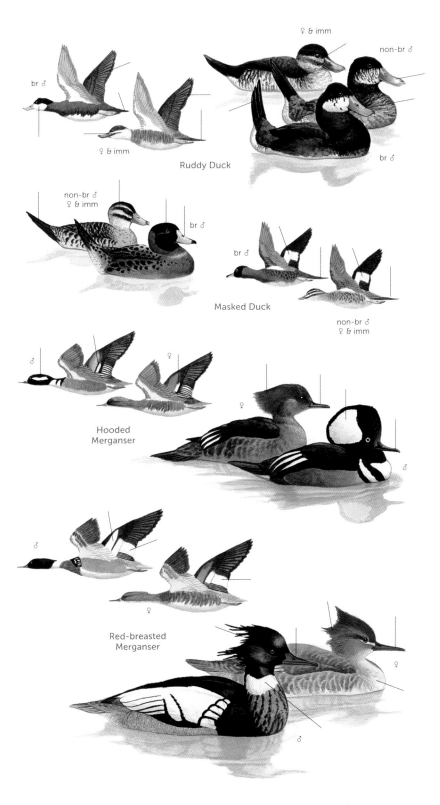

br ♂

♀ & imm

♀ & imm

non-br ♂

br ♂

Ruddy Duck

non-br ♂
♀ & imm

br ♂

br ♂

non-br ♂
♀ & imm

Masked Duck

♂

♀

Hooded
Merganser

♀

♂

♂

♀

Red-breasted
Merganser

♀

♂

PLATE 33    DUCKS/DUCK-LIKE WATERBIRDS — Ducks Flying

**Black-bellied Whistling-Duck**
(see also Plate 28)

**Fulvous Whistling-Duck**
(see also Plate 28)

96

**West Indian Whistling-Duck**
(see also Plate 28)

**Northern Shoveler**
(see also Plate 31)

br ♂

adult ♀

Mallard
(see also Plate 30)

Wood Duck
(see also Plate 31)

♂

♀

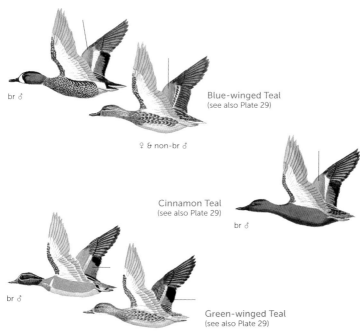

br ♂

♀ & non-br ♂

Blue-winged Teal
(see also Plate 29)

Cinnamon Teal
(see also Plate 29)

br ♂

br ♂

♀ & non-br ♂

Green-winged Teal
(see also Plate 29)

♂

♀

Gadwall
(see also Plate 29)

Ruddy Duck
(see also Plate 32)

br ♂

♀ & imm

br ♂

non-br ♂
♀ & imm

Masked Duck
(see also Plate 32)

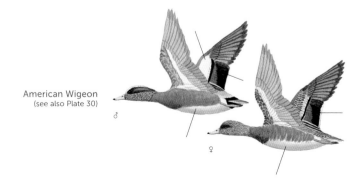

American Wigeon
(see also Plate 30)

♂

♀

Ring-necked Duck
(see also Plate 31)

♂

♀

Lesser Scaup
(see also Plate 31)

♂

♀

White-cheeked Pintail
(see also Plate 30)

Northern Pintail
(see also Plate 30)

br ♂

♀ & non-br ♂

Hooded Merganser
(see also Plate 32)

♂

♀

Red-breasted Merganser
(see also Plate 32)

♂

♀

**BUFF-BREASTED SANDPIPER** *Calidris subruficollis* (Playero canelo) 19–22cm (7.5–8.5in); 70g. **BEHAVIOR** *Favors grasslands.* **ADULT** Upperparts have scaled look. *Large dark eye framed by pale eye-ring on clean reddish-tan face*; thin black bill. Underparts pale tan with spots on sides; yellow legs and feet; short tail not extending beyond folded wings at rest. (Upland Sandpiper is larger, with longer neck, legs, and bill; streaked below.) **FLIGHT** White wing linings. **STATUS AND RANGE** A rare migrant in Puerto Rico and very rare in Virgin Islands, primarily late August–October. **HABITAT** Fields, pastures, short grass.

**UPLAND SANDPIPER** *Bartramia longicauda* (Playero batitú, Upland plover) 28–32cm (11–12.5in); 150g. **BEHAVIOR** *Favors grasslands.* Often perches on posts. **DESCRIPTION** *Orangish-yellow legs; thin, relatively short bill*; small head; long, slender neck; *long tail.* **FLIGHT** Dark primaries; long tail; stiff, shallow wingbeats. **STATUS AND RANGE** Irregular, but generally a rare and local migrant in Puerto Rico, St. Croix, and among British Virgin Islands, primarily southbound August–early October, less frequent northbound April–May. Very rare on other US Virgin Islands. Sometimes occurs in numbers. **HABITAT** Grasslands, pastures, and savannas.

**CATTLE EGRET** *Bubulcus ibis* (Garza ganadera, Garza africana, Cattle gaulin) 48–64cm (19–25in); wingspan 90cm (3ft); 340g. **BEHAVIOR** Flocks. The only *upland heron* in region. **DESCRIPTION** Small, with short, thick, yellowish bill. **BREEDING** Reddish legs and eyes; reddish-tinted bill. *Tan wash on crown, breast, and upper back.* **NON-BREEDING** Black legs and yellow bill. Tan wash reduced. (Great Egret much larger and aquatic, infrequent away from water. Bill yellower and larger.) **VOICE** Much guttural squawking around roosting and breeding colonies. **STATUS AND RANGE** Very common year-round resident throughout Puerto Rico and Virgin Islands. **HABITAT** Pastures and fields. Often around cattle or tractors. Roosts in mangroves or dense woods, but sometimes in large trees in towns like Frederiksted, St. Croix. (See also Plate 15.)

100

**KILLDEER** *Charadrius vociferus* (Chorlito sabanero, Playero sabanero, Soldier bird, Ploward) 25cm (9.75in); 100g. *Two black bands on breast.* **FLIGHT** Reddish-brown rump. **VOICE** Plaintive, high-pitched *kee* and *dee-de.* **STATUS AND RANGE** A common year-round resident in Puerto Rico and Virgin Islands. Migrants augment local numbers, primarily September–March. **HABITAT** Wet fields, short grass, mud holes, freshwater pond edges, cultivated areas, and open country. (See also Plate 25.)

Buff-breasted
Sandpiper

adult

Upland
Sandpiper

br

non-br
adult

Cattle Egret
(not to scale)

Killdeer

adult

PLATE 36    BIRDS OF PREY — Falcons

Possess slender, pointed wings and long, narrow tails. They are swift fliers and rarely soar.

**MERLIN** *Falco columbarius* (Halcón migratorio, Falcón migratorio, Esmerejón, Pigeon hawk) 25–34cm (10–13.5in); wingspan 64cm (2ft); male 160g, female 220g. Small falcon. Upperparts dark gray in male, dark brown in female. Underparts heavily streaked, tail barred black. *Pale tan eyebrow stripe.* **FLIGHT** Fast and agile; *pointed wings;* long, narrow tail. **STATUS AND RANGE** An uncommon migrant in October and somewhat scarcer non-breeding resident until April in Puerto Rico and Virgin Islands. **HABITAT** Coastal lakes and lagoons where shorebirds abound, also open and semiopen areas, woodlands, and forests.

**PEREGRINE FALCON** *Falco peregrinus* (Halcón peregrino, Falcón peregrino, Duck hawk) 36–58cm (14–23in); wingspan 75–120cm (29–47in); male 600g, female 1kg. *Large falcon*, with *masklike head pattern.* **ADULT** Dark gray above; cream-colored with dark bars below. **IMMATURE** Brown above; underparts cream-colored with heavy brown streaks. **FLIGHT** *Fast, powerful, and agile; wings pointed;* tail long, narrow. **STATUS AND RANGE** A generally uncommon to rare and local migrant and non-breeding resident in Puerto Rico, but somewhat more frequent in the Virgin Islands. Occurs primarily October–April. **HABITAT** Offshore cays and rocks with seabirds; wetlands with shorebirds or waterfowl. Sometimes inland and in towns, where it may perch on high buildings and communication towers.

**AMERICAN KESTREL** *Falco sparverius* (Falconcito, Halcón común, Falcón común, Killy-killy, Killy hawk, Bastard hawk, Sparrow hawk) 23–30cm (9–12in); wingspan 51–61cm (20–24in); male 80–140g, female 85–165g. **BEHAVIOR** *Hovers.* **DESCRIPTION** *Small falcon*, with *reddish-brown back.* Reddish tail with broad black terminal band; *two black facial bars.* Underparts whitish. **ADULT MALE** Blue-gray wings. **ADULT FEMALE** Reddish-brown wings. **IMMATURE** Dark breast streaks. **FLIGHT** Pointed wings; long, slender tail; hovers. **VOICE** High-pitched *killi-killi-killi.* **STATUS AND RANGE** A common permanent resident in Puerto Rico and Virgin Islands. It is the most common bird of prey on the latter islands. **HABITAT** Dry, open lowlands with adequate perches. Also towns and forest edges in mountains. Often seen on exposed perch from which it hunts.

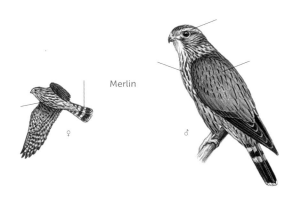

Merlin

♀

♂

Peregrine
Falcon

imm

adult

American
Kestrel

adult ♀

adult ♂

PLATE 37    BIRDS OF PREY — Hawks

Possess broad wings with rounded tips. Those with relatively shorter, fan-shaped tails and broader wings tend to soar more frequently.

**NORTHERN HARRIER** *Circus hudsonius* (Gavilán de ciénaga, Aguilucho pálido) 46–61cm (18–24in); wingspan 1–1.2m (3–4ft); male 360g, female 510g. Large, with long, slender wings and tail; *white rump*. **ADULT MALE** *Grayish-blue*. **ADULT FEMALE** Brown above; white below, heavily streaked with brown. **IMMATURE** Brown above; entirely reddish-brown below with dark brown streaks on breast. **FLIGHT** Low over ground with heavy flaps and distinctive tilting glides; *wings held well above horizontal*. **STATUS AND RANGE** Irregular, but generally a rare and local migrant and non-breeding resident, primarily October–April in Puerto Rico and Anegada, and very rare or vagrant elsewhere in Virgin Islands. **HABITAT** Marshes, swamps, and open savannas.

**SWALLOW-TAILED KITE** *Elanoides forficatus* (Elanio tijereta) 51–66cm (20–26in); wingspan 120cm (4ft); 440g. **BEHAVIOR** Flocks. **DESCRIPTION** A black-and-white kite with a *long, deeply forked tail. White head and underparts contrast with black back, wings, and tail*. **FLIGHT** When hunting, glides slowly close to ground with steady wings but tail constantly balancing. **STATUS AND RANGE** A very rare visitor to Puerto Rico, including Vieques, occurring with increased frequency in recent years. A vagrant to St. Croix in Virgin Islands. Most likely to occur August–October. **HABITAT** Coastal swamps, savannas, and river mouths.

**RED-TAILED HAWK** *Buteo jamaicensis* (Guaraguao colirrojo, Chicken hawk) 48–64cm (19–25in); wingspan 1.2m (4ft); male 1kg, female 1.2kg. Large. **ADULT** Dark brown above; white below, *dark belly stripes; tail reddish*. **IMMATURE** Tail faintly barred grayish-brown; more heavily streaked underparts. **FLIGHT** Soars on broad, rounded wings and fanned tail. **VOICE** Raspy *keeer-r-r-r*, slurring downward. **STATUS AND RANGE** A common permanent resident in Puerto Rico and Virgin Islands, where often seen soaring overhead. **HABITAT** Open country, woodlands, forests, towns, at all elevations.

**BROAD-WINGED HAWK** *Buteo platypterus* (Guaraguao de bosque) 34–44cm (13–17in); wingspan 86cm (34in); male 420g, female 490g. Medium-sized, chunky. **ADULT** *Tail boldly banded black and white*; underparts barred reddish-brown. (Red-tailed Hawk much larger; white breast with dark belly streaks. Sharp-shinned Hawk has similar color pattern but has long, narrow tail lacking bold bands.) **IMMATURE** Underparts white, streaked dark brown; tail bands more numerous, but less distinct. **FLIGHT** Alternates soaring and flapping on broad, rounded wings and fan-shaped tail. Often soars above forest canopy. **VOICE** Thin, shrill squeal, *pweeeeeeeeee*. **STATUS AND RANGE** Generally rare and very local year-round resident in Puerto Rico, though common in haystack hills of Río Abajo. Very rare visitor or perhaps migrant in Virgin Islands, primarily in November. The Puerto Rico race is threatened. **HABITAT** Dense broadleaf, mixed, and plantation forests at all elevations, less frequently open woodlands.

adult ♂

Northern Harrier

adult ♀

adult ♂

Swallow-tailed Kite

adult

imm

adult

imm

Red-tailed Hawk

Broad-winged Hawk

adult

adult

imm

adult

imm

PLATE 38    BIRDS OF PREY — Hawks and Vulture

**SHARP-SHINNED HAWK** *Accipiter striatus* (Gavilán de sierra, Falcón de sierra) Male 24–27cm (9.5–10.5in), female 29–34cm (11.5–13.5in); wingspan male 42–58 (17–23in), female 58–68 (23–27in); male 80–115g, female 150–220g. A small forest hawk. *Short, rounded wings*; small head; *long, narrow, squared-off tail, boldly barred with black.* (Broad-winged Hawk is larger, chunkier, with shorter, broadly banded tail and broader wings.) **ADULT** Dark steel-blue above; narrow reddish bars below. **FEMALE** Larger than male. **IMMATURE** Brown above; whitish below, streaked dark brown. **FLIGHT** *Rapid, alternately flapping and gliding*, rarely soars. **VOICE** Leisurely, high-pitched *que-que-que-que* ... **STATUS AND RANGE** A rare and increasingly local permanent resident in Puerto Rico. Occurs primarily in and around the commonwealth forests of Toro Negro and Maricao. The former population in the Luquillo Mountains is nearly gone. A few migrants occur in the Virgin Islands, particularly on St. John, where rare, and doubtless in Puerto Rico as well, primarily November–April. The Puerto Rico race is critically endangered. **HABITAT** Mature mountain forests.

Osprey
The only species in this family, it is well adapted to catching fish. Its claws are large and the soles of its feet are studded with spines for gripping its slippery prey. It captures fish by hovering and then plunging, feet first, into the water.

**OSPREY** *Pandion haliaetus* (Águila pescadora, Águila de mar, Guincho, Fish hawk, Eagle, Sea eagle) 53–61cm (21–24in); wingspan 1.5–1.8m (5–6ft); male 1.4kg, female 1.6kg. **BEHAVIOR** *Hovers and dives for fish.* **DESCRIPTION** *White head, dark bar behind eye*, contrast of primarily white underparts and dark upperparts. Vagrant Bahamas race has entirely white head. **FLIGHT** *Wings characteristically bent at wrist, dark wrist patch.* **VOICE** Piercing whistles. **STATUS AND RANGE** Common in Puerto Rico and Virgin Islands, where migrants and non-breeding residents occur primarily September–April. Some remain throughout the year. Some individuals of migratory race have successfully bred in Puerto Rico and attempted to do so on St. Croix and Anegada. **HABITAT** All calm freshwater or saltwater bodies.

106

American Vulture
A small Western Hemisphere family, these large birds possess unfeathered heads and necks. They are excellent soarers and all feed primarily on carrion.

**TURKEY VULTURE** *Cathartes aura* (Aura tiñosa, Buzzard) 68–80cm (27–32in); wingspan 1.6–1.8m (5.3–6ft); 1–2.4kg. **BEHAVIOR** Feeds on carrion. **DESCRIPTION** *Large.* Blackish-brown, with *small, bare head.* **ADULT** Head red. **IMMATURE** Head blackish. (See Black Vulture.) **FLIGHT** Soars. *Dark two-toned wings held well above horizontal in broad V.* **STATUS AND RANGE** Common but local permanent resident in southwestern Puerto Rico, uncommon in northwest and on north coast, rare in east. Recent reports from Vieques. **HABITAT** Open areas at all elevations.

imm

adult

**Sharp-shinned Hawk**
(Not to scale)

adult

N. American race

Osprey

Bahamas race

adult

imm

Turkey Vulture

Plate not to scale

PLATE 39    BIRDS OF PREY — Owls

Birds of prey; most are nocturnal. Possess a distinctive facial disk, a large head with eyes directed forward, and silent flight.

**BARN OWL** *Tyto alba* (Lechuza) 30–43cm (12–17in); 520g. **BEHAVIOR** Nocturnal. **DESCRIPTION** Large owl with *flat, heart-shaped face*, large *dark eyes*, and *white underparts*. **VOICE** Loud hissing screech, and loud clicking sounds. **STATUS AND RANGE** A very rare and local permanent resident in Puerto Rico, where now nesting. Has occurred regularly on northwest and north-central coast. Numbers appear to be slowly increasing. **HABITAT** Open woodlands, fields with scattered trees, native palm groves, in and around human settlements, as well as relatively open areas from coast to mountains.

**SHORT-EARED OWL** *Asio flammeus* (Múcaro real, Múcaro sabanero, Búho) 35–43cm (14–17in); 350g. **BEHAVIOR** Most active dawn and dusk, perches on posts. **DESCRIPTION** Large owl, tan below, breast heavily streaked. Yellow eyes; distinct facial disk. **FLIGHT** Conspicuous black wrist patches on pale underwings and large tan patches on upperwings. Erratic flaps and glides low over ground. **VOICE** Short, emphatic *bow-wow*. Also distinct wing clap. **STATUS AND RANGE** An uncommon and local permanent resident in Puerto Rico. In Virgin Islands it is an uncommon resident on Tortola, Anegada, Beef Island, and Guana Island and is very rare on St. Thomas. Numbers are increasing in region. **HABITAT** Open lowlands including pastures, short-grass marshlands, and airport edges. Also open mangrove areas, salt flats, scrub, and infrequently forests at middle to high elevations.

● **PUERTO RICAN OWL** *Gymnasio nudipes* (Mucarito, Múcaro común, Múcaro de Puerto Rico, Cuckoo bird, Puerto Rican screech-owl) 23–25cm (9–10in); 103–154g. **BEHAVIOR** Nocturnal. **DESCRIPTION** *Small owl*. Two color morphs. Red Morph—Usually brown above with varying amounts of reddish; underparts marked with heavy brown streaks. Gray Morph—Grayer overall, lacks reddish tint. Ear-tufts not noticeable except when bird is alarmed. **VOICE** Tremulous trill; sometimes a chatter, whoop, or maniacal laugh. **STATUS AND RANGE** A Puerto Rico/Virgin Islands endemic, it is common and widespread in Puerto Rico. This is the only small owl of the island. In Virgin Islands a few individuals survive on St. John, while reports persist from St. Thomas, Tortola, and Guana Island. The Virgin Islands share an endemic subspecies that previously existed on Culebra and likely Vieques, from which it is long extirpated. The rare gray morph in Puerto Rico inhabits dry forests of the southwest. The Virgin Islands race is critically endangered. The genus is endemic to Puerto Rico. **HABITAT** Forests and wooded areas from coast to mountains, including shade coffee plantations and human settlements.

Barn Owl

Short-eared Owl

grey morph

Puerto Rican Owl

red morph

Nocturnal birds with large mouths that engulf flying insects on the wing. All have mottled plumages for camouflage. Some rest and nest on the ground.

● **PUERTO RICAN NIGHTJAR** *Antrostomus noctitherus* (Guabairo de Puerto Rico, Puerto Rican Whip-poor-will) 22cm (8.5in); 36g. **BEHAVIOR** Nocturnal. **DESCRIPTION** Small nightjar, mottled gray, brown, and black. Black throat edged with pale band. **MALE** White throat band and portion of outertail feathers. **FEMALE** Pale gray throat band and tips of outertail feathers. (Chuck-will's-widow larger, more reddish-brown plumage, and less white in tail of male.) **VOICE** Emphatic, repeated whistle, *whip, whip, whip* ... Also emphatic clucking. **STATUS AND RANGE** Endemic to Puerto Rico, where locally common on southwest coast eastward to Guayama. The range of this species has expanded in recent decades and there are now reports as far east as Naguabo, El Yunque, and Carolina. Officially classified as endangered, though perhaps no longer so, this bird was thought extinct from 1888 to 1961. **HABITAT** Primarily dry semideciduous forests with open understory and dense leaf litter. Infrequently moist and wet forest.

**CHUCK-WILL'S-WIDOW** *Antrostomus carolinensis* (Guabairo migratorio, Guabairo de la Carolina) 31cm (12in); 120g. **BEHAVIOR** Nocturnal, sometimes perches on roads. Difficult to locate during day unless flushed from hiding among deep thickets. **DESCRIPTION** Large nightjar, mottled reddish-brown; breast primarily blackish; white throat band; throat mottled brown. **MALE** White inner webs on outertail feathers. **FEMALE** Outertail feathers tipped pale gray, blend to dark. **VOICE** Whistles its name, the first syllable weakest, *chuck, will's-wid-ow*. Seldom calls in region. **STATUS AND RANGE** A rare migrant and non-breeding resident in Puerto Rico and rare to very rare in Virgin Islands September–May. **HABITAT** Woodlands from coast to midelevations; also cave entrances.

**ANTILLEAN NIGHTHAWK** *Chordeiles gundlachii* (Querequequé antillano, Gaspayo, Capacho, Mosquito hawk, Piramidig, Killy-dadick, Gi-me-me-bit) 20–25cm (8–10in); 50g. **BEHAVIOR** Flocks, active dusk and dawn. **DESCRIPTION** Dark, hawklike, with slender, pointed wings and *conspicuous white wing patch*. Nearly identical to Common Nighthawk; distinguished with certainty only by call. All other species of similar appearance lack white wing patches. **FLIGHT** *Erratic and darting*. **VOICE** Loud, raspy *que-re-be-bé*. **STATUS AND RANGE** A locally common breeding resident in Puerto Rico and Virgin Islands, primarily April–August. It migrates out of region subsequent to breeding, but non-breeding grounds are unknown. Migrants from other Greater Antillean islands and Bahamas pass through region in spring and fall, increasing local numbers. A few nighthawks occur near urban areas November–March. **HABITAT** Open fields, pastures, and coastal fringes. Also urban areas where lights are kept on all night, such as shopping centers and industrial complexes. Many nest on buildings with flat, gravel-covered roofs.

**COMMON NIGHTHAWK** *Chordeiles minor* (Querequequé migratorio) 20–25cm (8–10in); 55–95g. **BEHAVIOR** Flocks, active dusk and dawn. **DESCRIPTION** Extremely similar to Antillean Nighthawk, which has tan rather than blackish wing linings and is sometimes tanner below and paler above, but these are not consistent field marks. Also, the Common Nighthawk appears to have longer wings. Identified with certainty only by call. **FLIGHT** Erratic and darting. **VOICE** Distinctive, nasal *nyeet*. Rarely calls during migration. **STATUS AND RANGE** An uncommon migrant to Puerto Rico and likely in Virgin Islands September–October and April–May. Often congregates in large flocks at dusk, moving on the next day. **HABITAT** Open areas such as agricultural fields, pastures, and savannas, including human settlements.

Puerto Rican Nightjar

♂

♂

Chuck-will's-widow

♀

Antillean Nighthawk

Common
Nighthawk

pale northern
migrant ♂

♀

♂

dark northern
migrant ♂

PLATE 41    LAND BIRDS — Aerial Birds

## Swifts

The most aerial of land birds, they pursue flying insects on the wing throughout the day without landing to rest. Flight is fast and erratic, propelled by shallow, rapid flapping of their stiff, bow-shaped wings.

**BLACK SWIFT** *Cypseloides niger* (Vencejo negro, Black swallow, Rain bird) 15–18cm (5.75–7in); 50g. **BEHAVIOR** Aerial, flocks. **DESCRIPTION** *Fairly large*, black swift, with *slightly forked tail*. (Chimney swift is smaller, with shorter tail, more darting flight, and quicker wingbeats.) **VOICE** A soft *tchip, tchip* in flight. **STATUS AND RANGE** An uncommon breeding resident mid-March through September in Puerto Rico, it migrates off the island and is rarely seen during intervening months. Migrants are very rare in Virgin Islands. Sometimes joins swallow flocks. **HABITAT** Primarily mountains, less frequently lowlands.

**CHIMNEY SWIFT** *Chaetura pelagica* (Vencejo de chimenea) 12–14cm (4.75–5.5in); 25g. **BEHAVIOR** Aerial, flocks. **DESCRIPTION** Medium-sized; dark; pale brown chin and throat. *Short, rounded tail barely visible in flight*. (Black Swift larger; has more conspicuous tail, which is slightly forked.) **VOICE** Loud, rapid twittering in flight. **STATUS AND RANGE** An irregular but generally rare migrant in Puerto Rico, very rare on St. Croix, and a vagrant elsewhere in Virgin Islands. Occurs primarily August–November and April–May. **HABITAT** Above cities and towns. Also above open fields and woodlands.

● **ANTILLEAN PALM-SWIFT** *Tachornis phoenicobia* (Vencejillo antillano) 10–11cm (4–4.25in); 9g. **BEHAVIOR** Aerial, flocks. **DESCRIPTION** Small, primarily white below, with *white rump, black breast band*. (Bank Swallow lacks white rump.) **STATUS AND RANGE** A decidedly rare visitor in Puerto Rico, including Mona Island. Occurs primarily on coast. Endemic to West Indies. **HABITAT** Open cultivated areas, palm groves, and urban zones.

## Martins and Swallows

Characterized by short, broad bills; long, pointed wings; and their habit of feeding on flying insects on the wing. They are very gregarious and can often be seen in large numbers over fields and marshes or perched on wires. The highly aerial swifts display much longer wings; shallower and more frequent wing strokes; and more rapid flight.

**NORTHERN ROUGH-WINGED SWALLOW** *Stelgidopteryx serripennis* (Golondrina alirrasposa, Golondrina aserrada) 12.5–14cm (5–5.5in); 16g. **BEHAVIOR** Flocks. **DESCRIPTION** Brown above, with white underparts blending to pale brown on throat. **STATUS AND RANGE** Irregular, but generally a rare migrant and non-breeding resident in Puerto Rico and Virgin Islands, particularly on St. John and Anegada. Southbound migrants occur primarily in October and non-breeding residents remain through February. It is very rare as a northbound migrant March–April. Sometimes occurs in numbers. **HABITAT** Open fields and wetlands.

Black Swift

Chimney
Swift

Antillean
Palm-Swift

Northern
Rough-winged
Swallow

**PURPLE MARTIN** *Progne subis* (Golondrina púrpura) 20–22cm (8–8.5in); 50g.
**BEHAVIOR** Flocks. **ADULT MALE** Entirely bluish-purple. Indistinguishable from male Cuban Martin. **ADULT FEMALE AND IMMATURE** Scaled pattern on grayish-brown breast; pale gray patch on side of neck; indistinct border between darker breast and whitish belly. (Female Caribbean Martin has brown wash on breast, rather than scaled pattern. See Cuban Martin.) **VOICE** Gurgling, including high *twick-twick*. Also high, melodious warble. **STATUS AND RANGE** An irregular but generally very rare migrant in Puerto Rico and St. Croix in Virgin Islands, though not recorded on latter island since 1980s. Occurs primarily during spring migration March–July. May occur in numbers during migration. **HABITAT** Towns and open areas.

**CUBAN MARTIN** *Progne cryptoleuca* (Golondrina cubana) 20–22cm (8–8.5in).
**BEHAVIOR** Flocks. **MALE** Bluish-purple overall. Indistinguishable from male Purple Martin. **FEMALE** White belly and abdomen contrast sharply with brown breast, sides, throat, and chin. (Female Purple Martin paler brown on breast; throat and chin blend gradually into whitish belly; also has pale gray patch on side of neck. Both sexes of Caribbean Martin similar to female Cuban Martin in pattern of underparts, but white below restricted to lower belly and abdomen. Also, female Caribbean Martin has less contrast between white and dark of underparts.) **VOICE** Gurgling, including high-pitched *twick-twick*, like a vibrating wire. Also strong, melodious warble. **STATUS AND RANGE** A very rare migrant in Puerto Rico, where reported primarily in February–May during northbound migration. Less frequent southbound in September. Some summer records. May occur in numbers during migration. Breeds only in Cuba. **HABITAT** Cities and towns. Also swamp borders and open areas, particularly in lowlands.

**CARIBBEAN MARTIN** *Progne dominicensis* (Golondrina de iglesias, Swallow) 20cm (8in); 40g. **BEHAVIOR** Flocks. **DESCRIPTION** Bicolored martin. **MALE** Upperparts, head, and throat blue; belly and abdomen white. **FEMALE AND IMMATURE** Blue of underparts replaced by brownish wash that blends into white of belly. (See Cuban Martin and Purple Martin.) **VOICE** Gurgling, including high *twick-twick*. Also melodious warble and gritty *churr*. **STATUS AND RANGE** A fairly common breeding resident in Puerto Rico and Virgin Islands January–September. During non-breeding season likely migrates to South America. **HABITAT** Towns, open areas, freshwater bodies, and coastal rock promontories.

**BANK SWALLOW** *Riparia riparia* (Golondrina parda) 12.5–14cm (5–5.5in); 15g.
**BEHAVIOR** Flocks. **DESCRIPTION** *Dark breast band*; dark brown upperparts. (Antillean Palm-Swift has white rump; longer, narrower wings; more rapid, darting flight.) **STATUS AND RANGE** Irregular, but generally an uncommon to rare migrant in Puerto Rico, primarily September–November and April–May, but a few occur as non-breeding residents December–February. In Virgin Islands it is rare during same seasons. Sometimes occurs in numbers, particularly on Anegada. **HABITAT** Primarily open coastal areas.

Purple Martin/
Cuban Martin

adult ♂

adult ♀

Cuban
Martin

adult ♂

Caribbean
Martin

Bank
Swallow

PLATE 43    LAND BIRDS — Aerial Birds

**TREE SWALLOW** *Tachycineta bicolor* (Golondrina bicolor) 12.5–15cm (5–5.75in); 20g. **BEHAVIOR** Flocks. **ADULT** Blue-green above, with *entirely white underparts* and slightly notched tail. Wing linings pale gray. **IMMATURE** Brown upperparts. **VOICE** Mostly silent in region. **STATUS AND RANGE** Irregular but generally a rare migrant and non-breeding resident in Puerto Rico and very rare to vagrant in Virgin Islands, primarily November–May, but occurring September–June. **HABITAT** Open areas, swamps, marshes, and other wetlands.

**BARN SWALLOW** *Hirundo rustica* (Golondrina horquillada, Swallow) 15–19cm (5.75–7.5in); 16g. **BEHAVIOR** Flocks. **ADULT** Primarily *tan underparts*; dark reddish-brown throat; *deeply forked tail* with white spots. **IMMATURE** Throat and upper breast tan; remainder of underparts white; tail less deeply forked. **VOICE** Thin, unmusical *chit*. **STATUS AND RANGE** A generally common and sometimes abundant migrant in Puerto Rico and Virgin Islands, primarily September–October and April–May. Some remain as non-breeding residents November–March, and fewer occur June–August. **HABITAT** Open areas over fields and swamps, primarily along coast.

**CAVE SWALLOW** *Petrochelidon fulva* (Golondrina de cuevas) 12.5–14cm (5–5.5in); 20g. **BEHAVIOR** Flocks. **DESCRIPTION** *Dark reddish-brown rump and forehead; pale reddish-brown ear-patch, throat, breast, and sides*; slightly notched tail. (Cliff Swallow has dark reddish-brown throat and ear-patch and lighter forehead.) **VOICE** Chattering or twittering. Also rather musical *twit*. **STATUS AND RANGE** A common permanent resident in Puerto Rico, but a vagrant in Virgin Islands. **HABITAT** Primarily over fields, wetlands, cliffs, and towns.

**CLIFF SWALLOW** *Petrochelidon pyrrhonota* (Golondrina de peñasco) 12.5–15cm (5–5.75in); 22g. **BEHAVIOR** Flocks. **DESCRIPTION** Dark reddish-brown chin, throat, and ear-patch; *pale tan forehead and rump*; slightly notched tail. (Cave Swallow has darker forehead and much paler ear-patch and throat.) **VOICE** Short, melodious, repeated note. **STATUS AND RANGE** A rare migrant and non-breeding resident in Puerto Rico and Virgin Islands. Peaks during southbound migration September–November, but occurs in late August and some remain through March. Infrequent spring migrant in April–May. **HABITAT** Primarily along coast.

116

adult

imm

Tree Swallow

adult

Barn Swallow

imm

Cave Swallow

Cliff Swallow

Ground-dwelling Fowl-like Birds

**HELMETED GUINEAFOWL** *Numida meleagris* (Guinea torcaz, Common guineafowl, Guinea bird, Guinea hen) 53cm (21in); 1.3kg. **BEHAVIOR** Terrestrial and flocks. **DESCRIPTION** *Unusual body shape; dark gray feathering with white spots; nearly naked head and neck.* **VOICE** Wild cackles. **STATUS AND RANGE** Introduced in region, where widespread domestically in farmyards, but locally feral. In feral state, uncommon locally in Puerto Rico and widely through the Virgin Islands. **HABITAT** Primarily dry scrubland.

**RED JUNGLEFOWL** *Gallus gallus* (Gallina [female], Gallo [male], Chicken [female], Rooster [male], Domestic fowl) Male 71cm (28in), female 43cm (17in); weight variable. **BEHAVIOR** Terrestrial. **MALE (ROOSTER)** *Resplendent plumage; red comb head wattle; long, bushy tail.* **FEMALE (HEN)** Smaller *comb and wattle;* brownish plumage. **VOICE** Universally recognized *cock-a-doodle-doo.* **STATUS AND RANGE** A well-known bird widely introduced in region. Feral very locally in Puerto Rico (particularly Mona Island) and widely in Virgin Islands, including St. Thomas, St. John, Tortola, Virgin Gorda, Anegada, and Jost Van Dyke. Semiferal and domesticated birds common on farms throughout region. **HABITAT** Dry and moist forests.

Pigeons and Doves
Plump, short-legged birds; doves are generally smaller and longer-tailed than pigeons.

**RUDDY QUAIL-DOVE** *Geotrygon montana* (Paloma perdiz rojiza) 25cm (10in); 110g. Difficult to locate. **BEHAVIOR** Terrestrial. **DESCRIPTION** Plump, *predominantly reddish-brown* with *pale tan stripe beneath eye.* **FEMALE** Less ruddy than male. (Other quail-doves in region have a white rather than tan stripe below eye and have whiter underparts.) **VOICE** Mournful coo gradually fading in strength and sometimes pitch, like blowing across mouth of bottle. Very ventriloquial. **STATUS AND RANGE** A fairly common permanent resident in Puerto Rico. In Virgin Islands rare on St. John and very rare or vagrant on other large islands. In early morning found on trails and road edges. **HABITAT** Primarily closed-canopy forests and shade coffee plantations in hills and mountains, also locally on coast.

⬤ **BRIDLED QUAIL-DOVE** *Geotrygon mystacea* (Paloma perdiz de Martinica, Paloma perdiz bigotuda, Marmy dove, Partridge, Wood dove, Barbary dove) 30cm (12in); 230g. Difficult to locate. **BEHAVIOR** Terrestrial. **DESCRIPTION** *White streak below eye; brown upperparts* (except for crown and neck); *reddish-brown limited to patch on wing.* Underparts grayish-brown. **FEMALE** Less iridescence on hindneck and upper back. **VOICE** Mournful *who-whóoo,* on one pitch or descending toward the end, loudest in middle of second syllable and then trailing off. Sometimes first syllable omitted. Similar to Key West Quail-Dove. **STATUS AND RANGE** Locally fairly common permanent resident on larger forested Virgin Islands. It is uncommon or absent on smaller ones, except Guana Island, where abundant and tame. Extremely rare and local in Puerto Rico except for Monte Pirata on Vieques, where uncommon. Endemic to West Indies. **HABITAT** Dense mountain forests with thick undergrowth; sometimes coastal forests.

⬤ **KEY WEST QUAIL-DOVE** *Geotrygon chrysia* (Paloma perdiz áurea) 28–30cm (11–12in); 170g. Difficult to locate. **BEHAVIOR** Terrestrial. **DESCRIPTION** *White line under eye; reddish-brown back and wings; primarily white underparts.* (Bridled Quail-Dove has browner upperparts and is much darker below. Ruddy Quail-Dove has more reddish-brown underparts and a duller streak below eye.) **VOICE** A mournful moan on one pitch, or sometimes descending at end. Call gradually increases in volume and then fades rapidly. Very ventriloquial. Similar to call of Bridled Quail-Dove. **STATUS AND RANGE** Fairly common permanent resident locally in Puerto Rico. Endemic to West Indies. **HABITAT** Dense woods and scrubby thickets with ample leaf litter, primarily arid and semiarid zones, but also in moist and wet mountain forests with undisturbed understory.

118

Helmeted Guineafowl

Red Junglefowl

♂

♀

♀

Ruddy Quail-Dove

♂

Bridled Quail-Dove

Key West Quail-Dove

Quail-Doves not to scale

● **PLAIN PIGEON** *Patagioenas inornata* (Paloma sabanera) 38–40cm (15–16in); 250g. **BEHAVIOR** Arboreal and gregarious. **DESCRIPTION** Paler than other large pigeons; *white edge to wing-coverts*, reddish-brown on wings and breast. **IMMATURE** Darker and browner than adult. **FLIGHT** Thin white band across wing. (White-winged Dove is smaller, browner, and has more pronounced white wing band.) **VOICE** Deep, deliberate *whóo, wo-oo* or *who, oo-óo*, and other variations. **STATUS AND RANGE** A rare and local permanent resident in Puerto Rico, where found almost exclusively on eastern third of island. Endangered. Endemic to West Indies. **HABITAT** Primarily open woodlands in mountains to moderate elevations. Sometimes coastal areas. Savannas, open woodlands, coastal scrub, dry limestone forests, and forest edges in moist and wet forests. It is usually associated with creeks and rivers with bamboo and African tulip trees (*Spathodea campanulata*).

● **SCALY-NAPED PIGEON** *Patagioenas squamosa* (Paloma turca, Paloma rubia, Red-necked pigeon, Mountain pigeon, Blue pigeon, Red head) 36–40cm (14–16in); 250g. **BEHAVIOR** Arboreal and gregarious. **ADULT** Appears entirely slate-gray. At close range head, neck, and breast have purplish-red tint. **IMMATURE** More reddish-brown than adult. (Plain Pigeon has reddish-brown wings and abdomen, and a white band on leading edge of wing.) **VOICE** Sounds like *Who are yoú!* **STATUS AND RANGE** A common permanent resident in Puerto Rico and Virgin Islands. Often seen flying rapidly over forest canopy. Endemic to West Indies. **HABITAT** Typically mountain forests; sometimes well-wooded lowlands, including wooded suburban gardens.

● **WHITE-CROWNED PIGEON** *Patagioenas leucocephala* (Paloma cabeciblanca, Blue pigeon, White head, Baldpate) 33–36cm (13–14in); 250g. **BEHAVIOR** Arboreal; flocks. **DESCRIPTION** Dark gray with *white crown*. **VOICE** *Whó took two?* (Faster and less deliberate than Scaly-naped Pigeon.) **STATUS AND RANGE** Locally common year round in Puerto Rico and St. Croix. Uncommon to rare on other Virgin Islands, though successfully reintroduced on Guana Island. Has daily foraging movements and moves among islands as conditions warrant. Nearly endemic to West Indies. Threatened. **HABITAT** Coastal woodlands and mangroves when breeding, sometimes mountains when not breeding.

**ROCK PIGEON** *Columba livia* (Paloma casera, Paloma común, Rock dove, Domestic pigeon) 33–36cm (13–14in); 350g. **BEHAVIOR** Flocks. **DESCRIPTION** Very variable coloration. Often gray with *black tail band* and *white rump*. **VOICE** Gentle cooing. **STATUS AND RANGE** Introduced. Common and feral in Puerto Rico and Virgin Islands. **HABITAT** Tame resident of towns and cities.

**COMMON GROUND DOVE** *Columbina passerina* (Rolita, Tortolita, Stone dove, Tobacco dove, Common dove) 15–18cm (5.75–7in); 30g. **BEHAVIOR** Primarily terrestrial. **DESCRIPTION** The only *tiny* dove in region. **MALE** Bluish-gray crown and hindneck; pinkish tint on underparts. **FEMALE** More uniformly gray. **FLIGHT** Flashes *reddish-brown wing patch*. **VOICE** Monotonous, often repeated call of either single or double notes, *coo, coo, coo, coo* ... or *co-coo, co-coo, co-coo* ... or *hoop, hoop, hoop* ... in staccato fashion. **STATUS AND RANGE** A very common permanent resident in Puerto Rico and Virgin Islands. Most frequent in arid regions. **HABITAT** Most dry lowland habitats, including urban areas. Less frequent at elevation, and absent from heavily wooded areas.

Plain Pigeon

Scaly-naped Pigeon

imm

White-crowned
Pigeon

adult ♂

Rock Pigeon

Common
Ground Dove

♀

♂

**WHITE-WINGED DOVE** *Zenaida asiatica* (Tórtola aliblanca, Cubanita) 28–30cm (11–12in); 150g. **BEHAVIOR** Usually gregarious. **DESCRIPTION** *Large, white central wing patch*. Tail tip white. (Zenaida Dove has white band on trailing edge of secondaries. Plain Pigeon is much larger, with less distinct white band crossing wing.) **VOICE** Single pitch, like *Twó bits for twó*. Also yodel-like cooing between two notes. **STATUS AND RANGE** A common permanent resident in Puerto Rico and Virgin Islands. It was first recorded in Puerto Rico in 1943 and subsequently among Virgin Islands in 1999. Numbers continue to increase. **HABITAT** Scrubland, mangroves, open woodlands, and urban gardens.

● **ZENAIDA DOVE** *Zenaida aurita* (Tórtola cardosantera, Mountain dove) 25–28cm (10–11in); 160g. *White band on trailing edge of secondaries; white-tipped, rounded tail.* (Mourning Dove lacks white in wing and has longer, pointed tail.) **VOICE** Gentle cooing, almost identical to Mourning Dove, *coo-oo, coo, coo, coo*, second syllable rising sharply. Rendered as "Mar-y boil brown rice." **STATUS AND RANGE** Generally a common permanent resident in Puerto Rico and Virgin Islands. Nearly endemic to West Indies. **HABITAT** Open areas, gardens, and hotel grounds. Also open woodlands, scrub thickets, and pine woods with dense understory.

**MOURNING DOVE** *Zenaida macroura* (Tórtola rabiche, Tórtola rabilarga) 28–33cm (11–13in); 120g. **BEHAVIOR** Often flocks. **DESCRIPTION** *Long, wedge-shaped tail fringed with white*. Lacks white in wing. (Zenaida and White-winged Doves have white wing markings.) **VOICE** Mournful cooing almost identical to Zenaida Dove, *coo-oo, coo, coo, coo*, second syllable rising sharply. **STATUS AND RANGE** A common permanent resident in Puerto Rico. Strangely, a vagrant in Virgin Islands although it occurs on Vieques and Culebra off eastern Puerto Rico. It was unknown from Puerto Rico prior to 1935. **HABITAT** Primarily lowland open country, dry coastal forests, and agricultural lands, often near freshwater. Also agricultural areas in mountains.

**EURASIAN COLLARED-DOVE** *Streptopelia decaocto* (Tórtola collarina euroasiática, Tórtola turca) 28–30cm (11–12in); male 150–260g, female 112–196g. Medium-sized dove, pale gray with dark primaries and *black collar around hindneck*. Gray undertail-coverts. (See African Collared-Dove.) **VOICE** Repeated three-syllable *kuk-koooooooó-kook*, with brief pauses between phrases. Harsh, nasal *mew* in flight or upon landing. (African Collared-Dove has two-syllable throaty call.) **STATUS AND RANGE** Introduced or expanded to region probably in late 1900s from introduced populations elsewhere. A common permanent resident in Puerto Rico, where numbers are increasing in east. The species is common on Tortola, Beef Island, and Virgin Gorda. It is uncommon on St. Croix and Anegada and is rare elsewhere in Virgin Islands. Increasing in numbers. **HABITAT** Urban areas and agricultural fields, especially near stock feed.

**AFRICAN COLLARED-DOVE (RINGED TURTLE-DOVE, BARBARY DOVE)** *Streptopelia roseogrisea* (Tórtola collarina africana) 25–28cm (10–11in); 130–160g. Medium-sized dove, light tan above and white below, with *black collar around hindneck*. Tail long and rounded. (Eurasian Collared-Dove darker, with gray rather than whitish undertail-coverts and much darker primaries.) **VOICE** Two-syllable throaty call and variable soft cooing. **STATUS AND RANGE** Introduced. This domesticated dove has escaped from captivity. It is common in semidomesticated state in rural Puerto Rico, where it breeds in wild. Well established in southwest corner: Ponce to Salinas, and in Río Piedras. Expanding eastward. It is rare on St. Croix. Interbreeds with Eurasian Collared-Dove. **HABITAT** Around rural habitations, mangroves, swamps, and woodlands.

White-winged
Dove

Zenaida
Dove

Mourning
Dove

Eurasian
Collared-Dove

African
Collared-Dove

## Cuckoos

Slender birds with long tails and long, thin, down-turned bills. Their movements are slow and deliberate, and their flight is direct.

● **PUERTO RICAN LIZARD-CUCKOO** *Coccyzus vieilloti* (Pájaro bobo mayor) 40–48cm (16–19in); male 75–83g, female 88–110g. Large, with *very long tail* and *two-toned underparts* with gray on chin and breast, cinnamon on belly and undertail coverts. (Mangrove Cuckoo much smaller, has black ear-patch.) **IMMATURE** Breast washed cinnamon rather than gray. **VOICE** Emphatic, lengthy *ka-ka-ka-ka* ... accelerating, becoming louder, sometimes with altered syllables at end. Also soft caws and other call notes. **STATUS AND RANGE** Endemic to Puerto Rico, where fairly common at all elevations. **HABITAT** Dense forests and shade coffee plantations.

**YELLOW-BILLED CUCKOO** *Coccyzus americanus* (Pájaro bobo piquiamarillo, Rain bird, Rain crow) 28–32cm (11–12.5in); 60g. *White underparts*; long tail; down-curved bill, yellow at base. *Reddish-brown wing patch.* **VOICE** Throaty *ka-ka-ka-ka-ka-ka-ka-ka-ka-kow, kow, kow, kow* (or *kowp, kowp, kowp, kowp* at end); volume increases, then slows substantially at end. **STATUS AND RANGE** An uncommon breeding resident May–August in Puerto Rico. A few birds summer in Virgin Islands, but breeding not recorded. Southbound migrants are generally common in Puerto Rico and uncommon to rare in Virgin Islands, September–October. Northbound migrants are rare in Puerto Rico and very rare in Virgin Islands, March–April. A few birds overwinter December–February. Highly variable abundance annually. Sometimes large flocks occur during migration. **HABITAT** Lowland scrub and dry forests.

**MANGROVE CUCKOO** *Coccyzus minor* (Pájaro bobo menor, Mani coco, Cow bird, cat bird, Dumb bird, Rain bird, Maybird, Four o'clock bird, Coffin bird, Gogo) 28–30cm (11–12in); 60g. *Black ear-patch* and *tan abdomen*. Slender. Long tail; long, down-curved bill, yellow at base. (All other cuckoos lack black ear-patch.) **VOICE** Slower, more nasal than Yellow-billed Cuckoo. **STATUS AND RANGE** Fairly common permanent resident in Puerto Rico and Virgin Islands. **HABITAT** Dry scrub, mangroves, thickets, shade coffee plantations, parks, woodlands, and most areas with substantial forests at all elevations, but less frequent in high mountains.

## Waxwings

A small family, all of which have crests and possess red, waxy structures on the tips of their secondaries. They are arboreal and feed primarily on berries, though they sometimes sally for insects.

**CEDAR WAXWING** *Bombycilla cedrorum* (Ampelis americano, Picotera) 18–18.5cm (7–7.25in); 30g. **BEHAVIOR** Flocks. **DESCRIPTION** *Tan overall* with *distinct crest, yellow-tipped tail*. **IMMATURE** Streaked underparts. **VOICE** Clear, short, high-pitched trill. Also unmusical *che-che-check*. **STATUS AND RANGE** Highly irregular, but generally very rare in Puerto Rico, primarily December–March. May occur in numbers. **HABITAT** Mountain rain forests to lowland cultivated edges and urban gardens.

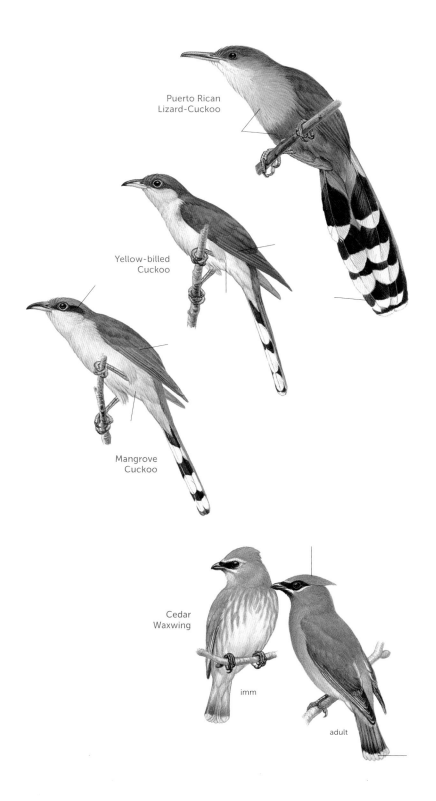

Puerto Rican
Lizard-Cuckoo

Yellow-billed
Cuckoo

Mangrove
Cuckoo

Cedar
Waxwing

imm

adult

PLATE 48    LAND BIRDS — Hummingbirds

Tiny birds with extremely rapid wingbeats and the ability to hover to feed. They can also fly backward. Most are brilliantly iridescent but appear black in poor light. They have long, pointed bills for probing into flowers. Hummers can be very aggressive around feeding territories.

● **PUERTO RICAN EMERALD** *Riccordia maugaeus* (Zumbadorcito de Puerto Rico, Fork-tailed hummingbird) Male 8.5–9.5cm (3.3–3.7in), female 7.5–8.5cm (3–3.3in); 3.4–3.8g. Small hummer with *forked tail* and no crest. **MALE** Green above and below, with black tail and pinkish base on lower mandible. **FEMALE** Underparts white, bill entirely black, outertail feathers tipped white. Tail may be forked, notched, or even-edged. (Antillean Crested Hummingbird has crest and rounded tail. See Green Mango.) **VOICE** Series of *tics* and a trill with buzz at the end. **STATUS AND RANGE** Endemic to Puerto Rico, where common in mountains and irregular on coast, particularly drier south coast. **HABITAT** Forests and edges, including shade coffee, also lowland wooded areas.

● **ANTILLEAN CRESTED HUMMINGBIRD** *Orthorhyncus cristatus* (Zumbadorcito crestado, Little doctorbird) 8.5–9.5cm (3.3–3.7in); 3.5g. Tiny; adults possess a *crest*. **ADULT MALE** Pointed crest; underparts blackish. **ADULT FEMALE** Crest less evident; underparts pale gray. **IMMATURE** Lacks crest. **VOICE** Emphatic notes. **STATUS AND RANGE** A common permanent resident throughout Virgin Islands, Vieques, Culebra, and on Puerto Rico's eastern coastal plain. Genus endemic to West Indies. **HABITAT** Primarily lowland openings, gardens, forest edges, and arid habitats.

● **ANTILLEAN MANGO** *Anthracothorax dominicus* (Zumbador dorado, Colibrí dorado, Doctorbird) 11–12.5cm (4.3–5in); 4–8g. Large hummer with down-curved black bill. **ADULT MALE** *Primarily black below*; throat green. **FEMALE** Whitish below and on tail tips. **IMMATURE MALE** Black stripe down center of whitish underparts. (Female Puerto Rican Emerald is smaller; has paler lower mandible and greener outertail feathers.) **VOICE** Unmusical thin trill, quite loud. Also sharp chipping notes. **STATUS AND RANGE** Common and widespread in Puerto Rico. Occurs primarily on coast to midelevations in mountains. Increasingly rare in Virgin Islands, where now believed absent from most islands except a few birds surviving on St. Thomas and offshore islets of Tortola. Endemic to West Indies. **HABITAT** Clearings and scrub. Also gardens and shade coffee plantations.

● **GREEN MANGO** *Anthracothorax viridis* (Zumbador verde, Colibrí verde) 11.5cm (4.5in); 6.6–7.2g. Large hummer with entirely emerald-green underparts; black, down-curved bill; and rounded tail. (Male Puerto Rican Emerald is smaller; has a shorter, straighter bill and a forked tail. **VOICE** Trill-like twitter; loud, harsh rattling or chattering notes; a hard *tic*. **STATUS AND RANGE** Endemic to Puerto Rico, where common in central and western mountains. It is decidedly uncommon in eastern mountains and on coast. **HABITAT** Mountain forests and shade coffee plantations, less frequent in moist and dry haystack hills (karst).

● **GREEN-THROATED CARIB** *Eulampis holosericeus* (Zumbador pechiazul, Doctorbird) 11.5–12cm (4.5–4.7in); 5–8g. Large hummer with slightly down-curved bill and *green breast*, though breast often appears black in poor light. Blue breast mark visible only in good light. (Male Antillean Mango has black breast.) **VOICE** Sharp *chewp* and loud wing rattle. **STATUS AND RANGE** A common and widespread permanent resident throughout the Virgin Islands. It is similarly so in lowlands of eastern Puerto Rico, becoming decidedly less abundant westward along the southern coast, and it is rare along the northwest coast. Species and genus endemic to West Indies. **HABITAT** In Virgin Islands, gardens and forests at all elevations. In Puerto Rico, primarily coastal.

126

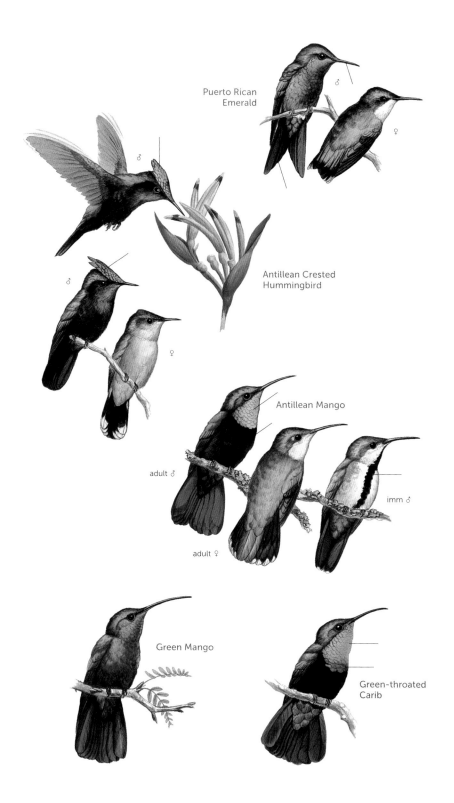

Puerto Rican
Emerald

♂

♀

♂

♀

Antillean Crested
Hummingbird

Antillean Mango

adult ♂

adult ♀

imm ♂

Green Mango

Green-throated
Carib

PLATE 49    LAND BIRDS — Hummingbirds, Tody, and Woodpeckers

● **VERVAIN HUMMINGBIRD** *Mellisuga minima* (Zumbadorcito menor) 6cm (2.5in); 2.4g. **BEHAVIOR** *Often hovers with tail cocked up.* **DESCRIPTION** *Tiny* hummer, much smaller than others in region, with *straight black bill.* Chin and throat sometimes flecked; sides and flanks dull green. **ADULT MALE** Tail deeply notched. **ADULT FEMALE** Tail rounded, tipped white. **VOICE** Loud, rhythmic, high-pitched, metallic squeaks. Also throaty buzz. **STATUS AND RANGE** Very rare on Mona Island, where it nested. A vagrant to Puerto Rico mainland. Genus endemic to West Indies. **HABITAT** All open areas with small flowers, open woodlands, and shade coffee.

### Todies

Small, chunky birds with green upperparts, a red throat, and a long, broad bill. Todies frequently sally from twigs for short distances to snatch insects. This bird family is endemic to the West Indies.

● **PUERTO RICAN TODY** *Todus mexicanus* (San Pedrito, Papagayo, Medio peso) 11cm (4.3in); 6g. Tiny, chunky; *bright green above; red throat; long, broad, reddish bill.* Flanks yellow. **VOICE** Loud, nasal *beep* or *bee-beep.* Wing rattles in flight. **STATUS AND RANGE** Endemic to Puerto Rico, where common and widespread from coast to mountains. **HABITAT** Forested areas from wet to dry, including dense thickets.

### Woodpeckers

Use their chisel-like bills to bore into trees for insects and to excavate nest cavities. The stiff tail serves as a prop while climbing. Males of most species have red marks on the head. Cavities excavated by woodpeckers provide important nest sites for other birds such as flycatchers, which cannot excavate their own cavities.

128  **YELLOW-BELLIED SAPSUCKER** *Sphyrapicus varius* (Carpintero pechiamarillo, Carpintero de paso) 20–23cm (8–9in); 50g. Difficult to detect. **BEHAVIOR** Drills distinctive series of horizontal holes in live trees. **DESCRIPTION** *Large white wing patch* shows as white wing-coverts in flight. **ADULT** Red forehead and crown, rarely black. Black-and-white facial pattern, black breast band. **ADULT MALE** Red throat. **ADULT FEMALE** White throat. **IMMATURE** Pale brown plumage, lightly spotted. Faint facial stripes. **VOICE** A plaintive *mew*, but rarely calls in region. **STATUS AND RANGE** A rare migrant and non-breeding resident in Puerto Rico and Virgin Islands from coast to mountains, primarily October–April. **HABITAT** Forests, forest edges, woodlands, and gardens.

● **PUERTO RICAN WOODPECKER** *Melanerpes portoricensis* (Carpintero de Puerto Rico) 23–27cm (9–10.5in); 45–70g. *Red throat and breast; white rump and forehead; blackish upperparts.* **ADULT MALE** Underparts primarily red with grayish-brown sides. **ADULT FEMALE AND IMMATURE** Less red on underparts. **FLIGHT** Undulating. **VOICE** Wide variety of calls, most commonly *wek, wek, wek-wek-wek-wek-wek* ... becoming louder and faster. Other vocalizations include *kuk* notes like a hen and *mew* notes. **STATUS AND RANGE** Endemic to Puerto Rico, including Vieques, where common and widespread. **HABITAT** Coastal coconut plantations and wooded urban parks to mountain forests, but primarily hills and lower mountains, including shade coffee.

♂

Vervain Hummingbird
(not to scale)

♀

adult

imm

Puerto Rican
Tody

adult ♀

Yellow-bellied
Sapsucker

adult ♂

imm

♀

Puerto Rican
Woodpecker

♂

PLATE 50    LAND BIRDS — Parrots

## Parrots, parakeets, and allies

Easily recognized by their raucous calls, large heads, and extremely heavy bills, which they often use to assist their movements among tree branches. All are gregarious, and all native species in the region are green. Flight is direct, with rapid, shallow wingbeats.

● **PUERTO RICAN PARROT** *Amazona vittata* (Cotorra puertorriqueña, Puerto Rican Amazon) 30cm (12in); 320g. **BEHAVIOR** Flocks. **DESCRIPTION** Bright green overall, *white eye-ring, red forehead*. (See Red-crowned Parrot.) **FLIGHT** Blue primaries and secondaries. **VOICE** Raucous squawks, including distinct bugling flight call. **STATUS AND RANGE** Endemic to Puerto Rico, where rare and very local. Reintroduced population around Río Abajo was expanding, but hurricanes of 2017 reduced numbers to fewer than 100 birds in the wild. The hurricanes also nearly extirpated original population in Luquillo Mountains. Hundreds of captive-bred birds survive in aviaries and presumably will be released in both localities. In 1975 only 13 birds were known to survive in the wild. Critically endangered. **HABITAT** Midelevation wet forests and northwestern limestone hills.

**RED-CROWNED PARROT** *Amazona viridigenalis* (Cotorra coronirroja, Green-cheeked Amazon) 30–33cm (12–13in); 295–345g. **BEHAVIOR** Flocks. **DESCRIPTION** Green overall, with *red forecrown* and *light green cheeks*. **FLIGHT** *Orange-red wing patch* and blue primaries. (Puerto Rican Parrot has red only on forehead and lacks orange-red wing patch.) **VOICE** Distinctive, not as raspy and raucous as most parrots: *keet, kau-kau-kau-kau*. **STATUS AND RANGE** Introduced to Puerto Rico, probably in late 1960s. Now rare and very local. Occurs primarily around the Central Aguirre Historic District at Jobos Bay on southern coast. **HABITAT** Lowland moist forests and scrub.

**ORANGE-WINGED PARROT** *Amazona amazonica* (Cotorra alianaranjada, Orange-winged Amazon) 32cm (12.5in); 300–470g. **BEHAVIOR** Flocks. **DESCRIPTION** Green overall, with *yellow cheeks and crown*; blue lores and eyebrow stripe. **FLIGHT** *Orange-red wing patch* and blue primaries. **VOICE** Call *kweet, kweet, kweet, kweet* is higher-pitched, weaker, and less raucous than in most other parrots in Puerto Rico. **STATUS AND RANGE** Introduced to Puerto Rico, probably in late 1960s. Presently, uncommon and very local. Occurs primarily in Ciales and Morovis. **HABITAT** Lowland second-growth forests and urban areas with ornamental trees. Infrequently in mountains.

**WHITE-FRONTED PARROT** *Amazona albifrons* (Cotorra frentiblanca) 22–26cm (8.7–10.3in); 180–240g. **BEHAVIOR** Flocks. **DESCRIPTION** Smallest *Amazona*. White forehead with blue lining behind white; red spectacles; tail tipped red; bill yellow. **MALE** Red feathers on shoulders. **FEMALE** Lacks red on shoulders. **IMMATURE** Duller overall, with yellowish forehead and reduced red on face. **FLIGHT** Fast and shallow wingbeats. Blue primaries and secondaries. **VOICE** Distinctive, higher pitched than most parrots, raspy and raucous *keet, kree-kaeet-kaeet-kaeet*. **STATUS AND RANGE** Introduced to Puerto Rico, probably in late 1960s. Now rare and very local, primarily around Mayagüez. **HABITAT** Lowland moist secondary forests and urban areas with large trees.

Puerto Rican Parrot

Red-crowned Parrot

Orange-winged Parrot

♂　　　♀

adult ♀

imm

adult ♂

White-fronted Parrot

**TURQUOISE-FRONTED PARROT** *Amazona aestiva* (Cotorra frentiazul) 35–37cm (13.8–14.6in); 350–450g. **BEHAVIOR** Flocks. **DESCRIPTION** Large parrot; blue forehead; yellow face and crown; red and yellow feathers on shoulders; red on tip of tail feathers; bill black. **FLIGHT** Fast and shallow wingbeats. Red wing patch and blue primaries. **VOICE** Distinctive, raspy, and raucous: *keet, krau-krau-krau-krau*. **STATUS AND RANGE** Introduced to Puerto Rico, probably in late 1960s. Now rare and very local in Old San Juan, Río Piedras, and Guaynabo. **HABITAT** Lowland second-growth forests and urban areas with trees.

**MONK PARAKEET** *Myiopsitta monachus* (Perico monje, Quaker parakeet, Quaker conure, Gray-breasted parakeet) 28cm (11in); 130g. **BEHAVIOR** Flocks. **DESCRIPTION** Fairly large, with *gray crown, throat, and breast; long, pointed tail;* flight feathers blue. **VOICE** Raucous squawks. **STATUS AND RANGE** Introduced to Puerto Rico, probably in 1950s, where now common, particularly in San Juan metropolitan area and to lesser extent on coast. There is a small flock on Tortola and reports of same on St. Thomas in Virgin Islands. **HABITAT** Coastal palm groves, urban gardens.

**ROSY-FACED LOVEBIRD** *Agapornis roseicollis* (Inseparable de Namibia) 17–18cm (7–7.5in); 45–60g. A very small green parrot with a *pinkish-red face, throat, and upper breast. Blue rump.* **VOICE** Various squeaky calls. **STATUS AND RANGE** Introduced to Puerto Rico, perhaps in late twentieth century. Now local around coastal plain and foothills, particularly Guaynabo, Bayamón, and San Juan, where increasing. **HABITAT** Open fields and urban areas.

**BUDGERIGAR** *Melopsittacus undulatus* (Periquito australiano, Parakeet, Budgie) 18cm (7in); 22–32g. **BEHAVIOR** Flocks. **DESCRIPTION** The typical pet shop parakeet or "budgie." Natural coloration green below, yellow head, and back heavily barred with black. Blue, white, and other color variations. **VOICE** Sharp screech. **STATUS AND RANGE** Introduced. Regularly escapes or is released, but not known to be established. Rare in Puerto Rico, primarily in San Juan and Ponce metropolitan areas. Numerous reports from Tortola, and a few from several other Virgin Islands. **HABITAT** Open areas with short grass, urban areas, golf courses.

Turquoise-fronted
Parrot

Monk
Parakeet

Rosy-faced
Lovebird

Budgerigar

PLATE 52    LAND BIRDS — Parrots

**ORANGE-FRONTED PARAKEET** *Eupsittula canicularis* (Periquito frentianaranjado, Halfmoon conure, Orange-fronted conure) 23–24cm (9–9.5in); 70g. **BEHAVIOR** Flocks. **DESCRIPTION** Medium-sized, primarily green with *orange forehead, white eye-ring, and blue primaries. Long, pointed tail.* **VOICE** Raspy squawks. **STATUS AND RANGE** Introduced to Puerto Rico, probably in 1960s, where now uncommon and local. Occurs primarily in extreme northeast and to lesser extent between San Juan and Caguas. **HABITAT** Wooded pastures and urban areas with ornamental trees.

**BROWN-THROATED PARAKEET** *Eupsittula pertinax* (Periquito carisucio, Periquito gargantimoreno, Periquito pertinaz, Parakeet, Caribbean parakeet, Brown-throated conure) 23–28cm (9–11in); 80–100g. **BEHAVIOR** Flocks. **DESCRIPTION** Fairly large, primarily green with *yellowish-orange face and forehead;* throat and breast dull yellowish-brown; primaries blue. *Long, pointed tail.* **VOICE** Raucous squawks. **STATUS AND RANGE** Introduced on St. Thomas reportedly from Curaçao, apparently in 1800s; it is now an uncommon and local permanent resident. Small numbers occur on St. John and Tortola. Formerly occurred on Jost Van Dyke in small numbers, and perhaps Virgin Gorda. In 1970s occurred on eastern tip of Puerto Rico, Culebra, and Vieques, but now extirpated. **HABITAT** On St. Thomas, wooded thickets in hills.

**WHITE-WINGED PARAKEET (CANARY-WINGED PARAKEET)** *Brotogeris versicolurus* (Periquito aliblanco, Periquito aliamarillo, Bee bee parrot, Canary-winged bee bee) 23cm (9in); 70g. **BEHAVIOR** Flocks. **DESCRIPTION** Small, but larger than Budgerigar. Green overall, with ivory-colored bill; *yellow band bordering wing. Tail long and pointed.* **FLIGHT** Wings flash *large whitish-yellow triangular patches.* **VOICE** High-pitched squawks. **STATUS AND RANGE** Introduced to Puerto Rico, probably in 1950s, where now locally common. **HABITAT** Woodlands from coast to foothills. Also towns and urban areas.

**RED-MASKED PARAKEET** *Psittacara erythrogenys* (Perico carirrojo) 33cm (13in); 165–200g. **BEHAVIOR** Flocks. **DESCRIPTION** Large parakeet, green overall; *face and crown primarily red, eye-ring white. Long, pointed tail.* **FLIGHT** *Red under leading edge of wing.* **VOICE** Nasal squawks. **STATUS AND RANGE** Introduced in Puerto Rico, probably in early 1970s, where now uncommon and local. Occurs along north coast, particularly Caño Tiburones, and a small flock in Arecibo. Species was decimated by 2017 hurricanes. **HABITAT** Lowlands, often around treed urban areas.

Orange-fronted
Parakeet

imm

adult

Brown-throated
Parakeet

White-winged
Parakeet

Red-masked
Parakeet

PLATE 53    LAND BIRDS — Parrots

**COCKATIEL** *Nymphicus hollandicus* (Cacatiel, Cacatúa ninfa) 30–33cm (12–13in); 80–100g. A *crested* parrot, *primarily gray* with a *large white wing mark* and an *orange circle behind eye. Tail long and pointed.* **MALE**  Head yellow or white. **FEMALE**  Head pale gray. **VOICE**  Various whistles and screeches. **STATUS AND RANGE**  Introduced apparently fairly regularly in recent decades. Occurs locally in small numbers in Puerto Rico, and in Virgin Islands on Tortola and Virgin Gorda. Not known with certainty to be established. **HABITAT**  Urban areas and human settlements.

**BLUE-AND-YELLOW MACAW** *Ara ararauna* (Guacamayo azul y amarillo) 80–85cm (32–34in); 1–1.2kg. **BEHAVIOR**  Flocks. **DESCRIPTION**  A *huge* parrot, *primarily blue above and yellow below.* **VOICE**  Loud squawks. **STATUS AND RANGE**  Introduced to Puerto Rico, likely in the 1970s. Now locally uncommon in San Juan metropolitan area, Guaynabo, and Bayamón. Occasional individuals seen on Tortola in British Virgin Islands. **HABITAT**  Forests, open areas with palms, and among human habitations.

**WHITE COCKATOO (UMBRELLA COCKATOO)** *Cacatua alba* (Cacatúa blanca) 46–61cm (18–24in); 550g. **BEHAVIOR**  Flocks. **DESCRIPTION**  Medium-sized, *entirely white* cockatoo with a usually flattened but *noticeable crest,* which makes head seem very large. Crest can be fanned. Bill black. **FEMALE**  Smaller body, head, and bill; reddish-brown eye (male's eye dark brown or black). **FLIGHT**  Pale yellow underwings and undertail. **VOICE**  Nasal *keh* or *keeh-ah* calls. **STATUS AND RANGE**  Introduced in Puerto Rico, perhaps in late twentieth or early twenty-first century. Now very local between Bayamón and Guaynabo. **HABITAT**  Forests, woodlands, clearings, areas with fruiting trees.

136

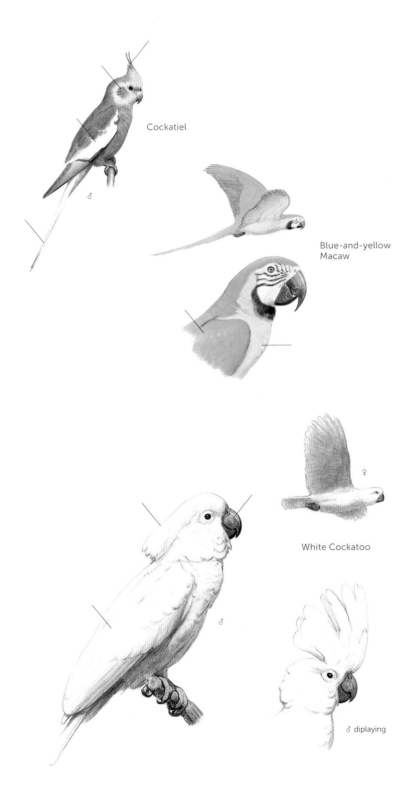

Cockatiel

♂

Blue-and-yellow
Macaw

White Cockatoo

♀

♂

♂ diplaying

PLATE 54    LAND BIRDS — Tyrant Flycatchers

Most are dull plumaged with a colorful crown patch that is usually concealed. Many species typically sit on exposed perches from which they sally to snare flying insects. Their broad bills, with bristles at the base, are well adapted for this purpose. Some are highly aggressive to other birds, even hawks.

● **PUERTO RICAN FLYCATCHER** *Myiarchus antillarum* (Jui de Puerto Rico) 18.5–20cm (7.25–8in); 22–25g. **BEHAVIOR** Sallies for insects. **DESCRIPTION** Medium-sized, with faint wing bars. Light brownish-gray underparts, lighter toward tail; lacks yellow wash. *Best identified by call.* (Caribbean Elaenia is smaller; with two whitish wing bars and a conspicuous yellow wash on belly. Puerto Rican Kingbird is much larger, with a distinctly two-toned body pattern and larger bill.) **VOICE** The most characteristic call is a plaintively whistled *whee*, from which its Spanish name is derived. Also a dawn song, *whee-a-wit-whee*, the two middle syllables of which are unmusical and sometimes sung independently during the day. Other calls include an emphatic *huit, huit*, a rolling *pee-r-r-r*, and a rasping note. **STATUS AND RANGE** A Puerto Rico/Virgin Islands endemic, it is a common permanent resident in Puerto Rico. In Virgin Islands, uncommon on St. John, Anegada, and Beef Island, rare on other islands. **HABITAT** Wooded areas, including mangrove borders, arid scrub, shade coffee plantations, haystack hills, and mountain forests. Absent from higher elevations, except Cerro Maravilla. On St. John favors dry forest.

**GRAY KINGBIRD** *Tyrannus dominicensis* (Pitirre, Petchary, Chicherry) 22–25cm (8.5–10in); 45g. **BEHAVIOR** Sallies from exposed perch for insects. **DESCRIPTION** Gray above, pale gray-white below, with distinct *dark mask* extending under eye; slightly notched tail. Crown patch rarely visible. (Puerto Rican Kingbird has a dark crown extending below the eye, and distinctive calls.) **VOICE** Emphatic *pi-tirr-ri*, or *chi-che-ry*. Also a sharp *peet* burr and *tir-ré*. **STATUS AND RANGE** Conspicuous and common throughout Puerto Rico and Virgin Islands. Migrants from other Greater Antillean islands augment local numbers October–November. **HABITAT** Open areas, including urban zones, with scattered trees in lowlands and mountains.

138

● **PUERTO RICAN KINGBIRD (LOGGERHEAD KINGBIRD)** *Tyrannus taylori* (Clérigo, Puerto Rican petchary) 24–26cm (9.5–10in); 45g. **BEHAVIOR** Sallies from exposed perch for insects. **DESCRIPTION** *Distinctively two-toned*: dark above and white below. *Crown blackish*, with rarely seen yellow patch. Nearly square tail. Bill large. (See Puerto Rican Flycatcher and Gray Kingbird.) **IMMATURE** Gray above, pale tan below, with tan wing-coverts. **VOICE** A wide variety of calls including emphatic, mallet-like chattering notes in a series, or other vocalizations with a *bzze-beep* or *bee-beep* in them such as *joú-bee-béep*. Also a melodious laugh like an unenthusiastic version of a Puerto Rican Woodpecker call. **STATUS AND RANGE** Endemic to Puerto Rico, including Vieques, where fairly common and widespread though uncommon in Luquillo Mountains. Considered a subspecies of Loggerhead Kingbird by AOS. **HABITAT** Forested areas, including shade coffee plantations. Also haystack hills and some mangrove swamps.

**FORK-TAILED FLYCATCHER** *Tyrannus savana* (Tijereta sabanera) Male 37–40cm (14.5–16in) with tail, female 28–30cm (11–12in) with tail; 30g. **BEHAVIOR** Flocks. **ADULT MALE** Black head; *pale gray back*; blackish-brown wings; white underparts. In breeding plumage *tail very long* with white-edged streamers; shorter during molt. **ADULT FEMALE AND IMMATURE** Duller; tail shorter. **STATUS AND RANGE** A very rare visitor to Puerto Rico and a vagrant to St. Croix in Virgin Islands. Most likely to occur July–August, but could occur any month. Could occur in numbers. **HABITAT** Open areas, savannas, pastures, airports, and mangroves.

Puerto Rican
Flycatcher

Gray Kingbird

Puerto Rican Kingbird

adult ♀
& imm

Fork-tailed Flycatcher

adult ♂

**CARIBBEAN ELAENIA** *Elaenia martinica* (Jui blanco, Pee whistler, John Phillip) 15.5–18cm (6–7in); 22g. *Throat and lower belly whitish with light yellowish wash*; breast pale gray; lower mandible pinkish; *two whitish wing bars*. Slight crest; displays crown patch when agitated. **VOICE** A distinctive and repetitious *jui-up, wit-churr*, last syllable softest. Song drawn-out *pee-wee-reereeree*. Calls well into day. **STATUS AND RANGE** Generally common and widespread permanent resident in Virgin Islands. In Puerto Rico, common in northeast and southwest and uncommon to rare in remainder of island. **HABITAT** Woodlands, coastal scrub, and forests. Primarily dry lowlands, but sometimes in mountains.

● **PUERTO RICAN PEWEE** *Contopus blancoi* (Bobito de Puerto Rico) 15cm (5.75in); 10g. **BEHAVIOR** Sallies from exposed perch for insects. **DESCRIPTION** Small flycatcher with brownish-olive upperparts and blackish wings and tail. *Underparts cinnamon-colored*; wings and tail nearly black. Lower mandible pale at base. Considered subspecies of Lesser Antillean Pewee by AOS. **VOICE** Sweet, high-pitched trill sometimes rising up the scale, reminiscent of water filling a glass, *pree-e-e-e-e*. Also a repeated *peet-peet-peet*. **STATUS AND RANGE** Endemic to Puerto Rico, where fairly common but local. Generally, it is more abundant in western half of the island. This pewee is absent from the Virgin Islands. **HABITAT** Moist midelevation mountain forests and woods, particularly shade coffee plantations. Occurs sparingly in lower and drier forests, mangroves, and scrub near sea level.

**EASTERN WOOD-PEWEE** *Contopus virens* (Pibí oriental) 16cm (6.25in); 14g. **ADULT** *Two whitish wing bars; whitish underparts washed dark gray on sides and breast*; sometimes complete breast bar. Generally lacks eye-ring, but may show hint of one. Dull orange lower mandible; undertail coverts sometimes yellowish. Relatively long wings extend halfway down tail. **VOICE** Plaintive whistle, *pee-a-wee*, slurring down, then up. **STATUS AND RANGE** Very rare in Puerto Rico and a vagrant on St. John and St. Croix in Virgin Islands. Most likely to occur September–October, less so November–April. **HABITAT** Mixed and coastal woodlands, forests, forest edges, scrub, open areas, and gardens.

Vireos
Olive-green birds that resemble warblers but have thicker bills, hooked at the tip. Their movements are sluggish as they move along branches, carefully inspecting twigs and undersides of leaves for insects.

**YELLOW-THROATED VIREO** *Vireo flavifrons* (Vireo gargantiamarillo) 12.5cm (5.5in); 18g. Difficult to locate. **BEHAVIOR** Found in forest canopy. **DESCRIPTION** *Yellow spectacles; two white wing bars*; dark eye. *Chin, throat, and breast yellow.* (White-eyed Vireo has white chin, throat, and breast.) **VOICE** Wheezy *chee-wee, chee-woo, u-wee, chee-wee ...* , also scolding *chi-chi-chur-chur-chur-chur-chur*. **STATUS AND RANGE** Irregular, ranging from locally fairly common to a very uncommon migrant and non-breeding resident in Puerto Rico and St. John September–April. It is rare (Guana Island) to vagrant (St. Croix) on other Virgin Islands. **HABITAT** Widespread in many forest types including natural forests, coastal scrub, woodlands, beach ridge forests, and second growth.

**WHITE-EYED VIREO** *Vireo griseus* (Vireo ojiblanco) 12.5cm (5in); 11g. Difficult to locate. **DESCRIPTION** Whitish below; *yellow sides and spectacles; two white wing bars*. **ADULT** *White eye.* (Yellow-throated Vireo has yellow chin, throat, and breast.) **IMMATURE** Duller; dark eye. **VOICE** Loud, slurred, three to seven syllables, such as *chip-a-tee-weeo-chip*, repeated with variations. Also churring note. **STATUS AND RANGE** Generally a fairly common migrant and non-breeding resident in Puerto Rico. It is rare on St. John and very rare on the other Virgin Islands. Occurs primarily October–April. Likely more frequent than records indicate. **HABITAT** Undergrowth, scrub, coastal thickets, and brushy woodlands.

Caribbean
Elaenia

Puerto Rican
Pewee

Eastern
Wood-Pewee

Yellow-throated Vireo
(not to scale)

adult

White-eyed Vireo
(not to scale)

PLATE 56    LAND BIRDS — Vireos (without wing bars) and Bananaquit

● **PUERTO RICAN VIREO** *Vireo latimeri* (Bienteveo) 12.5cm (5in); 10–15g.
**BEHAVIOR** Forages at all levels, but most frequently near ground. **DESCRIPTION** Distinguished by its *two-toned underparts*: throat and breast pale gray, belly and abdomen pale yellow; and by its *incomplete white eye-ring* and brown eye. **VOICE** Melodious whistle, usually three to four syllables repeated for several minutes, then changed; also a chattering *chur-chur-churr-rrr*. Contact note a *tup, tup*; also issues a hoarse, grating, catlike *mew*.
**STATUS AND RANGE** Endemic to Puerto Rico, where common. Most common in haystack hills of north coast and forested valleys of south coast. **HABITAT** Forests of all types and all elevations, including mangroves, dry coastal scrub, moist limestone hills, and wet mountain forests. Perhaps least frequent in higher elevations of Luquillo Mountains.

**RED-EYED VIREO** *Vireo olivaceus* (Vireo ojirrojo) 15cm (5.75in); 17g. Difficult to locate. **DESCRIPTION** Gray cap; *white eyebrow stripe* bordered by *black eye-line and crown stripe. Lacks black "whisker."* (Black-whiskered Vireo has black whisker stripe, tanner underparts; duller green on back, and paler gray on crown.) **ADULT** Red eye.
**IMMATURE** Brown eye, yellower tints on flanks and undertail-coverts. **VOICE** Calls primarily in April. Nasal, high *chway*. Also abrupt phrases, often repeated. (Black-whiskered Vireo has longer phrases.) **STATUS AND RANGE** Irregular, ranging from a locally fairly common to very uncommon southbound migrant in Puerto Rico and Virgin Islands, primarily September–October. Fewer birds pass through northbound in April–May, and even fewer overwinter in November–March. Likely more frequent than records indicate. **HABITAT** Dry and wet forests, open woodlands, scrub, and gardens, primarily on coast but less frequently in mountains.

**BLACK-WHISKERED VIREO** *Vireo altiloquus* (Julián chiví, John-chew-it, John Phillip, Greenlet) 15–16.5cm (5.75–6.5in); 18g. *Whitish eyebrow stripe; dark eye-line; black mustache stripe; lacks wing bars.* **ADULT** Red eye. **IMMATURE** Brown eye, browner plumage, and a faint wing bar. (No other vireos in region have black mustache stripe.)
**VOICE** Monotonous, throughout day. Short, melodious two- to three-syllable phrases, each different, separated by pauses. Also a complaining *shway*. **STATUS AND RANGE** Common breeding resident in Puerto Rico, fairly common on St. Croix, St. John, and Anegada, and uncommon on remaining Virgin Islands. Occurs February–August. Birds arrive en masse in early February and depart southward just as rapidly in late August or early September. Some birds present year-round in Puerto Rico and St. Croix. **HABITAT** All forest types at all elevations.

**PHILADELPHIA VIREO** *Vireo philadelphicus* (Vireo de Filadelfia) 11.5–13cm (4.5–5in); 10–16g. **BEHAVIOR** Usually forages high in tree foliage. **DESCRIPTION** Gray crown; gray-olive upperparts; *pale yellow throat and upper breast*, variable in intensity. Dark lores; whitish eyebrow stripe; brown eye; lacks wing bars. (Warbling Vireo has whiter breast and lacks dark lores. Tennessee Warbler has slenderer bill; in non-breeding plumage, has yellowish eyebrow stripe and greenish crown. In breeding plumage, much whiter below.)
**VOICE** A complaining *shway*. **STATUS AND RANGE** A rare southbound migrant and non-breeding resident in Puerto Rico October–March. A very rare northbound migrant April–May. **HABITAT** Forests, woodlands, and gardens.

**BANANAQUIT** *Coereba flaveola* (Reinita común, Sugar bird, Yellow bird, Yellow breast, Bahaman honeycreeper) 10–12.5cm (4–5in); 9g. Note the *curved bill; white eyebrow stripe and wing spot; yellow breast, belly, and rump.* **IMMATURE** Duller; eyebrow stripe yellowish. **VOICE** A thin, ascending, insect-like buzz that tumbles into a short warble. Call note an unmusical *tsip*. **STATUS AND RANGE** A very common and conspicuous permanent resident in Puerto Rico and Virgin Islands. **HABITAT** All habitats except driest lowlands and open pastures.

Puerto Rican Vireo

Red-eyed Vireo

adult

Black-whiskered Vireo

adult

Philadelphia Vireo

imm

adult

Bananaquit

imm

## DARK STREAKS BELOW; LITTLE OR NO YELLOW/ORANGE IN BREEDING ADULTS
### New World Warblers
Small, insectivorous birds with thin, pointed bills. Most are migratory.

● **ELFIN-WOODS WARBLER** *Setophaga angelae* (Reinita de bosque enano) 12.5–13.5cm (5–5.25in); 7.5–8.5g. **ADULT** *Thin white eyebrow stripe; white patches on ear-coverts and neck; incomplete eye-ring; black crown.* **IMMATURE** Grayish-green on back and yellowish-green on head and underparts. (Black-and-white Warbler has broad white crown stripes and creeps along trunks.) (See Plate 64.). **VOICE** Short, rapid, unmusical notes on one pitch, swelling and terminating with short double syllables slightly lower. **STATUS AND RANGE** Endemic to Puerto Rico, where uncommon and extremely local. Limited to two locations: in and around Luquillo and Maricao forests. Threatened. **HABITAT** Dense vines of canopy in humid mountain forests; sometimes at lower elevations.

**BLACKPOLL WARBLER** *Setophaga striata* (Reinita rayada) 12.5–14cm (5–5.5in); 13g. **BREEDING MALE** *Black cap, white cheek.* **BREEDING FEMALE** Grayish above, whitish below; lightly streaked sides; white wing bars and undertail-coverts. **NON-BREEDING ADULT AND IMMATURE** White wing bars and undertail-coverts; faint side streaks; pale legs. (Non-breeding adult and immature Bay-breasted Warbler unstreaked below, with pale tan rather than white undertail-coverts, and black legs.) (See Plate 64.) **VOICE** Thin, high-pitched *zeet-zeet-zeet-zeet* ... , also, distinctive *zheet*. **STATUS AND RANGE** Abundance varies year to year, but generally a fairly common migrant in Puerto Rico October–November and May. A rare nonbreeding resident December–April. It varies from common to uncommon in Virgin Islands, primarily October–November. **HABITAT** Mangroves, brush, scrub forests, open areas with trees, mixed woodlands, and upland forests.

**BLACK-AND-WHITE WARBLER** *Mniotilta varia* (Reinita trepadora) 12.5–14cm (5–5.5in); 11g. **BEHAVIOR** *Forages up and down tree trunks, often upside down.* **DESCRIPTION** *Black-and-white striped crown.* **MALE** Black cheek patch. **FEMALE** Whiter, particularly on cheek, throat, and sides. **VOICE** Thin *tee-zee, tee-zee, tee-zee, tee-zee,* varying in length. Also, buzzy *chit*. **STATUS AND RANGE** A fairly common migrant and non-breeding resident in Puerto Rico and St. John, uncommon on other Virgin Islands. Occurs primarily August–April. **HABITAT** Forests and wooded areas at all elevations.

**NORTHERN WATERTHRUSH** *Parkesia noveboracensis* (Pizpita de mangle) 12.5–15cm (5–5.75in); 18g. **BEHAVIOR** *Bobs and teeters;* terrestrial. **DESCRIPTION** *Pale tan below* with dark brown streaks. *Prominent pale tan eyebrow stripe that narrows behind eye, and fine blackish-brown streaks on throat.* (See Louisiana Waterthrush.) **VOICE** Sharp, emphatic *tchip*. **STATUS AND RANGE** A common migrant and non-breeding resident in Puerto Rico and Virgin Islands, primarily September–April. **HABITAT** Borders of standing water, primarily saline and brackish, in or near mangroves and coastal scrub forests.

**LOUISIANA WATERTHRUSH** *Parkesia motacilla* (Pizpita de río) 14.5–16cm (5.5–6.25in); 20g. **BEHAVIOR** *Bobs and teeters;* terrestrial. **DESCRIPTION** *White below,* with dark brown streaks. *White eyebrow stripe broadens behind eye;* lacks streaks on throat. (Northern Waterthrush has fine streaks on throat, and pale tan eyebrow stripe does not broaden behind eye.) **VOICE** Sharp *chink,* higher and more ringing than Northern Waterthrush. **STATUS AND RANGE** A fairly common to uncommon migrant and non-breeding resident August–March in Puerto Rico. It is uncommon on St. John and rare on other Virgin Islands. **HABITAT** Near or along flowing freshwater in wooded areas.

**OVENBIRD** *Seiurus aurocapilla* (Pizpita dorada) 14–16.5cm (5.5–6.5in); 19g. **BEHAVIOR** Bobs and tilts tail up; terrestrial. **DESCRIPTION** *Orange crown bordered with blackish stripes; bold white eye-ring;* white underparts heavily marked with large dark streaks. **FEMALE** Slightly duller. (Wood Thrush is larger, lacks blackish crown stripes, and is spotted rather than streaked.) **VOICE** A loud, sharp *chek*. **STATUS AND RANGE** A fairly common migrant and non-breeding resident in Puerto Rico and most forested Virgin Islands; it is rare on St. Croix. Occurs August–May. **HABITAT** Principally woodlands, shade coffee, and primary forest floors, often near streams or pools. Also occurs in mangrove thickets and scrub.

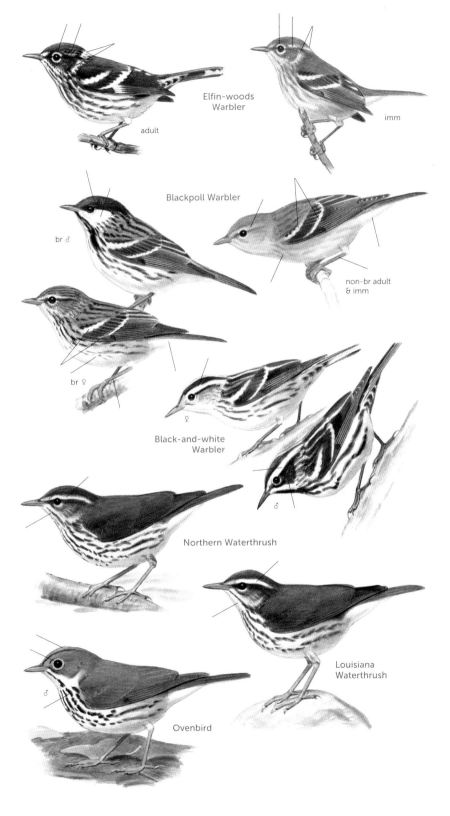

Elfin-woods Warbler

adult

imm

Blackpoll Warbler

br ♂

non-br adult & imm

br ♀

Black-and-white Warbler

♀

♂

Northern Waterthrush

Louisiana Waterthrush

♂

Ovenbird

DARK MARKINGS BELOW; YELLOW/ORANGE IN PLUMAGE

**MAGNOLIA WARBLER** *Setophaga magnolia* (Reinita manchada) 11.5–12.5cm (4.5–5in); 10g. *White tail markings* are diagnostic in most plumages; white eyebrow stripe and wing bars; yellow throat and rump. **NON-BREEDING ADULT AND IMMATURE** Pale eyebrow stripe; white eye-ring; gray head. Yellow underparts, tan band nearly across breast. (See Plate 64.) **BREEDING MALE** Cheek black, underparts heavily striped black. **BREEDING FEMALE** Substantially paler. (All other warblers with yellow rumps lack conspicuous white tail markings. Yellow-rumped Warbler has some white in tail but has a white rather than yellow throat.) **VOICE** Hard, sonorous *tseek*. **STATUS AND RANGE** Generally fairly common to uncommon southbound migrant in Puerto Rico and St. John, and rare on other Virgin Islands. Occurs primarily September–May, but less frequent as a non-breeding resident November–March. **HABITAT** Open woodlands in lowlands, swamp edges, overgrown pasture, and bushes. Sometimes in mangroves, gardens, and mountains.

**CAPE MAY WARBLER** *Setophaga tigrina* (Reinita tigre) 12.5–14cm (5–5.5in); 11g. In all plumages, heavy striping on breast and yellowish rump help identification. Usually has a diagnostic *yellow neck patch*. (Magnolia Warbler lacks yellow neck patch.) **ADULT MALE** Reddish-brown cheek; large white wing patch. **ADULT FEMALE** Duller; cheek grayish-olive; single white wing bar. **IMMATURE** Striped breast; yellowish rump; tan patch behind cheek. (See Plate 64.) **VOICE** A very thin, short *tsit*. **STATUS AND RANGE** An uncommon migrant and non-breeding resident in Puerto Rico and Virgin Islands September–April. **HABITAT** Mountain forests to coastal thickets, mangroves, and gardens. Almost anywhere plants are flowering; it is a habitat generalist.

**BLACK-THROATED GREEN WARBLER** *Setophaga virens* (Reinita verdosa) 12.5cm (5in); 9g. In all plumages, *yellowish-gray cheeks surrounded by characteristic yellow band*. **ADULT MALE** Black chin, throat, upper breast, and side streaks. **ADULT FEMALE AND IMMATURE MALE** Duller; chin yellowish. **IMMATURE FEMALE** Yellowish-gray cheek; faint side streaks. (Immature female Blackburnian Warbler has yellower throat and breast and whitish back stripes.) (See Plate 64.) **VOICE** Short, crisp *tsip*. **STATUS AND RANGE** An uncommon to rare and local migrant and non-breeding resident in Puerto Rico, and very rare on St. John, St. Croix, and St. Thomas in Virgin Islands. Occurs September–May. **HABITAT** Primarily mid- to high-elevation broadleaf and pine forests as well as shade coffee. May occur at all elevations. Sometimes mangroves, woodlands, and gardens.

**BLACKBURNIAN WARBLER** *Setophaga fusca* (Reinita de fuego) 13cm (5in); 10g. **ADULT FEMALE, NON-BREEDING MALE, AND IMMATURE MALE** Bright *orange-yellow throat, breast, eyebrow stripe, and sides of neck*. *White back stripes* and wing bars; dark side stripes. **BREEDING MALE** Orange throat and facial markings. **IMMATURE FEMALE** Yellowish throat, breast, eyebrow stripe, and sides of neck; white back stripes and wing bars. (Immature Black-throated Green Warbler has tan throat and breast and lacks whitish stripes on back.) (See Plate 64.) **VOICE** Fine, weak *tsseek, tsseek*. **STATUS AND RANGE** A very rare migrant in Puerto Rico and in Virgin Islands, where reported from St. John, Tortola, and Guana and Mosquito Islands. Occurs primarily September–October and April–May, but a few remain November–March. **HABITAT** Primarily pines, also tall trees, and botanical gardens.

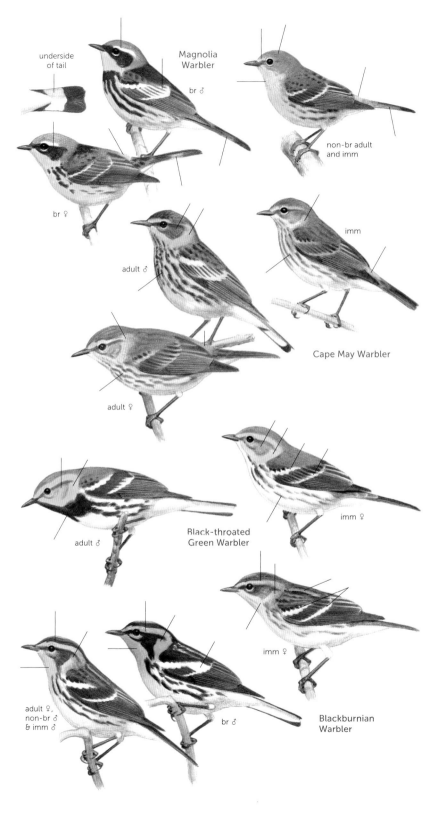

underside
of tail

Magnolia
Warbler

br ♂

non-br adult
and imm

br ♀

adult ♂

imm

Cape May Warbler

adult ♀

Black-throated
Green Warbler

imm ♀

adult ♂

imm ♀

adult ♀,
non-br ♂
& imm ♂

br ♂

Blackburnian
Warbler

MARKINGS BELOW; YELLOW IN PLUMAGE

**PRAIRIE WARBLER** *Setophaga discolor* (Reinita galana) 12cm (4.75in); 8g.
**BEHAVIOR** *Bobs tail*. **DESCRIPTION** Yellow underparts; *black side streaks*. **IMMATURE FEMALE** Yellow underparts; blackish streaks on sides; pale facial markings. (See Plate 64.)
**VOICE** A dry, husky *chip*. **STATUS AND RANGE** A fairly common to common migrant and non-breeding resident in Puerto Rico, St. Croix, and St. John; uncommon on other Virgin Islands. Occurs late August—April. **HABITAT** Dry coastal forests, thickets, pastures with scattered trees, mangroves, pine forests, and gardens, at all elevations.

**PALM WARBLER** *Setophaga palmarum* (Reinita palmera) 12.5—14cm (5—5.5in); 10g.
**BEHAVIOR** *Bobs tail*, often on ground. **DESCRIPTION** Note yellowish undertail-coverts, olive-colored rump, faint eyebrow stripe, and brownish back. **BREEDING** Dark reddish-brown crown. **NON-BREEDING** Yellowish undertail-coverts; olive-colored rump; faint eyebrow stripe; brownish back. (See Plate 64.) **VOICE** A distinctive *tsick*. **STATUS AND RANGE** An uncommon migrant and non-breeding resident in Puerto Rico and locally on St. John, primarily October—April. It is uncommon to rare on St. Croix and rare on other Virgin Islands. **HABITAT** Generally brush and bushes near coast or bordering wetlands, including mangrove fringes. Also open areas with sparse brush, and gardens.

**YELLOW-THROATED WARBLER** *Setophaga dominica* (Reinita gargantiamarilla) 13cm (5in); 9g. **BEHAVIOR** Often forages in tree crowns, among epiphytes, and sometimes picks insects off human structures. **DESCRIPTION** Note yellow throat and upper breast; white eyebrow stripe, *neck patch*, belly, and abdomen; sides streaked. **FEMALE** Black slightly reduced. **VOICE** A series of sweet notes descending in pitch toward end. Also high-pitched, slightly metallic *tsip*. **STATUS AND RANGE** Generally an uncommon migrant and non-breeding resident in Puerto Rico. Rare in Virgin Islands. Occurs primarily August—March. **HABITAT** Pine forests, gardens, developed areas, Australian pine (*Casuarina*), lowland forests, and coconut palms.

**YELLOW-RUMPED WARBLER** *Setophaga coronata* (Reinita coronada, Myrtle warbler) 14cm (5.5in); 12g. In all plumages, *yellow rump and patch on side of breast*, along with *white throat* are distinctive. A yellow-throated form could occur as a vagrant. **IMMATURE** Duller. (See Plate 64.) (Magnolia Warbler has a yellow rather than white throat.) **VOICE** Hard, characteristic *check*. **STATUS AND RANGE** Generally an uncommon and local migrant and non-breeding resident in Puerto Rico, St. John, St. Croix, and Anegada. It is rare on other Virgin Islands. Occurs primarily November—April. Of very irregular occurrence year to year. **HABITAT** Gardens, woodlands, thickets, areas with scattered vegetation. Also mangroves and swamp edges. Especially where fruits present.

**CANADA WARBLER** *Cardellina canadensis* (Reinita de Canadá) 12.5—15.5cm (5—5.75in); 10g. **ADULT MALE** Bluish-gray upperparts; *bold yellow spectacles*; yellow underparts with *black stripes forming a necklace*. **ADULT FEMALE** Duller than male. (See Plate 64.) **IMMATURE** Olive-brown wash on upperparts; virtually no necklace. **VOICE** A low *tchup*. **STATUS AND RANGE** A very rare migrant in Puerto Rico. Occurs primarily September and October. **HABITAT** Primarily lowlands in moderately open vegetation among scattered trees, usually near swamps or other standing water.

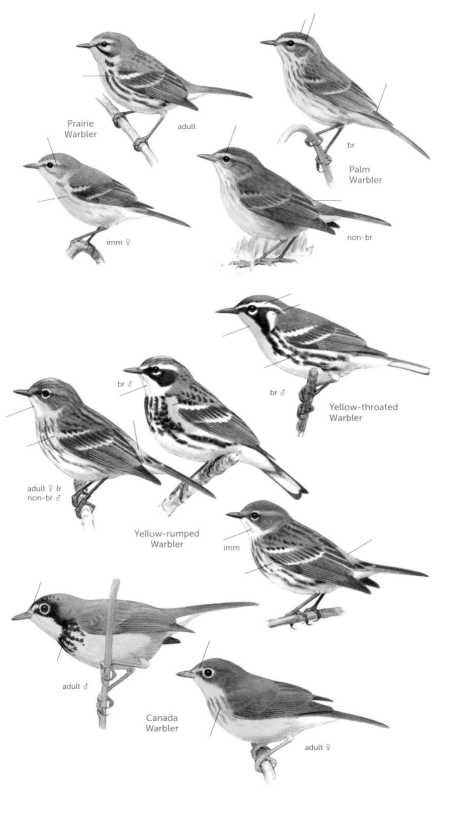

Prairie
Warbler

adult

br

Palm
Warbler

imm ♀

non-br

Yellow-throated
Warbler

br ♂

br ♂

adult ♀ &
non-br ♂

Yellow-rumped
Warbler

imm

adult ♂

Canada
Warbler

adult ♀

## BLACK/GRAY FACE OR HEAD; YELLOW BELOW; NO STREAKS BELOW

**KENTUCKY WARBLER** *Geothlypis formosa* (Reinita de Kentucky) 12.5–14.5cm (5–5.75in); 14g. Difficult to locate. **ADULT MALE** *Yellow spectacles; black facial mark and crown*; yellow underparts. **ADULT FEMALE AND IMMATURE MALE** Less black on face and crown. **IMMATURE FEMALE** Black on face absent, replaced by gray on lores. (See Plate 65.) **VOICE** A sharp *check*. **STATUS AND RANGE** A rare migrant and non-breeding resident in Puerto Rico and St. John, late August–April. It is very rare or vagrant on other Virgin Islands. **HABITAT** Dense undergrowth and thickets in moist mature broadleaf forest understory.

**HOODED WARBLER** *Setophaga citrina* (Reinita encapuchada) 12.5–14.5cm (5–5.75in); 10g. **BEHAVIOR** *Flicks and fans tail, showing white outertail feathers.* **MALE** *Distinctive black hood; yellow forehead and cheeks.* **ADULT FEMALE** Variable hood, from almost complete to black markings only on crown. (See also Plate 65.) **IMMATURE FEMALE** Lacks hood; yellow face sharply demarcated. (Adult female and immature Wilson's Warblers smaller, with yellow eyebrow stripe and no white in tail.) **VOICE** A metallic *chink*. **STATUS AND RANGE** An uncommon migrant and non-breeding resident in Puerto Rico September–April. Fairly common on St. John, uncommon on St. Croix, and rare on other Virgin Islands. **HABITAT** Moist mature broadleaf forest, mangroves, and sometimes undergrowth. Primarily lowlands, but also uplands.

**COMMON YELLOWTHROAT** *Geothlypis trichas* (Reinita picatierra) 11.5–14cm (4.5–5.5in); 10g. **ADULT MALE** Conspicuous *black facial mask*, edged above by whitish; throat and breast yellow. **ADULT FEMALE** Lacks facial mask; bright yellow throat and breast contrast with whitish belly; narrow whitish eye-ring; usually pale, whitish eyebrow stripe. (See also Plate 65.) **IMMATURE** Duller and browner than adult female. **VOICE** A sharp, gravelly *tchit*. The clear song *witchity, witchity, witchity, witch* is heard rarely before northward migration. **STATUS AND RANGE** A common migrant and non-breeding resident in Puerto Rico and uncommon in Virgin Islands. Occurs primarily October–early May. **HABITAT** Wet, thick, grassy areas usually on edges of freshwater swamps, ponds, or canals. Sometimes brush, overgrown fields, and abandoned pastures.

**CONNECTICUT WARBLER** *Oporornis agilis* (Reinita de Connecticut) 13.5–15cm (5.25–5.75in); 15g. Difficult to locate. **BEHAVIOR** Usually terrestrial; *bobs up and down*. **DESCRIPTION** Large, stocky, with *distinctive hood and white eye-ring. Dull yellow from belly to undertail-coverts, which extend nearly to end of tail.* (Mourning Warbler sometimes has eye-ring, but this is thin and broken in front; undertail-coverts shorter.) **ADULT MALE** *Hood bluish-gray.* **ADULT FEMALE AND IMMATURE** Hood pale gray-brown; whitish throat. (See also Plate 65.) **VOICE** A nasal, raspy *witch*. **STATUS AND RANGE** A very rare migrant in Puerto Rico, it occurs primarily in October. A vagrant in Virgin Islands. **HABITAT** Moist woodland understory, usually near water.

**MOURNING WARBLER** *Geothlypis philadelphia* (Reinita enlutada) 13–14.5cm (5–5.75in); 10–18g. Difficult to locate. **BEHAVIOR** Low to ground. **ADULT MALE** *Bluish-gray hood; black breast patch; lacks eye-ring.* **ADULT FEMALE** *Hood pale gray or brownish;* incomplete eye-ring; whitish throat; no black on breast. **IMMATURE** Hood pale gray or brownish; incomplete whitish eye-ring; throat yellowish. (See Plate 65.) (Connecticut Warbler has bold white, complete eye-ring and longer undertail-coverts.) **VOICE** A distinctive, metallic *jink*. **STATUS AND RANGE** Very rare in Puerto Rico as a southbound migrant in October, but a few may remain as non-breeding residents. Found most frequently in southwest corner of island. **HABITAT** Wet thickets, second growth, and swamp edges.

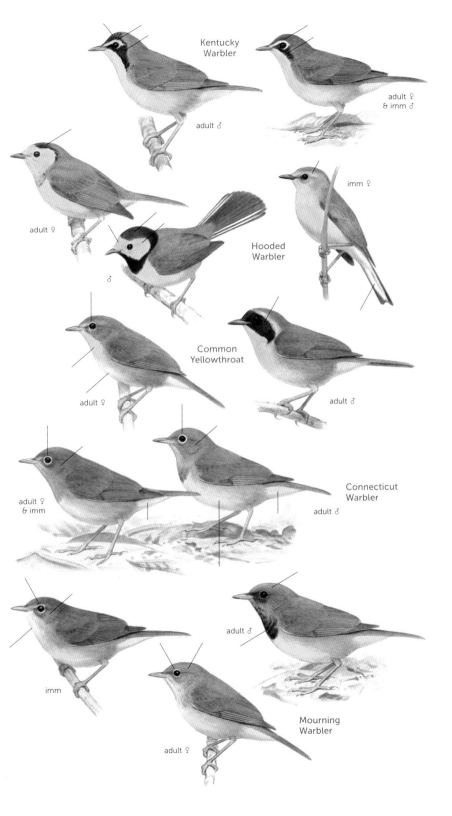

Kentucky Warbler

adult ♂

adult ♀
& imm ♂

adult ♀

Hooded
Warbler

♂

imm ♀

Common
Yellowthroat

adult ♀

adult ♂

Connecticut
Warbler

adult ♀
& imm

adult ♂

imm

Mourning
Warbler

adult ♂

adult ♀

YELLOW BELOW; LITTLE OR NO BLACK ON HEAD OR FACE

**YELLOW WARBLER** *Setophaga petechia* (Canario de mangle, Reinita amarilla, Canary, Mangrove canary) 11.5–13.5cm (4.5–5.25in); 13g. **ADULT MALE** Yellow overall including outertail feathers; reddish streaks on breast and sides. **BREEDING FEMALE** Yellow overall. Faintly streaked or unstreaked below; no reddish-brown on head. (See Wilson's Warbler.) **NON-BREEDING FEMALE** Underparts with some pale tan. (See Plate 64.) **IMMATURE** Upperparts olive-gray; underparts grayish-white; yellow in wings. (See Plate 64.) (Female and immature Wilson's Warblers have an eyebrow stripe rather than an eye-ring; show more greenish upperparts; lack tail spots or markings on underparts. Saffron Finch is larger; has heavier bill; occurs in grassy habitats.) **VOICE** Variable; typically loud, clear, and rapid *sweet-sweet-sweet-ti-ti-ti-weet*. Also thin *zeet* and hard *chip*. **STATUS AND RANGE** A common permanent resident in Puerto Rico on south, southwest, and east coasts, but uncommon to rare elsewhere. Numbers are declining at an alarming rate, likely because of the Shiny Cowbird. It is common to fairly common among all Virgin Islands. Migrants augment local numbers September–April. **HABITAT** Primarily mangroves, but sometimes coastal scrub, freshwater swamps, and shade trees, usually near water. Infrequent in mountains.

**NORTHERN PARULA** *Setophaga americana* (Reinita pechidorada) 10.5–12cm (4–4.75in); 9g. Grayish-blue above with *greenish-yellow back*; yellow throat and breast; white wing bars; incomplete white eye-ring. **NON-BREEDING ADULT AND IMMATURE** May have *faint black and reddish band across breast*. **BREEDING MALE** *Breast band conspicuous*. (Adelaide's Warbler has yellow eyebrow stripe and lacks greenish-yellow patch on back.) **VOICE** Ascending insect-like buzz with sharp note or warble at end; heard March–May. Call note a sweet *toip*. **STATUS AND RANGE** A common migrant and non-breeding resident in Puerto Rico and fairly common in Virgin Islands August–May. **HABITAT** All forest habitat at all elevations, including trees in urban parks. Also lowland scrub and gardens with large trees.

152

**BLUE-WINGED WARBLER** *Vermivora cyanoptera* (Reinita aliazul) 12cm (4.75in); 8g. Overall bright yellow with *bluish wings, white wing bars, and black eye-line*. (Prothonotary Warbler lacks white wing bars and black eye-line.) **VOICE** A sharp, loud *jeet*. **STATUS AND RANGE** Generally an uncommon migrant and non-breeding resident on St. John, and rare on other larger Virgin Islands and Puerto Rico. Occurs primarily October–April. **HABITAT** Primarily mature moist forests, but sometimes mangroves, thickets, and bushes.

**PROTHONOTARY WARBLER** *Protonotaria citrea* (Reinita pronotaria) 13.5cm (5.25in); 15g. **MALE** *Golden-yellow overall except blue-gray wings* and tail. **FEMALE** Golden-yellow face, throat, and breast; blue-gray wings and tail. (See Plate 65.) (See Blue-winged Warbler. Saffron Finch is larger; has heavier bill; wings are not gray; occurs in grassy habitat.) **VOICE** A metallic *tink*, similar to waterthrushes. **STATUS AND RANGE** Numbers vary year to year, but generally an uncommon migrant and less frequent non-breeding resident in Puerto Rico and rare in Virgin Islands. Occurs primarily September–April. **HABITAT** In or near mangrove swamps, but also other moist forests, including in uplands; also thickets near water.

● **ADELAIDE'S WARBLER** *Setophaga adelaidae* (Reinita mariposera) 12.5cm (5in); 6–10g. Bluish-gray upperparts; yellow throat and breast; yellow and white eyebrow stripe and crescent below eye. **FEMALE** Similar, but duller facial markings; less white in tail. (Female Northern Parula has yellowish-green patch on back and lacks yellow eyebrow stripe.) **VOICE** Loud trill, variable in pitch and speed. Also medium-strength *chick*. **STATUS AND RANGE** Formerly endemic only to Puerto Rico, where common and widespread, and to Vieques, where fairly common. It recently expanded its range to Culebra as well as to St. John and St. Thomas in Virgin Islands. On St. John, small numbers remain at a few locations following the two 2017 hurricanes. Its present status on St. Thomas is unclear. Adelaide's Warbler is now a Puerto Rico/Virgin Islands endemic. This is an unusual biogeographical event. **HABITAT** Primarily dry coastal scrubland and thickets and moist limestone forests of haystack hills.

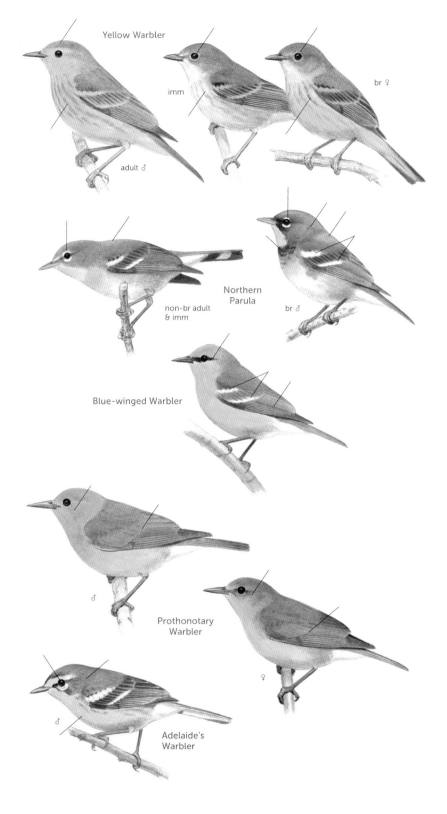

Yellow Warbler

imm

br ♀

adult ♂

Northern Parula

non-br adult & imm

br ♂

Blue-winged Warbler

♂

Prothonotary Warbler

♀

Adelaide's Warbler

♂

PLATE 62   LAND BIRDS — Warblers

## LITTLE OR NO YELLOW OR STREAKS BELOW IN ADULT BREEDING BIRDS

**AMERICAN REDSTART** *Setophaga ruticilla* (Candelita) 11–13.5cm (4.25–5.25in); 8g. **BEHAVIOR** Flicks and spreads tail. **ADULT MALE** Black upperparts, throat, and breast; *large orange patches in wings and tail*. **ADULT FEMALE** Head gray; upperparts greenish-gray; *large yellow patches in wings and tail*. **IMMATURE** Head greenish-gray; yellow patches reduced. **VOICE** Song variable but most often a series of increasingly loud notes, sometimes slurred or accented at end. Call note a loud *tschip*, also *srelee*. **STATUS AND RANGE** A common migrant and non-breeding resident in Puerto Rico and fairly common in Virgin Islands. Occurs primarily late August–early May. **HABITAT** Usually forests and woodlands from coast to mountains. Also gardens and shrubby areas.

**GOLDEN-WINGED WARBLER** *Vermivora chrysoptera* (Reinita alidorada) 12.5cm (5in); 9g. **BEHAVIOR** Prefers tree canopies. **DESCRIPTION** Note the *yellow wing patch; gray or black throat and cheek patch*. Forehead yellow; underparts whitish. **ADULT MALE** Throat and cheek patch black. **FEMALE AND IMMATURE** Paler and more subdued. Throat and cheek patch gray. **VOICE** A rather strong *chip*. **STATUS AND RANGE** A decidedly rare migrant and non-breeding resident in Puerto Rico and Tortola; it is very rare in other Virgin Islands. Occurs primarily September–April. **HABITAT** Primarily high mountain forests, including haystack hills with tall canopy. Sometimes lowland forests including mangroves.

**BAY-BREASTED WARBLER** *Setophaga castanea* (Reinita castaña) 12.5–15cm (5–5.75in); 13g. **BEHAVIOR** Slow-moving canopy dweller. **BREEDING MALE** *Reddish-brown cap and band on chin, throat, and sides; pale tan neck patch*. **BREEDING FEMALE** Duller. **NON-BREEDING ADULT AND IMMATURE** Back greenish-gray; unstreaked tannish below, including undertail-coverts; tannish flanks; white wing bars; usually blackish legs. (Non-breeding adult and immature Blackpoll Warbler finely streaked below, with pale legs; white undertail-coverts. Pine Warbler has unstreaked back.) (See Plate 64.) **VOICE** Weak *tsee-tsee-tsee*. Also a sharp *jeet*. **STATUS AND RANGE** Irregular but generally a decidedly rare migrant in Puerto Rico, primarily October–November and April–May. It is very rare on St. Croix and vagrant to other Virgin Islands. **HABITAT** Forest edges, woodlands, gardens, and open areas with scattered trees.

**CHESTNUT-SIDED WARBLER** *Setophaga pensylvanica* (Reinita flanquicastaña) 11.5–13.5cm (4.5–5.25in); 9g. **BEHAVIOR** Often cocks tail. **BREEDING MALE** *Yellow cap; reddish band along sides; white underparts*. **BREEDING FEMALE** Duller. **NON-BREEDING ADULT AND IMMATURE** Yellowish-green above; white eye-ring; pale gray underparts; two yellowish wing bars. (See Plate 65.) **VOICE** A harsh *tschip*. **STATUS AND RANGE** Irregular, but generally an uncommon to rare migrant and non-breeding resident in Puerto Rico, St. John, Tortola, and Guana Island. Very rare on other Virgin Islands. Occurs September–May. **HABITAT** Open woodlands, gardens with trees and shrubs.

American Redstart

adult ♀

adult ♂

Golden-winged
Warbler

adult ♂

Bay-breasted
Warbler

br ♀

br ♂

non-br adult
& imm

Chestnut-sided
Warbler

br ♂

non-br adult
& imm

PLATE 63    LAND BIRDS — Warblers

## NO YELLOW OR STREAKS BELOW IN ADULT BIRDS

**TENNESSEE WARBLER** *Leiothlypis peregrina* (Reinita de Tennessee) 11.5–12.5cm (4.5–5in); 7–18g. **NON-BREEDING ADULT** Olive-green above, yellowish below; yellowish eyebrow stripe, noticeable eye-line. **BREEDING MALE** Bright olive-green above, white below; gray crown; white eyebrow stripe, pale gray line through eye. **BREEDING FEMALE** Crown duller and greenish; breast with yellowish wash. **IMMATURE** Olive-green above; yellowish-green below except for white undertail-coverts. (See Plate 65.) **VOICE** Short, fine *tseet-tseet-tseet* ... repeated frequently. **STATUS AND RANGE** A very rare migrant in Puerto Rico, primarily September–October but also April–May. May occur in numbers. Vagrant on St. John. **HABITAT** Woodlands, gardens, and scrub.

**BLACK-THROATED BLUE WARBLER** *Setophaga caerulescens* (Reinita azul) 12–14cm (4.75–5.5in); 10g. **MALE** *Blue above;* black face and band along sides; *white wing spot.* **FEMALE** Narrow whitish eyebrow stripe; white wing spot, sometimes absent in young females. (See Plate 65.) **VOICE** A dull *chip.* Before migrating north rarely sings a wheezy, rising *zur, zur, zree.* **STATUS AND RANGE** A common migrant and non-breeding resident in Puerto Rico, uncommon on St. John, and rare on other Virgin Islands. Occurs September–May. **HABITAT** Forests, forest edges, shade coffee, and woodlands, primarily in mountains. Also moist to wet lowlands. Infrequent in dry forests.

**SWAINSON'S WARBLER** *Limnothlypis swainsonii* (Reinita de Swainson) 14cm (5.5in); 19g. Very difficult to locate. **BEHAVIOR** Primarily terrestrial. **DESCRIPTION** Head brownish-gray with *brown crown, whitish eyebrow stripe,* and blackish line through eye. Back, wings, and tail unmarked olive grayish-brown. Underparts whitish, grayer on sides. **VOICE** Sharp, metallic *chip.* **STATUS AND RANGE** A very rare migrant and non-breeding resident in Puerto Rico and St. John in Virgin Islands. Occurs September–April. **HABITAT** Heavy leaf litter in canebrakes, thickets, dense woodland understory, and wet limestone forests.

**WORM-EATING WARBLER** *Helmitheros vermivorum* (Reinita gusanera) 14cm (5.5in); 13g. **BEHAVIOR** Often forages among dead leaves at all levels in forest. **DESCRIPTION** Plain greenish-gray upperparts, wings, and tail; tan head with *black stripes on crown and through eye;* underparts pale tan, whiter on throat and belly. **VOICE** Rarely heard song is a rapid, thin trill, somewhat insect-like. Call note a thin, slightly musical *thip* or *thip-thip.* **STATUS AND RANGE** An uncommon migrant and non-breeding resident in Puerto Rico and St. John, while rare on other Virgin Islands. Occurs September–April. **HABITAT** Dense forests at all elevations.

156

br ♂

Tennessee Warbler

imm

♂

Black-throated
Blue Warbler

♀

Swainson's
Warbler

Worm-eating
Warbler

COMPARISON PLATE. STREAKS BELOW, SOMETIMES VERY FINE

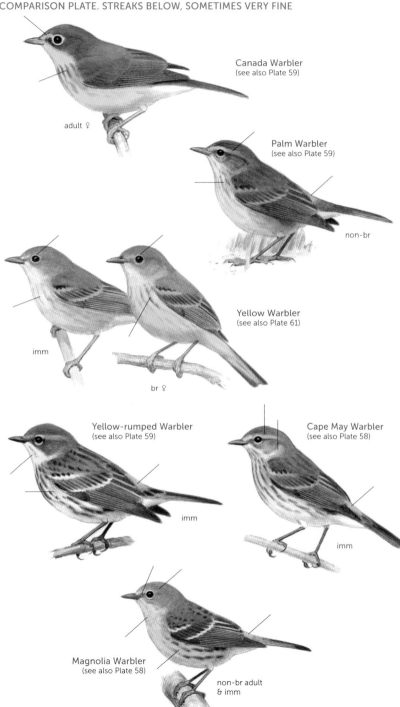

Canada Warbler
(see also Plate 59)

adult ♀

Palm Warbler
(see also Plate 59)

non-br

158

imm

Yellow Warbler
(see also Plate 61)

br ♀

Yellow-rumped Warbler
(see also Plate 59)

imm

Cape May Warbler
(see also Plate 58)

imm

Magnolia Warbler
(see also Plate 58)

non-br adult
& imm

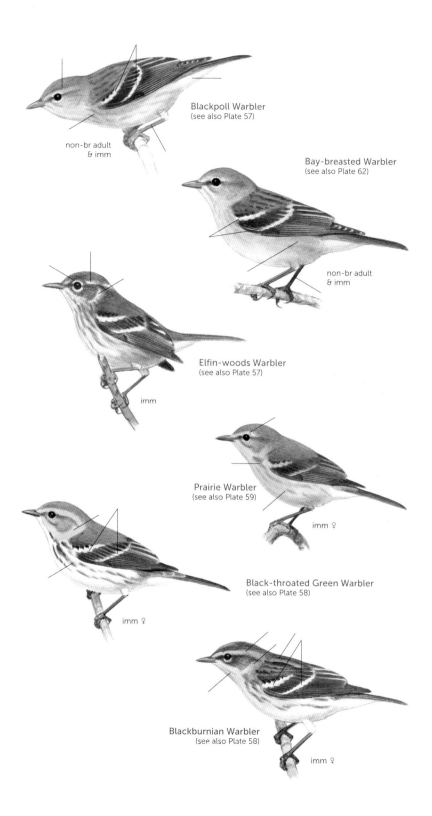

Blackpoll Warbler
(see also Plate 57)

non-br adult
& imm

Bay-breasted Warbler
(see also Plate 62)

non-br adult
& imm

Elfin-woods Warbler
(see also Plate 57)

imm

Prairie Warbler
(see also Plate 59)

imm ♀

Black-throated Green Warbler
(see also Plate 58)

imm ♀

Blackburnian Warbler
(see also Plate 58)

imm ♀

PLATE 65    LAND BIRDS — Confusing Warblers

COMPARISON PLATE. NO STREAKS BELOW

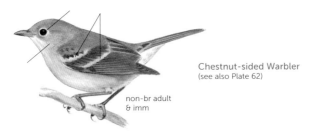

Chestnut-sided Warbler
(see also Plate 62)

non-br adult
& imm

Tennessee Warbler
(see also Plate 63)

imm

160

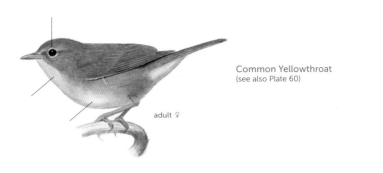

Common Yellowthroat
(see also Plate 60)

adult ♀

Black-throated Blue Warbler
(see also Plate 63)

♀

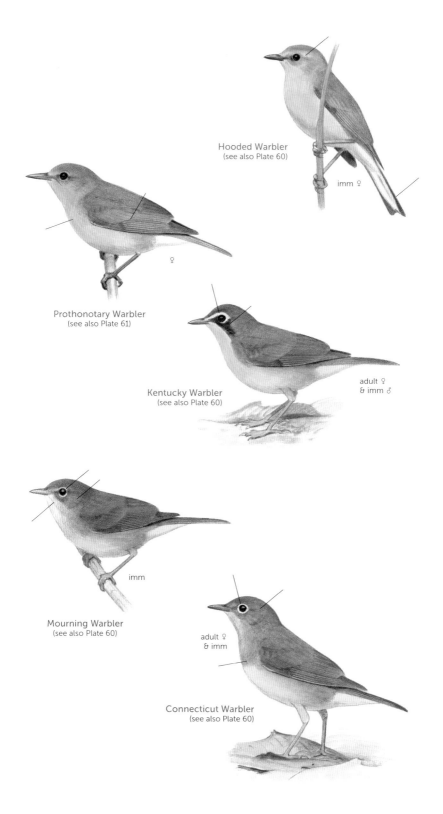

Hooded Warbler
(see also Plate 60)

imm ♀

Prothonotary Warbler
(see also Plate 61)

♀

Kentucky Warbler
(see also Plate 60)

adult ♀
& imm ♂

Mourning Warbler
(see also Plate 60)

imm

adult ♀
& imm

Connecticut Warbler
(see also Plate 60)

## MEDIUM-SIZED, WITH SPOTS OR STREAKS BELOW

**SWAINSON'S THRUSH** *Catharus ustulatus* (Zorzalito de Swainson) 17.5cm (7in); 35g. Difficult to detect. **BEHAVIOR** Moderately terrestrial. **DESCRIPTION** Grayish-brown above; whitish below, with brownish spots on breast. *Whitish eye-ring and lores give spectacled appearance.* (Veery, and Gray-cheeked and Bicknell's Thrushes lack conspicuous eye-ring. Hermit Thrush has less conspicuous eye-ring and has reddish-brown tail.) **VOICE** Generally silent in West Indies. **STATUS AND RANGE** Generally a very rare migrant in Puerto Rico. Occurs regularly and at times in numbers on Guana Island in British Virgin Islands; consequently, likely occurs more regularly on other islands. Occurs primarily in October but found September–November and March–May. Abundance fluctuates year to year. **HABITAT** Open woods and tree clumps with much leaf litter and little undergrowth. Also gardens.

**BICKNELL'S THRUSH** *Catharus bicknelli* (Zorzalito de Bicknell) 16–19cm (6.25–7.5in); 26–33g. Difficult to locate and identify. **BEHAVIOR** Highly terrestrial in dense vegetation. **DESCRIPTION** Brownish upperparts; white underparts and sides of throat; breast tan, boldly spotted black. *Grayish cheeks* and lores; dark reddish-brown tail. (Gray-cheeked Thrush slightly larger, grayer above, with darker lores, whiter breast, and pinkish rather than yellow on lower mandible, but characters overlap. Too similar to separate accurately.) **VOICE** Generally silent in West Indies. **STATUS AND RANGE** A decidedly uncommon to rare and local migrant and non-breeding resident in Puerto Rico, occurring late September–early May. Very rare on Vieques. Its stealthy behavior indicates it is likely more frequent than records indicate. Threatened elsewhere in its range. **HABITAT** Broadleaf forests, generally at higher elevations. Also woods or gardens with large trees.

162   ● **PEARLY-EYED THRASHER** *Margarops fuscatus* (Zorzal pardo, Chucho, Thrushie, Sour-sop bird) 28–30cm (11–12in); 75g. Upperparts brown; *underparts white, streaked with brown. White eye; large yellowish bill;* large white patches on tail tip. **VOICE** Series of one- to three-syllable phrases with lengthy pauses between. Also many raucous call notes. Often sings well into the day and during clear nights. **STATUS AND RANGE** A common permanent resident in Puerto Rico and Virgin Islands. Genus nearly endemic to West Indies. **HABITAT** Thickets, woodlands, and forests at all elevations from mangroves and coastal palm groves to mountaintops. Also urban areas. Sometimes a nuisance around human settlements in Virgin Islands.

Swainson's Thrush

Bicknell's Thrush

Pearly-eyed Thrasher

MEDIUM-SIZED, WITH LONG, COCKED TAILS

**NORTHERN MOCKINGBIRD** *Mimus polyglottos* (Ruiseñor) 23–28cm (9–11in); 50g. **BEHAVIOR** *Cocks tail.* **DESCRIPTION** Gray above, grayish-white below. *Wings and tail conspicuously marked with white; long tail.* (Gray Kingbird lacks white wing and tail patches and does not cock its shorter tail. Vagrant Bahama Mockingbird larger; lacks white in wings.) **VOICE** Clear, melodious phrases, each repeated several times. Also loud, scolding *tchack*. It sometimes imitates other birds. **STATUS AND RANGE** A common permanent resident in Puerto Rico and Virgin Islands, though unknown from latter prior to 1916. **HABITAT** Open country with scattered bushes or trees, including semiarid scrub, open mangrove forests, gardens, parks, and settled areas. Primarily lowlands, but ranges into mountains.

**GRAY CATBIRD** *Dumetella carolinensis* (Maullador gris, Pájaro gato gris) 23cm (9in); 40g. Difficult to locate. **BEHAVIOR** Often cocks tail slightly upward. **DESCRIPTION** *Entirely gray, with black cap, reddish-brown undertail-coverts, and long tail.* **VOICE** Distinctive soft, catlike *mew*. Also *pert-pert-pert*. Song disconnected phrases including mews, imitations, and pauses. **STATUS AND RANGE** A rare migrant and non-breeding resident in Puerto Rico. Occurs primarily October–May. A vagrant in Virgin Islands. **HABITAT** Thickets, dense undergrowth, urban gardens, particularly areas with abundant fruit.

● **RED-LEGGED THRUSH** *Turdus plumbeus* (Zorzal patirrojo, Zorzal azul) 25–28cm (10–11in); 66–86g. **BEHAVIOR** Often holds tail upward. **DESCRIPTION** *Gray upperparts; reddish legs and bill; red eye-ring; large white tail tips.* **VOICE** Low *wéecha*; rapid, distinctive, high-pitched *chu-wéek, chu-wéek, chu-wéek*; and loud *wheet-wheet*. Song melodious but monotonous one- to three-syllable phrases similar to Pearly-eyed Thrasher but more musical and with shorter pauses between notes. **STATUS AND RANGE** Common and widespread permanent resident in Puerto Rico. Often seen on mountain roads at dawn. Vagrant on St. John. Endemic to West Indies. **HABITAT** Woodlands and forests at all elevations, scrub, thick undergrowth, gardens, and shade coffee plantations.

adult

Northern Mockingbird

imm

adult

Gray Catbird

Red-legged Thrush

PLATE 68    LAND BIRDS — Slender-billed Birds

## BLACK AND ORANGE/REDDISH-BROWN BIRDS

**ORCHARD ORIOLE** *Icterus spurius* (Bolsero castaño) 16.5–18cm (6.5–7in); 20g.
**ADULT MALE** Primarily black with *reddish-brown breast, belly, lower back, and bend of wing.* **FEMALE** Grayish olive-green above; brighter on head and rump; dull yellow below. Note *two white wing bars* and *bright olive-green tail.* **IMMATURE MALE** Similar to female, but with black chin and throat. **STATUS AND RANGE** A very rare migrant in Puerto Rico in October and April–May. Less frequent as non-breeding resident November–March. A vagrant in Virgin Islands. **HABITAT** Woodlands and gardens.

**BALTIMORE ORIOLE** *Icterus galbula* (Bolsero de Baltimore, Calandria del norte, Northern oriole) 18–20cm (7–8in); 35g. **ADULT MALE** *Orange and black plumage; white wing bar; orange tail patches.* **ADULT FEMALE AND IMMATURE** Brownish above, *orange-yellow below with two whitish wing bars.* (Troupial larger, with more extensive black bib, an orange-yellow hindneck, and much more white in wings.) **STATUS AND RANGE** An uncommon to rare migrant and non-breeding resident in Puerto Rico, St. John, and Tortola; rare on St. Croix and very rare elsewhere in Virgin Islands. Occurs September–May. In Puerto Rico numbers peak during southbound migration in October, particularly on western half of island. Non-breeding residents often congregate in small numbers. In Virgin Islands, numbers peak strongly during northbound migration in April. **HABITAT** All elevations in gardens with trees, semiarid scrubland, open woodlands, swamps, and forest edges.

**● PUERTO RICAN ORIOLE (BLACK-COWLED ORIOLE)** *Icterus portoricensis* (Calandria de Puerto Rico) 20–22cm (8–8.5in); male 41g, female 37g. Black overall, with *yellow shoulders, rump, and undertail-coverts.* **IMMATURE** Upperparts brownish-gray with olive-yellow rump, underparts tawny brown with yellowish-brown throat. (Yellow-shouldered Blackbird has yellow confined to shoulder patch.) **VOICE** Infrequently heard dawn song of high-pitched whistles, some exclamatory, others questioning. Also sharp *keek* or *check*, sometimes sounding as if bird has a cold. **STATUS AND RANGE** Endemic to Puerto Rico, where fairly common. **HABITAT** Forests, forest edges, woodlands, and gardens from coast to midelevations, particularly near palms, which are used for nesting.

**VENEZUELAN TROUPIAL** *Icterus icterus* (Turpial venezolano, Bugler bird) 23–27cm (9–10.5in); 59–67g. *Large size, orange-yellow and black plumage, extensive white wing patch.* (See Baltimore Oriole.) **VOICE** Clear whistles, *troup, troup* ... or *troup-ial, troup-ial* ... **STATUS AND RANGE** Probably introduced in nineteenth century. A fairly common permanent resident throughout Puerto Rico, but particularly in the southwestern corner. Most frequent in lowlands, but also occurs in midelevations of Central Mountains. In Virgin Islands it is rare on St. Thomas, and very rare on Water Island and St. John. **HABITAT** Principally arid scrublands, but also human habitations.

imm ♂

adult ♂

Orchard Oriole

♀

Baltimore Oriole

adult ♂

♀ & imm

adult

Puerto Rican Oriole

imm

Venezuelan Troupial

## BLACK BIRDS

**SHINY COWBIRD** *Molothrus bonariensis* (Tordo lustroso, Glossy cowbird) 18–20cm (7–8in); male 40g, female 30g. **BEHAVIOR** Flocks. **DESCRIPTION** Medium-sized dark bird with conical bill. **ADULT MALE** *Uniformly glossy black with purplish sheen.* **ADULT FEMALE** *Drab grayish-brown upperparts; lighter brown underparts;* faint eyebrow stripe (see also Plate 76). **IMMATURE** Resembles adult female, but has pale eyebrow stripe and finely streaked underparts. (Greater Antillean Grackle much larger, with larger bill and tail.) **VOICE** Whistles followed by melodious trill. A soft unmusical *ka-wúk*, the second syllable rising and emphasized. Also, a variety of short call notes. **STATUS AND RANGE** Common permanent resident in Puerto Rico, but generally very rare in Virgin Islands. Colonized Puerto Rico naturally in 1950s. **HABITAT** Primarily open country and edges in lowlands. Favors dairies.

● **GREATER ANTILLEAN GRACKLE** *Quiscalus niger* (Mozambique, Chango) 25–30cm (10–12in); male 85g, female 60g. **BEHAVIOR** Flocks. **DESCRIPTION** Fairly large, with dark plumage, long tail, and conical, pointed bill. **ADULT MALE** Glossy metallic-blue to violet-black plumage; *yellow eye; deeply V-shaped tail.* **ADULT FEMALE** Duller; tail with smaller *V.* **IMMATURE** Dull brownish-black; tail flat; eye pale brown. (Great-tailed Grackle is larger in overall size, tail, and bill; plus has a more pronounced purplish sheen. All other black birds within range lack V-shaped tail.) **VOICE** Highly variable, including high *cling, cling, cling.* Notes vary from musical to wheezy gasps. Call note a *chuck.* **STATUS AND RANGE** A common permanent resident in Puerto Rico, very rare in Virgin Islands, where recorded from several islands, but has not become established. Endemic to West Indies. **HABITAT** Primarily open areas in lowlands, gardens, residential areas, and mangroves.

**GREAT-TAILED GRACKLE** *Quiscalus mexicanus* (Zanate mexicano) male 43cm (17in), female 33cm (13in); male 230g, female 125g. *Largest grackle;* long tail and pointed bill. Forms flocks. **ADULT MALE** Black with glossy purple sheen on head, back, and underparts; yellow eye; *very long, deep, V-shaped tail.* **ADULT FEMALE** *Brown overall, yellow eye.* **IMMATURE** Like adult female but dark eye, facial markings more distinct, dark barring on belly and abdomen. **VOICE** Very vocal; wide variety of clear whistles such as an ascending *kriiik;* also rattles and snaps. **STATUS AND RANGE** An increasingly frequent visitor to Puerto Rico, where first reported around 2003. Presently, single individuals found at several locations around coast including Cataño, Arecibo, and Guayama. Its range is expanding, and this grackle is very likely to become established. **HABITAT** Urban areas.

168

● **YELLOW-SHOULDERED BLACKBIRD** *Agelaius xanthomus* (Mariquita, Capitán) 20–23cm (8–9in); male 41g, female 35g. **BEHAVIOR** Flocks. **ADULT** Entirely glossy black overall, with *yellow shoulder patch.* (Puerto Rican Oriole more extensively yellow.) **IMMATURE** Duller; abdomen brown. **VOICE** A wide variety of calls. Raspy *tnaaa* accented at beginning; whistled *tsuu*, descending scale; melodious *eh-up*, second syllable lower and accented; various *chucks, chinks,* and *checks.* **STATUS AND RANGE** Endemic to Puerto Rico, where common only very locally at La Parguera and to lesser extent at Cabo Rojo salt flats. Rare and local elsewhere in Puerto Rico proper. Also, locally common on Mona Island. Critically endangered. **HABITAT** Primarily open mangroves and arid scrublands.

**EUROPEAN STARLING** *Sturnus vulgaris* (Estornino europeo, Estornino pinto) 22cm (8.5in); 75g. **BEHAVIOR** Flocks. **DESCRIPTION** Glossy black; with slender, pointed bill and short tail. **BREEDING ADULT** *Bill yellow.* **NON-BREEDING ADULT** *Underparts heavily flecked with white spots;* dark bill. **FLIGHT** Straight, unlike other black birds in region. Wings distinctively swept back. **VOICE** Wide variety of whistles, squeaks, and raspy notes. **STATUS AND RANGE** A recent colonist in region, discovered in Puerto Rico in 1973, when eight birds were found breeding near Boquerón. Small numbers are periodically found near Fajardo, but not in recent years. There are a few reports from St. Croix prior to Hurricane Hugo in 1989. Introduced in 1890s to North America from Europe. **HABITAT** Primarily open lowlands, including pastures and gardens.

Shiny Cowbird

adult ♀

adult ♂

Greater Antillean Grackle

adult ♂

adult ♂

adult ♀

Great-tailed Grackle

Yellow-shouldered
Blackbird

adult

non-br
adult

European Starling

imm

br

MEDIUM-SIZED BIRDS

● **PUERTO RICAN TANAGER** *Nesospingus speculiferus* (Llorosa) 18–20cm
(7–8in); 29–40g. **ADULT** Olive-brown above, white below; pale brownish stripes on
breast; conspicuous *white wing spot*. **IMMATURE** Lacks wing spot and has brownish
underparts. **VOICE** Noisy. Harsh *chuck* or *chewp* frequently runs into chatter of varying
length, *chi-chi-chit*. Infrequently sings a sweet, warbling courtship song with quality of a
hummingbird call. Also a soft twitter, and a thin sigh like a heavy exhale. **STATUS AND
RANGE** Endemic to Puerto Rico, where common in higher mountains, but regular locally at
moderate altitudes. Family also endemic to Puerto Rico. **HABITAT** Undisturbed mountain
forests, also second growth.

**SCARLET TANAGER** *Piranga olivacea* (Piranga escarlata) 18cm (7in); 29g.
**FEMALE** Overall yellowish-green plumage; distinctive bill shape; white wing linings in flight.
**NON-BREEDING MALE** Similar to female, but *wings black*. (Female Baltimore Oriole more
yellowish, with more pointed bill and whitish wing bars. See Summer Tanager.) **BREEDING
MALE** *Red overall, with black wings* and tail. **STATUS AND RANGE** Irregular, but generally a
rare migrant in Puerto Rico and very rare in Virgin Islands, primarily St. Croix. In Puerto Rico
occurs far most frequently during southbound migration in October. In Virgin Islands occurs
far most frequently as a northbound migrant in April. Numbers appear to be increasing.
**HABITAT** Open woods, forest edges, and gardens with trees.

**SUMMER TANAGER** *Piranga rubra* (Piranga roja) 18–19.5cm (7–7.5in); 30g.
*Large-billed* tanager. **ADULT MALE** *Entirely red*, brighter below; wings slightly darker.
**FEMALE** Yellowish olive-green above; yellowish-orange below. **IMMATURE MALE** Similar to
female, but with reddish tinge. (Female Scarlet Tanager yellow-green below; lacks orange
tinge; has whitish rather than yellow wing linings; and smaller bill.) **VOICE** A sharp, quick
*pit-ti-tuck*. **STATUS AND RANGE** An irregular but generally rare to very rare migrant and
very rare non-breeding resident in Puerto Rico, St. Thomas, and St. John, September–May.
It is very rare elsewhere in Virgin Islands. **HABITAT** Woodlands, forest edges, and gardens,
primarily at midelevations.

170

Puerto Rican Tanager

non-br ♂

br ♂

Scarlet Tanager

♀

adult ♂

♀

Summer Tanager

PLATE 71     LAND BIRDS — Heavy-billed Birds

PRIMARILY BLACK BIRDS

● **PUERTO RICAN BULLFINCH** *Melopyrrha portoricensis* (Comeñame, Comegandul, Capacho, Gallito) 16.5–19cm (6.5–7.5in); 23–45g. **ADULT** Black overall, with *reddish-brown throat, crown band, and undertail-coverts.* (Lesser Antillean Bullfinch has minimal reddish-brown in crown. Ranges do not overlap.) **IMMATURE** Dark olive-green; only undertail-coverts reddish-brown. **VOICE** Two to ten distinctive rising whistles followed by buzz. Also whistled *coochi, coochi, coochi,* and medium-strength *check,* like hitting two stones together. Sings much of day. **STATUS AND RANGE** Endemic to Puerto Rico, where common and widespread. Genus endemic to West Indies. **HABITAT** Forests and dense thickets of all types and at all elevations.

● **LESSER ANTILLEAN BULLFINCH** *Loxigilla noctis* 14–15.5cm (5.5–6in); 13–23g. **MALE** All black with *reddish-brown chin, throat, above eye, and undertail-coverts.* **FEMALE AND IMMATURE** Brownish-olive above, gray below; orangish undertail-coverts. (See Puerto Rican Bullfinch.) **VOICE** Short, crisp trill; harsh *chuck;* five to ten thin *tseep* notes sometimes followed by a buzz. Also, a lengthy twitter. **STATUS AND RANGE** Generally, a locally common permanent resident in Virgin Islands, where it has spread and now occurs on all large islands and a number of smaller ones. It is uncommon on St. Croix. Naturally colonized Virgin Islands around 1960 from Lesser Antilles. Numbers and range are increasing. Genus endemic to West Indies. **HABITAT** Primarily dry forest and scrub, but also shrubbery, gardens, thickets, and forest understory at all elevations.

**BLACK-FACED GRASSQUIT** *Melanospiza bicolor* (Gorrión negro, Chamorro negro, Finch, Sinbird, Grass sparrow) 10–11.5cm (4–4.5in); 7–13g. **MALE** *Black head and underparts.* **FEMALE AND IMMATURE** Drab brownish-olive overall. (See Plate 76.) (Drabber than Yellow-faced Grassquit and lacks faint facial markings.) **VOICE** Emphatic buzz often followed by second, louder effort. Also soft, musical *tsip.* **STATUS AND RANGE** A very common permanent resident throughout Puerto Rico and Virgin Islands. Genus endemic to West Indies. **HABITAT** Open areas with grasses and shrubs, forest clearings, road edges, and gardens.

**SMOOTH-BILLED ANI** *Crotophaga ani* (Garrapatero, Judío, Black witch, Black parrot, Black daw, Long-tailed crow, Tickbird, Savanna blackbird, Old Arnold, Chapman bird) 30–33cm (12–13in); 100g. **BEHAVIOR** Small noisy flocks. **DESCRIPTION** Large, black overall, with *parrot-like bill and long, flat tail.* (Grackles have thin bills and V-shaped tails.) **FLIGHT** Straight with rapid, shallow wingbeats followed by short glides. **VOICE** A noisy bird. Loud, squawky whistle, *a-leep.* **STATUS AND RANGE** A common permanent resident in Puerto Rico and Virgin Islands. **HABITAT** Scattered trees and bushes, primarily in open lowlands, also forest edges.

imm

Puerto Rican Bullfinch

adult

♂

Lesser Antillean
Bullfinch

♀ & imm

Smooth-billed
Ani

Black-faced
Grassquit

♂

♀ & imm

## WITH YELLOW OR ORANGE

**● ANTILLEAN EUPHONIA** *Euphonia musica* (Jilguero, Canario del país, Blue-hooded euphonia) 12cm (4.75in); 13g. Difficult to locate. **DESCRIPTION** Small and compact, with *sky-blue crown and hindneck*. **MALE** Primarily dark above and *rich yellow below, on rump, and on forehead*. **FEMALE** Duller; greenish above, yellowish-green below; yellowish rump and forehead. **VOICE** Rapid, subdued, almost tinkling *ti-tit*; hard, metallic *chi-chink*; plaintive *whee*; jumbled, tinkling song mixed with explosive notes. **STATUS AND RANGE** Locally common in Puerto Rico. Endemic to West Indies. **HABITAT** Dense forests from dry lowlands to wet mountaintops. Often in canopy. Favors mistletoe berries.

**● PUERTO RICAN SPINDALIS (PUERTO RICAN STRIPE-HEADED TANAGER)** *Spindalis portoricensis* (Reina mora) 16.5cm (6.5in); 23–41g. **MALE** *Black head striped with white*. Underparts primarily yellow; reddish-orange wash on breast and hindneck. **FEMALE** Underparts dull whitish; *gray streaks on sides and flanks; whitish mustache stripe*; inconspicuous white eyebrow stripe. **VOICE** Variable thin, high-pitched whistle, *zeé-tit-zeé-tittit-zeé*, the *zee* syllable like an inhaling sound. A thin trill like beating a tiny hammer is rarely heard, as is a short twittering. Call note a soft *teweep*. **STATUS AND RANGE** Endemic to Puerto Rico, where common and widespread. A vagrant on Tortola. Family also endemic to West Indies. **HABITAT** Woodlands, forests, and gardens at all elevations.

**SAFFRON FINCH** *Sicalis flaveola* (Gorrión azafrán) 14–15cm (5.5–5.75in); 12–23g. **BEHAVIOR** Loose flocks. **ADULT** Medium-sized; *entirely yellow with an orange crown*. **MALE** Crown bright orange. **FEMALE** Crown yellowish-orange. **IMMATURE** Generally gray, paler below, with yellow undertail-coverts and, with age, a *yellow breast band*. (Yellow and Prothonotary Warblers smaller; with finer bill; not in grassy habitats.) **VOICE** Sharp *pink*; a whistled *wheat*; a fairly loud, melodious, but slightly harsh *chit, chit, chit, chi-chit* of differing durations. **STATUS AND RANGE** Introduced probably about 1960 in Puerto Rico; uncommon and local around Santurce, from Guaynabo to Aguadilla, and ascending to mountain towns. Also Mayagüez. **HABITAT** Lawns, roadsides and farmlands with seeding grasses.

**YELLOW-FACED GRASSQUIT** *Tiaris olivaceus* (Gorrión barba amarilla) 9.5–11.5cm (3.7–4.5in); 6–10g. **MALE** *Yellow throat and eyebrow stripe; black breast*. **FEMALE AND IMMATURE** Yellowish-olive coloration and usually faint yellowish eyebrow stripe, eye-ring, and chin. (See Plate 76.) (Female and immature Black-faced Grassquit less olive and lack facial markings.) **VOICE** Soft *tek*; also thin trill, sometimes sequentially at different pitches. **STATUS AND RANGE** Common permanent resident in Puerto Rico, including Vieques, where it is uncommon. **HABITAT** Primarily open grassy areas with scattered brush from lowlands to moderate elevations, sometimes high mountains.

**YELLOW-CROWNED BISHOP** *Euplectes afer* (Obispo Napoleón, Obispo coroni-amarillo) 11.5–12.5cm (4.5–5in); 11–20g. **BEHAVIOR** Flocks. **BREEDING MALE** *Yellow rump and crown; black underparts*. **FEMALE AND NON-BREEDING MALE** Mottled brown above, pale tan below. *Yellowish eyebrow stripe* contrasts sharply with *dark brown eye-line*. Breast and crown finely striped. (See Plate 76.) (Non-breeding Northern Red Bishop has paler cheek; pale eye-line; no yellow in eyebrow stripe. Grasshopper Sparrow has whitish central crown stripe.) **VOICE** Series of *sweet* and *chuck* notes similar to Northern Red Bishop. **STATUS AND RANGE** Introduced to Puerto Rico, probably in 1960s. Uncommon and very local. Very rare in Puerto Rico since hurricanes in 2017. Formerly on north coast and in southwest. **HABITAT** High grass and reeds near freshwater.

**DICKCISSEL** *Spiza americana* (Arrocero, Sabanero americano) 15–18cm (5.75–7in); male 29g, female 25g. **BEHAVIOR** Flocks. **DESCRIPTION** *Yellowish wash on breast; dull yellow eyebrow stripe; thick bill; reddish-brown bend of wing*. **NON-BREEDING MALE** Pale *black throat patch*. **FEMALE** Black on throat confined to few streaks. (See Plate 76.) **BREEDING MALE** Dark black throat patch; yellow below more extensive. **STATUS AND RANGE** Irregular year to year, but generally a rare to very rare migrant and non-breeding resident in Puerto Rico, primarily September–April. **HABITAT** Grasslands with scattered trees.

Antillean Euphonia

♀

♂

Puerto Rican
Spindalis

♀

♂

Saffron Finch

♂

imm

Yellow-faced
Grassquit

♂

♀ & imm

Yellow-crowned
Bishop

♀ & non-br ♂

br ♂

Dickcissel

♀

br ♂

PLATE 73  LAND BIRDS — Heavy-billed Birds

**ORANGE-CHEEKED WAXBILL** *Estrilda melpoda* (Veterano) 10cm (4in); 7–10g.
**BEHAVIOR** Flocks. **ADULT** Note the *orange cheek patch*; reddish bill and uppertail-coverts.
**IMMATURE** Lacks orange cheek; bill pale pink. **VOICE** Clear *pee*, singly or in series. Flocks
have characteristic twitter. Song, infrequently heard, is quite variable. **STATUS AND
RANGE** Introduced to Puerto Rico, probably during era of slavery. Likely a second
introduction in late 1950s. Common on coastal plain, less frequent in Central Mountains.
**HABITAT** Tall seeding grass in agricultural areas, and road edges.

**RED SISKIN** *Spinus cucullatus* (Cardenalito) 10cm (4in). **BEHAVIOR** Flocks.
**MALE** Primarily *orange-red with black hood*. **FEMALE** *Orange rump, wing markings, and
wash on breast*. **VOICE** High-pitched twitter and *chi-tit*, similar to Indian Silverbill. **STATUS
AND RANGE** Introduced to Puerto Rico, perhaps in the early 1900s, where rare and very
local in dry foothills of southeast. A 2017 record suggests it survives in small numbers. There
is a 2005 record of a single bird on Beef Island in British Virgin Islands. **HABITAT** Thick
scrub, often in dry ravines.

**NORTHERN RED BISHOP (ORANGE BISHOP)** *Euplectes franciscanus* (Obispo
anaranjado) 12.5cm (5in); 12–22g. **BEHAVIOR** Flocks. **BREEDING MALE** *Distinctive
orange-red plumage with black belly and crown*. **FEMALE AND NON-BREEDING
MALE** Mottled brown above and pale tan below with pale tan eyebrow stripe. Breast and
crown finely striped. (See Plate 76.) **IMMATURE** Like female, but more tannish. (Grasshopper
Sparrow has golden spot near bill and single, central whitish crown stripe. See Yellow-
crowned Bishop.) **VOICE** Breeding males sing sputtering song. **STATUS AND
RANGE** Introduced to Puerto Rico, probably in 1960s. Common in lowlands of southwest.
Prior to hurricanes of 2017 occurred around entire coast; likely to recolonize. Presently
locally common in southwest, absent in north and northeast. Uncommon and very local on
St. Croix. **HABITAT** Primarily agricultural fields, grassy borders, sometimes open areas.

**ROSE-BREASTED GROSBEAK** *Pheucticus ludovicianus* (Picogrueso rosado,
Picogrueso pechirrosado) 19–20cm (7.5–8in); 45g. **BEHAVIOR** Often flocks.
**MALE** *Pinkish-red breast; black head and back*; white wing bars; pink wing linings in flight.
**FEMALE** Large, with heavy bill, white crown stripes, white wing bars, and streaked
underparts. (See Plate 76.) **FLIGHT** Yellow wing linings. **STATUS AND RANGE** Irregular year
to year, but generally rare to very rare in Puerto Rico as a southbound migrant in October,
particularly in northwest corner of island. It is very rare in Virgin Islands as a northbound
migrant, primarily in April, and is even less frequent as a non-breeding resident November–
March. **HABITAT** Scrub, woodlands, forest edges, and shade coffee. Also gardens.

Orange-cheeked
Waxbill

imm

adult

Red Siskin

♂

♀

br ♂

♀ & non-br ♂

Northern Red
Bishop

Rose-breasted
Grosbeak

♀

♂

## MODERATE-SIZED BIRDS

**BOBOLINK** *Dolichonyx oryzivorus* (Chambergo) 18.5cm (7.25in); male 47g, female 37g. **BEHAVIOR** Flocks. **DESCRIPTION** Note larger size than birds of similar appearance. **NON-BREEDING ADULT** Central pale tan crown stripe; unmarked pale tan underparts; streaked sides; pointed tail. (See also Plate 76.) **BREEDING MALE** Black below, grayish-tan hindneck, white patches on wings and lower back. **BREEDING FEMALE** Similar, but with whitish throat. (Non-breeding adult Bobolink differs from various sparrows and bishops by its much larger size and streaked sides and abdomen.) **VOICE** Distinctive *pink*. **STATUS AND RANGE** Irregular, but generally an uncommon and local migrant in Puerto Rico and rare in Virgin Islands. Occurs during southward migration, primarily late September–October. Often occurs in numbers. Declining. **HABITAT** Sorghum fields, pastures, and grassy areas.

**INDIGO BUNTING** *Passerina cyanea* (Gorrión azul) 12.5cm (5in); 14g. **BEHAVIOR** Flocks. **NON-BREEDING MALE** Brown overall; *traces of blue in wings and tail*. **FEMALE** Dull brown overall; *very pale breast stripes and wing bars*; no conspicuous markings. Female's faint breast stripes and wing bars distinguish it from immature mannikins. (See Plate 76.) **BREEDING MALE** *Entirely blue*. **VOICE** Emphatic *twit*. Sometimes sings thin song of paired phrases. **STATUS AND RANGE** Highly variable year to year, but generally an uncommon to fairly common migrant and non-breeding resident locally in Puerto Rico, particularly in northwest corner of island, as well as on St. Croix. It is fairly common to common on the other larger Virgin Islands except Anegada, where it is uncommon. Sometimes occurs in numbers. Species is increasing in region. **HABITAT** Agricultural fields, grassy areas bounded by heavy thickets, rows of trees or woodlands, pasture edges, and scrub.

**BLUE GROSBEAK** *Passerina caerulea* (Picogrueso azul) 16.5–19cm (6.5–7.5in); 28g. **BEHAVIOR** Flicks and fans tail. **MALE** *Entirely blue, with reddish-brown wing bars*. **FEMALE** Brown overall; *large size*, with *heavy bill; reddish-brown wing bars*. Hints of blue sometimes on wings and rump. (See Plate 76.) **STATUS AND RANGE** Irregular, but generally a rare migrant and non-breeding resident in Puerto Rico. Very rare in Virgin Islands. As a migrant in Puerto Rico, occurs primarily in western portion of island during southbound migration in October–November. It occurs much less frequently northbound in March–April. As migrant in Virgin Islands displays reverse trend, occurring primarily northbound in March. **HABITAT** Agricultural fields, forest edges, Australian pine (*Casuarina*) groves, seeding grass near thickets or woodlands. Also gardens with trees.

**JAVA SPARROW** *Lonchura oryzivora* (Gorrión de Java, Gorrión arrocero, Java finch) 15–16.5cm (5.75–6.5in); 23–28g. **BEHAVIOR** Forages primarily on ground. Flocks. **ADULT** Primarily gray above and below. Note *broad, pinkish-red bill; white cheek patch; black crown*. **IMMATURE** Similar but duller bill, tannish-white cheeks, and brownish body. **VOICE** Hard, metallic *chink*. **STATUS AND RANGE** Introduced to Puerto Rico, probably in 1950s or early 1960s. Uncommon and declining in San Juan area. Rarely seen elsewhere on island. Nearly extirpated by hurricanes of 2017. **HABITAT** Primarily urban areas with short grass, such as athletic fields and large lawns where grass is seeding.

**HOUSE SPARROW** *Passer domesticus* (Gorrión inglés, Gorrión domestico) 15cm (5.75in); 28g. **BEHAVIOR** Flocks. **MALE** Distinguished by *black bib, gray crown, and pale cheek*. **FEMALE AND IMMATURE** *Pale tan eyebrow stripe and underparts; brown upperparts streaked with black*. (See Plate 76.) **VOICE** Distinctive *chirp*. **STATUS AND RANGE** Common and widespread in Puerto Rico and locally common in Virgin Islands. Probably arrived in Puerto Rico via a grain ship to Ponce in 1960s. Once established in Puerto Rico, likely island-hopped to Virgin Islands. **HABITAT** Urban and industrial areas, and human settlements at all elevations, but most frequent in lowlands. Also areas with livestock.

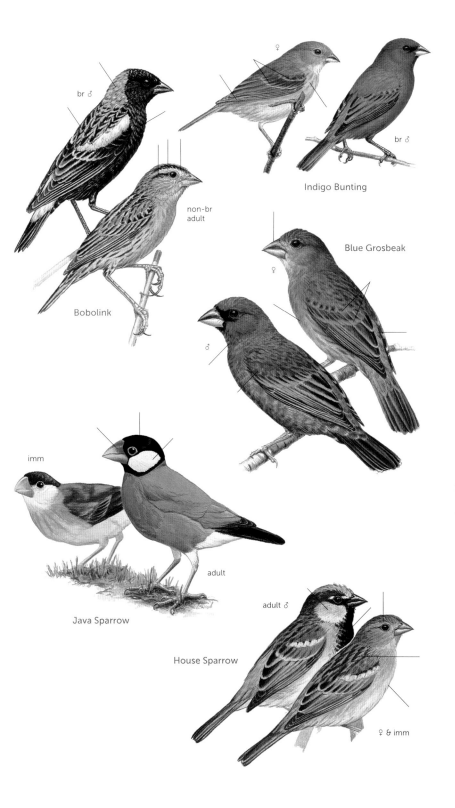

br ♂

non-br
adult

Bobolink

♀

Indigo Bunting

br ♂

Blue Grosbeak

♀

♂

imm

adult

Java Sparrow

adult ♂

House Sparrow

♀ & imm

PLATE 75    LAND BIRDS — Heavy-billed Birds

## SMALL BIRDS

**PIN-TAILED WHYDAH** *Vidua macroura* (Viuda colicinta) Breeding male 30–33cm (12–13in), female and non-breeding male 11.5cm (4.5in); 12–19g. **BEHAVIOR** Flocks. **BREEDING MALE** *Black and white, with long tail plumes and red bill.* **FEMALE AND NON-BREEDING MALE** Mottled reddish-brown above; *red bill; black-and-white facial stripes.* (See Plate 76.) **IMMATURE** More grayish-brown; whitish eyebrow stripe. Bill blackish, pinkish-red at base. **VOICE** Distinctive twittering, sometimes intermixed with loud chattering and whistles. Also emphatic *sweet.* **STATUS AND RANGE** Introduced to Puerto Rico, probably in 1960s. Uncommon and local on coast, less frequent in mountains. Hurricanes of 2017 decimated northern and eastern populations, which are slowly recovering. **HABITAT** Lawns and fields with short grass.

**INDIAN SILVERBILL (WARBLING SILVERBILL)** *Euodice malabarica* (Gorrión picoplata) 11.5cm (4.5in); 10–14g. **BEHAVIOR** Flocks. **DESCRIPTION** Overall light brown upperparts, *white underparts and rump*, and dark tail. Heavy bill is bluish. **VOICE** Usually quick, two-syllable *chit-tit.* Sometimes a medium-strength *chit*, one or in series. Rarely a loud, musical song. **STATUS AND RANGE** Introduced to Puerto Rico, probably in 1960s. Common on southwestern coast, uncommon along south coast, rare and local in metropolitan San Juan. Population recovering following decimation by hurricanes of 2017. **HABITAT** Arid scrub, pastures, and gardens where grass is in seed.

**SCALY-BREASTED MUNIA (NUTMEG MANNIKIN)** *Lonchura punctulata* (Gorrión canela, Spice finch) 11.5cm (4.5in); 14g. **BEHAVIOR** Flocks. **ADULT** Note the *cinnamon-colored hood and scalloped underparts.* **IMMATURE** Cinnamon-colored above; paler below. (Immature distinguished from several similar species by its heavy, blackish bill and light cinnamon coloration. It is not as pale below as immature Tricolored Munia.) **VOICE** Soft, plaintive, whistled *peet*, dropping in pitch and fading at end. **STATUS AND RANGE** Introduced to Puerto Rico, probably in 1960s. Locally common and spreading, particularly in lowlands, but increasing island-wide following decimation by hurricanes of 2017. Periodically recorded in Virgin Islands (St. Croix, Anegada) but not established. **HABITAT** Lowland open areas, such as pasturelands, road edges, and urban parks.

**BRONZE MANNIKIN** *Spermestes cucullata* (Diablito, Pandillero) 10cm (4in); 8–12g. **BEHAVIOR** Flocks. **ADULT** Distinguished by its *black hood*, dark grayish-brown back, and *white belly with scalloped pattern on sides and flanks.* **IMMATURE** Hood and scalloped markings faint or lacking. (Immature is darker and smaller than other mannikin species.) **VOICE** Coarse *crrit.* Much chattering within flocks. **STATUS AND RANGE** Introduced to Puerto Rico, probably during era of slavery. Common around coast. Eastern population reduced by hurricanes of 2017, but rebounding. **HABITAT** Fields, lawns, and wherever grass is in seed.

**TRICOLORED MUNIA (TRICOLORED MANNIKIN)** *Lonchura malacca* (Monjita tricolor, Chestnut mannikin, Black-headed nun) 11.5cm (4.5in); 10–14g. **BEHAVIOR** Flocks. **ADULT** Good field marks are *black hood, cinnamon-colored back, and white underparts with black belly patch.* **IMMATURE** Cinnamon-brown above and pale tan below. (Immature more cinnamon-colored and has paler bill and underparts than Scaly-breasted Munia.) **VOICE** Thin, nasal honk, *nyeat*; less plaintive, clear, and melodious than Scaly-breasted Munia. **STATUS AND RANGE** Introduced to Puerto Rico, probably in 1960s. Rare and local, primarily in lowlands. Population decimated by hurricanes of 2017. **HABITAT** High grass bordering dense vegetation. Also grasses of swampy areas and along canals.

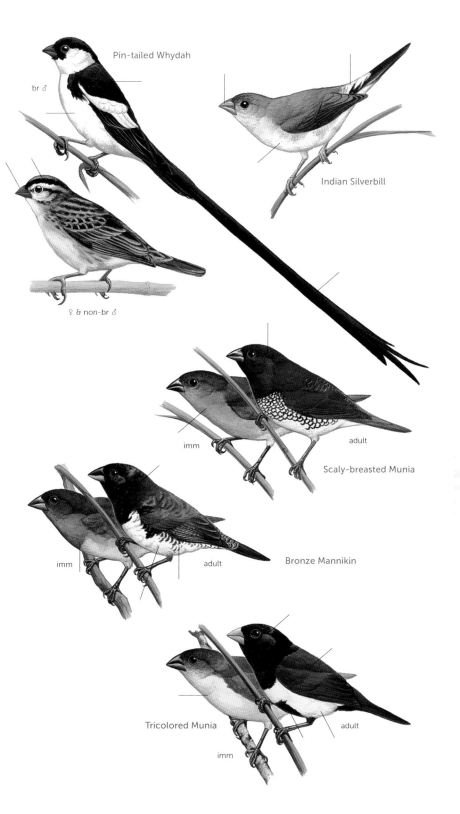

Pin-tailed Whydah

br ♂

♀ & non-br ♂

Indian Silverbill

imm

adult

Scaly-breasted Munia

imm

adult

Bronze Mannikin

Tricolored Munia

imm

adult

PLATE 76   LAND BIRDS — Heavy-billed Birds

## NON-DESCRIPT BROWN BIRDS

**LINCOLN'S SPARROW** *Melospiza lincolnii* (Gorrión de Lincoln) 13.5–15cm
(5.25–5.75in); 18g. Difficult to locate. **ADULT:** Note *pale gray central crown stripe,
eyebrow stripe, ear-patch, and sides of neck. Breast pale tan, finely streaked black.*
**IMMATURE:** Similar, but eyebrow stripe tannish-white. **STATUS AND RANGE:** A very rare
migrant in Puerto Rico in October and April. It is even less frequent as a non-breeding
resident November–March. **HABITAT:** Moist highland forest thickets, especially around
clearings. Also coastal thickets and borders of dense forests.

**GRASSHOPPER SPARROW** *Ammodramus savannarum* (Gorrión chicharra) 12.5cm
(5in); 17g. Difficult to locate. **ADULT** *Best field marks are golden mark forward of eyebrow
stripe; and whitish central crown stripe.* (Brown-plumaged Yellow-crowned and Northern
Red Bishops lack single central crown stripe.) **IMMATURE** Paler mark by bill; fine streaks on
breast and flanks. **VOICE** Long, thin, insect-like buzz, then hiccup. Also, a very thin,
high-pitched twitter or tinkling song. Call note a gritty, insect-like *kr-r-it*. **STATUS AND
RANGE** A fairly common but local permanent resident in Puerto Rico. **HABITAT** Weedy
fields, pastures with short grass, and hay fields, primarily along coast.

Lincoln's
Sparrow

Grasshopper
Sparrow

imm

adult

adult

182

Northern Red Bishop
For comparison.
(see also Plate 73)

♀ & non-br ♂

♀ & non-br ♂

Yellow-crowned Bishop
For comparison.
(see also Plate 72)

non-br
adult

Bobolink
For comparison.
(see also Plate 74)

♀

Indigo Bunting
For comparison.
(see also Plate 74)

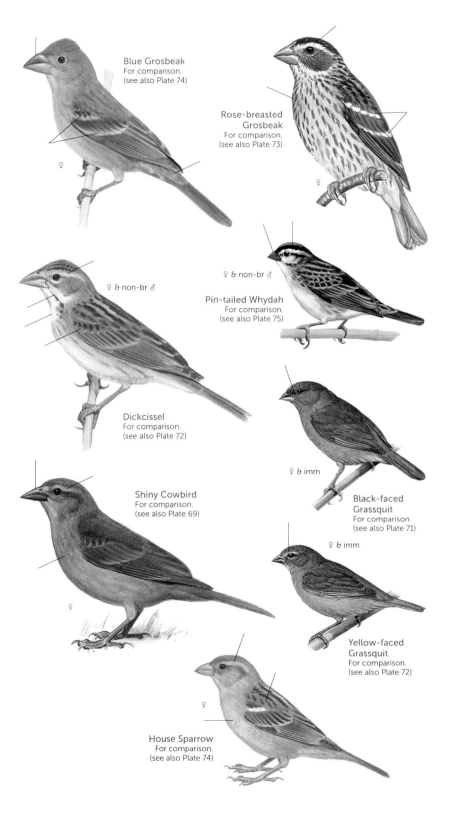

**Blue Grosbeak**
For comparison.
(see also Plate 74)

♀

**Rose-breasted Grosbeak**
For comparison.
(see also Plate 73)

♀

♀ & non-br ♂

♀ & non-br ♂

**Pin-tailed Whydah**
For comparison.
(see also Plate 75)

**Dickcissel**
For comparison.
(see also Plate 72)

**Shiny Cowbird**
For comparison.
(see also Plate 69)

♀

♀ & imm

**Black-faced Grassquit**
For comparison.
(see also Plate 71)

♀ & imm

**Yellow-faced Grassquit**
For comparison.
(see also Plate 72)

♀

**House Sparrow**
For comparison.
(see also Plate 74)

**TRINDADE PETREL** *Pterodroma arminjoniana* (Petrel de la Trindade) 35–39cm (14–15in); wingspan 88–100cm; 270–475g. Medium-sized. Wings long and narrow, beat faster than shearwaters. Coloration variable, with dark, light, and intermediate morphs. Dark morph—Similar to Sooty Shearwater, but tail longer, bill heavier, and *less white on underwings*. Light morph—Underparts white, but with dark patch nearly surrounding neck. Underwings darker than similar shearwaters in region with white underparts. Intermediate morph—Variable coloration between the dark and light morphs. **STATUS AND RANGE** A vagrant to Puerto Rico (off Culebra, 1976—photo). Frequents Gulf Stream. **HABITAT** At sea.

**SKUA** *Stercorarius* sp. The few skua records in the region were not identified to species. Either of two species is likely, and each occurs in different months. There are two skua records from off Puerto Rico and two off the Virgin Islands (dates unavailable).

**GREAT SKUA** *Stercorarius skua* (Págalo grande) 51–66cm (20–26in); wingspan 1.3–1.4m (4–4.5ft); 1.3–1.4kg. Large, bulky, powerful, gull-like. Dark brown; reddish-brown highlights; golden or reddish-brown streaks on head and neck. Underparts pale. Indistinct dark cap. (Extremely similar to South Polar Skua, which in all color phases is less reddish and has less streaking on back, wing-coverts, and underparts. Jaegers have more slender, pointed wings.) **FLIGHT** *White wing patch*, distinct hunchbacked appearance. **STATUS AND RANGE** Likely a vagrant off Puerto Rico and Virgin Islands at low frequencies, primarily November–March. **HABITAT** Well out at sea.

**SOUTH POLAR SKUA** *Stercorarius maccormicki* (Págalo polar, Págalo grande) 53cm (21in); wingspan 1.3–1.4m (4–4.5ft); 1–1.4kg. Extremely similar to Great Skua but slightly smaller. Three color phases. Dark phase—As above, but darker underparts and lacks reddish tones. Intermediate phase—Light brown head, neck, and underparts, light hindneck, may have dark cap. Light phase—Pale gray underparts, head, and neck. **FLIGHT** *White wing patch*, distinct hunchbacked appearance. **STATUS AND RANGE** Likely a vagrant off Puerto Rico and Virgin Islands at low frequencies migrating northbound, primarily April–June and to lesser extent southbound September–October. The few skua records in region were not identified to species; however, this species is a bit more to be expected. **HABITAT** Well out at sea.

**SABINE'S GULL** *Xema sabini* (Gaviota de Sabine) 27–33cm (11–13in); wingspan 84cm (33in); 85g. A small gull. In all plumages the *tricolored wing pattern in flight*, particularly the large *triangular white wing patch*, is diagnostic. Tail slightly forked. **BREEDING ADULT** Dark gray hood, *black bill with yellow tip*. **FIRST YEAR** Upperparts gray-brown, bill black, dark tail band. **STATUS AND RANGE** A vagrant to Puerto Rico, where recorded from Ponce (1992), San Juan Harbor (1992), and Barceloneta (2020—photo). **HABITAT** Generally at sea.

**RED PHALAROPE** *Phalaropus fulicarius* (Falaropo picogrueso) 21cm (8in); 50g. **BEHAVIOR** *Spins on water surface to feed.* **DESCRIPTION** Bill stout and black except for yellow spot at base of lower mandible. **NON-BREEDING ADULT** *Unstreaked pale gray above, underparts white.* Hindcrown blackish; broad black bar through eye to ear-coverts. **BREEDING FEMALE** Entirely dark reddish-brown below with a conspicuous white facial patch. **BREEDING MALE** Dull orangish-brown below with less distinct whitish facial patch. (Red is stockier than other phalaropes, with shorter and thicker bill, no stripes on back in any plumage, and noticeable wing stripe in flight.) **FLIGHT** Unstreaked pale gray above; white wing stripe. **STATUS AND RANGE** A vagrant to Puerto Rico (2011; 2016—photo) and Virgin Islands (1998), where most likely to occur October–April. **HABITAT** Usually out at sea; sometimes ponds and lagoons.

dark
morph

light
morph

light
morph

Trindade Petrel

Great
Skua

intermediate phase

light phase

dark phase

South Polar Skua

first year

Sabine's Gull

br

br

first year

Red Phalarope

br ♀

non-br

non-br

Plate not to scale

**WHITE-WINGED TERN** *Chlidonias leucopterus* (Fumarel aliblanco) 22–27cm (9–10.5in); wingspan 58–67cm (23–26in); 42–79g. Small tern, with slightly notched tail. **NON-BREEDING ADULT** Note black rear of crown and ear-spot; white rump; lacks dark neck mark. **BREEDING ADULT** Primarily black except for white tail and rear of body. Wings pale gray with black underwing linings; legs red. (Non-breeding Black Tern has gray rump, dark mark on side of neck, dark legs, and darker wings, especially upper forewing.) **STATUS AND RANGE** Vagrant in Puerto Rico (2001—photo) and St. Croix (1986; 2013—photo). **HABITAT** Inland freshwater bodies, coastal lagoons, and river mouths.

**NORTHERN JACANA** *Jacana spinosa* (Jacana norteña) 19–23cm (7.5–9in); male 80g, female 140g. Chicken-like, with large *yellow wing patches* and *extremely long, slender, greenish toes*. **ADULT** Deep reddish-brown; blackish head and neck. *Bill and forehead shield yellow.* **IMMATURE** Whitish below; white eyebrow stripe. **FLIGHT** Low over water with shallow wingbeats and dangling legs. Often raises wings after landing, displaying yellow undersides. **VOICE** Sharp, repeated cackle. **STATUS AND RANGE** A vagrant to Puerto Rico (1870s; specimen, 1986). Likely these are birds straying from Hispaniola. **HABITAT** Freshwater bodies with large-leaved floating vegetation.

**NORTHERN LAPWING** *Vanellus vanellus* (Avefría europea) 28–31cm (11–12in); 130–330g. Distinctive *crest and broad black breast band*. **IMMATURE** Crest and color pattern less conspicuous. **FLIGHT** Wingbeats slow and floppy. White band across base of upper tail and black patch at tip, contrasting white wing linings and black flight feathers, rounded wingtips. **VOICE** A whistled *pee-wit*. **STATUS AND RANGE** Vagrant to Puerto Rico (1978–79—photo). **HABITAT** Grasslands and tidal flats.

**NEOTROPIC CORMORANT (OLIVACEOUS CORMORANT)** *Phalacrocorax brasilianus* (Cormorán oliváceo) 63–69cm (25–27in); 1.2kg. **BEHAVIOR** *Sits with wings spread*, dives, flocks. **DESCRIPTION** Large; black; with long neck and *slender, hooked bill*. (Longer tail than more frequently occurring Double-crested Cormorant, especially noticeable in flight. Also decidedly greater bulk and heavier bill.) **BREEDING ADULT** Orangish-yellow base of bill; chin edged white. **NON-BREEDING ADULT** Base of bill yellowish; white edge reduced or absent. **IMMATURE** Brown, paler below; base of bill pale yellow. **STATUS AND RANGE** Vagrant in Puerto Rico (three sightings), and Peter Island (two sightings) in Virgin Islands. All but one sighting are since 1974. **HABITAT** Inland and calm coastal waters. Frequents freshwater more than Double-crested.

**WOOD STORK** *Mycteria americana* (Tántalo americano) 100cm (40in); wingspan 150cm (5ft); male 2.6kg, female 2.1kg. Large, with long legs, white coloration, black on wings, head dark. *Bill large, down-curved at tip*. **ADULT** *Head bald and blackish*, bill black. **IMMATURE** Head feathered and brownish, bill yellowish. **FLIGHT** Black trailing edge of wing; feet trail beyond tail. **STATUS AND RANGE** Vagrant to Vieques (2014—photo) off Puerto Rico. **HABITAT** Swamps, mangroves, and coastal mudflats. Also ponds and inland water bodies.

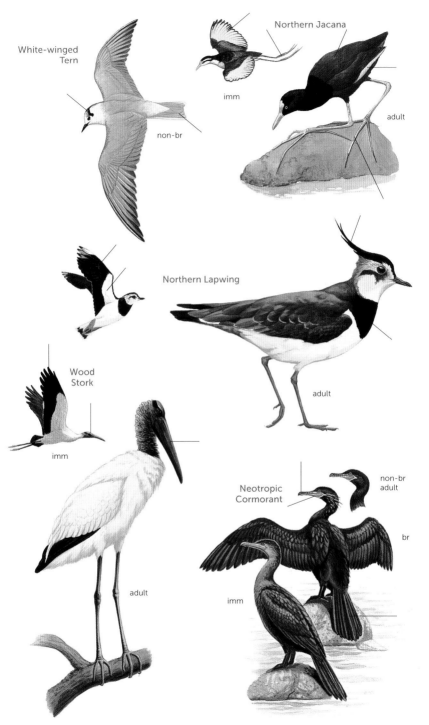

White-winged
Tern

non-br

Northern Jacana

imm

adult

Northern Lapwing

adult

Wood
Stork

imm

adult

Neotropic
Cormorant

non-br
adult

br

imm

Plate not to scale

**WHITE-FACED WHISTLING-DUCK** *Dendrocygna viduata* (Chiriría cariblanca) 38–48cm (15–19in); 500–820g. **ADULT** *White face*. **IMMATURE** Paler; face beige. **FLIGHT** Wings dark above and below; no white markings except on head. Head and feet droop; feet extend beyond tail. **VOICE** High-pitched, three-note whistle. **STATUS AND RANGE** Vagrant to Puerto Rico (Cartagena Lagoon, 2005—photo). **HABITAT** Open wetlands.

**BRANT** *Branta bernicla* (Ganso carinegro) 55–66cm (22–26in); wingspan 1.1–1.3m (3.6–4.3ft); 1–1.5kg. **BEHAVIOR** Surface feeder; flocks. **DESCRIPTION** A small, dark sea goose with a black head, neck, and breast. Note *small white patch on side of neck*. (Canada Goose is much larger, with white patch on face. It is also a more terrestrial and freshwater bird.) **FLIGHT** White uppertail-coverts. **STATUS AND RANGE** Vagrant to Puerto Rico (2009—photo). **HABITAT** Shallow bays and calm coastal waters.

**CANADA GOOSE** *Branta canadensis* (Ganso canadiense) 64–110cm (25–43in); wingspan 1.2–1.8m (4–6ft); 1.5–6kg. **BEHAVIOR** Flocks, grazes in open fields. **DESCRIPTION** Very large, with a long neck and short legs. Distinctive black head and neck, with *white band on cheeks and throat*. **FLIGHT** Dark wings with white band across uppertail-coverts. **STATUS AND RANGE** A vagrant in Puerto Rico, where likely to occur October–April. Records from 1977, 1981, 1984, 2003. Care must be taken to determine that birds are not escapees. **HABITAT** Wetland borders, grassy fields.

**TUNDRA SWAN** *Cygnus columbianus* (Cisne de tundra) 120–147cm (47.2–57.9in); wingspan 1.7m (5.5ft); 3.8–10.5kg. **BEHAVIOR** Surface feeder; flocks. **DESCRIPTION** A *huge* bird with a long neck and short legs. **ADULT** *White overall with black bill, sometimes yellow lores*. **IMMATURE** Pale grayish-brown overall with pinkish bill. (The domesticated Mute Swan, *Cygnus olor*, which sometimes escapes from captivity, has an orange bill with a black nob at its base.) **STATUS AND RANGE** Vagrant to Puerto Rico and Virgin Islands. Represented by only three records, including specimens, from Puerto Rico (1944, specimen; 2010, 2019), and one from St. Thomas (1983, specimen). **HABITAT** Shallow ponds and lagoons.

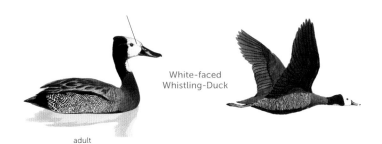

White-faced
Whistling-Duck

adult

Brant

Canada Goose

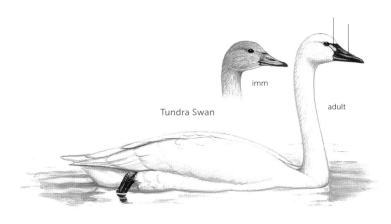

imm

Tundra Swan

adult

**BUFFLEHEAD** *Bucephala albeola* (Pato pinto) 33–38cm (13–15in); 230–600g.
**BEHAVIOR** Dives, flocks. **DESCRIPTION** Small. **MALE** *Primarily white plumage; large white head patch*; and white forewing are diagnostic. **FEMALE** Much browner, with with distinctive *white facial stripe*. (Hooded Merganser has a crest and a slender, hooked bill.) **FLYING MALE** White forewing and secondaries. **FLYING FEMALE** White secondaries. **STATUS AND RANGE** A vagrant to Puerto Rico (late 1800s, specimen). Likely to occur October–March. **HABITAT** Open bays and lagoons.

**EURASIAN WIGEON** *Mareca penelope* (Silbón europeo) 42–52cm (16.5–20in); 500–1,000g. **BEHAVIOR** Surface feeder. **MALE** Distinguished by dark *reddish-brown head; cream-colored crown stripe; pinkish breast*. **FEMALE** Gray phase—Brownish; gray head; light blue bill. Red phase—Similar; reddish tint to head and neck. (Gray phase female similar to American Wigeon but head darker gray. Red phase female decidedly redder on head. Both Eurasian phases have blackish flecks in wingpits.) **FLIGHT** *White patches on forewing*; green speculum; white belly; blackish flecks in wingpits. **STATUS AND RANGE** Vagrant in Puerto Rico (1958; 2004—photo; 2015—photo; 2016—photo) and St. Croix (2003). Likely to occur October–March. **HABITAT** Freshwater ponds.

**TUFTED DUCK** *Aythya fuligula* (Porrón moñudo) 40–47cm (16–19in); 0.6–1kg.
**BEHAVIOR** Dives. **MALE** Black head, breast, and upperparts, *entirely white flanks, long crest*, not always visible. (Very similar male Ring-necked Duck has only white vertical shoulder bar rather than entirely white flanks. It also lacks crest and has white ring on bill.)
**FEMALE** Brown overall, with *small but noticeable crest and limited white around bill*.
(Female Ring-necked Duck has eye-ring and white band around bill. Female Lesser Scaup has larger white facial shield.) **STATUS AND RANGE** A vagrant to Puerto Rico (2012—photo). **HABITAT** Primarily bodies of open freshwater.

**CANVASBACK** *Aythya valisineria* (Pato piquisesgado) 51–61cm (20–24in); 1–1.5kg.
**BEHAVIOR** Dives, flocks. **DESCRIPTION** *Sloping forehead profile* is distinctive.
**MALE** Reddish-brown head and neck. **FEMALE** Brown head and neck; less contrast in plumage. **FLIGHT** Elongated appearance. **FLYING MALE** White belly and underwings sandwiched between black breast and tail. **FLYING FEMALE** Whitish belly and underwings contrast with dark breast and tail. **STATUS AND RANGE** A vagrant in Puerto Rico, where known from five sight records (1998; other dates unavailable). Most likely to occur October–March. May occur in numbers. **HABITAT** Large, deep lagoons.

**AMERICAN BLACK DUCK** *Anas rubripes* (Pato oscuro) 53–64cm (21–25in); 0.7–1.7kg. **BEHAVIOR** Surface feeder. **DESCRIPTION** *Dark brown plumage and purple speculum* are important field marks. **MALE** Bill yellow. **FEMALE** Bill olive and mottled black. (Female Mallard is lighter brown and has white bands on either side of a blue speculum.) **FLIGHT** White underwings contrast with dark body; purple speculum. **STATUS AND RANGE** A vagrant to Puerto Rico (1935—specimen). Most likely to occur October–April. **HABITAT** Shallow water bodies.

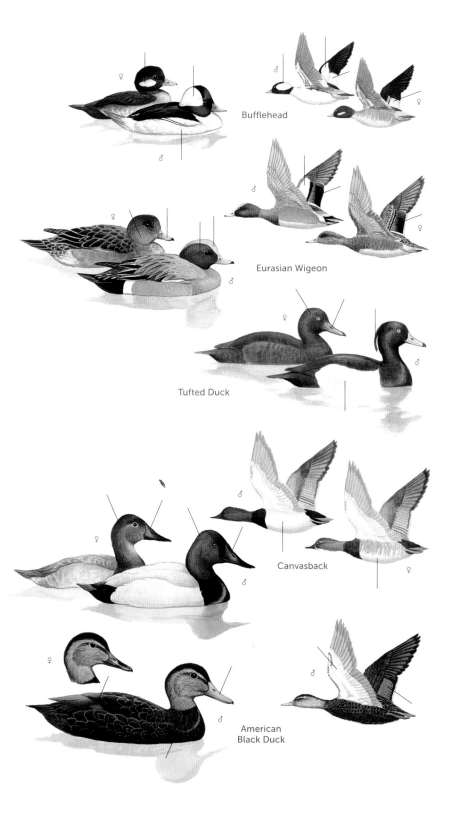

Bufflehead

Eurasian Wigeon

Tufted Duck

Canvasback

American
Black Duck

**APLOMADO FALCON** *Falco femoralis* (Halcón aplomado) 30–42cm (12–16.5in); wingspan 102–122cm (40–48in); male 200–300g, female 270–460g.
**BEHAVIOR** Frequently hovers. **DESCRIPTION** Moderate-sized, slender falcon with long, pointed wings and long, banded tail. Note *broad white eye-stripe and dark facial bar beneath eye. Throat and breast white, sides dark, sometimes connecting on breast; belly and abdomen reddish-brown.* **IMMATURE** Eye-stripe tan; throat and breast reddish-brown with moderate streaking. **STATUS AND RANGE** A vagrant to Puerto Rico (2008—photo). **HABITAT** Open grasslands in arid areas.

**WESTERN MARSH HARRIER (EURASIAN MARSH-HARRIER)** *Circus aeruginosus* (Aguilucho lagunero) 48–55cm (19–22in); wingspan 115–145cm (45–57in); male 560g, female 750g. A large hawk with long, slender wings and tail.
**MALE** Brown overall, heavily striped below; *gray wings and tail; rust-colored belly and abdomen*; pale tan head and breast. **FEMALE** Primarily dark brown overall, but *crown and throat contrasting pale tan.* (Northern Harrier has conspicuous white rump.) **FLIGHT** Male—Underwings gray with black tips, tail gray. Female—Wings brown, but leading edge of upperwing whitish. **STATUS AND RANGE** Vagrant to Puerto Rico (2004—photo; 2006—photo). Could occur on any island. **HABITAT** Marshes.

**BLACK VULTURE** *Coragyps atratus* (Zopilote negro) 58–68cm (23–26.5in); wingspan 140–160cm (4.5–5.3ft); 2–3kg. A large, entirely black raptor with a very short tail. **FLIGHT** Displays conspicuous *white wing patches*. Flight is labored, alternating rapid flapping with brief glides. Wings held horizontal. (Turkey Vulture lacks white wing patches, has a longer tail, and rocks as it soars, flapping only occasionally, with wings held well above the horizontal.) **STATUS AND RANGE** Vagrant to Puerto Rico (2018–19—photo). **HABITAT** Open lowlands; also urban areas, particularly dumps.

imm

adult

adult

Aplomado Falcon

♂

♂

♀

Western Marsh Harrier

Black Vulture

Not to scale

**VIOLET-GREEN SWALLOW** *Tachycineta thalassina* (Golondrina verdemar) 13cm (5.25in) 14g. **BEHAVIOR** Aerial, typically flocks. **DESCRIPTION** Note the *white patches on sides of rump, and white underparts extending up to cheek*. **MALE** Green crown and back. **FEMALE** Brown crown and green back. **STATUS AND RANGE** A vagrant in Puerto Rico (2010—photo) and St. Thomas (2018—photo). **HABITAT** Open woodlands, often with standing dead trees.

**SHORT-TAILED SWIFT** *Chaetura brachyura* (Vencejo rabón) 10cm (4in); 16–22g. **BEHAVIOR** Aerial, flocks. **DESCRIPTION** A small swift. Its *pale gray rump and undertail-coverts* contrast with blackish plumage. Tail very short. **FLIGHT** Fast and erratic. Shallow, rapid flapping on stiff, bow-shaped wings. **VOICE** Soft chipping in flight. **STATUS AND RANGE** A vagrant to Puerto Rico (date unavailable) and St. Croix in Virgin Islands (1936—specimen; 1987). **HABITAT** Over towns, open areas, and forests in lowlands and hills.

**COMMON SWIFT** *Apus apus* (Vencejo común) 17cm (6.5in); 40g. **BEHAVIOR** Aerial, flocks. **DESCRIPTION** A fairly large, dark swift with a *long, noticeably forked tail*. It has a *conspicuously whitish throat*. (The Black Swift has a much shorter, unnotched tail and a dark throat.) **FLIGHT** Fast and erratic. Shallow, rapid flapping on stiff, bow-shaped wings. **STATUS AND RANGE** A vagrant in Puerto Rico (2015—photo). **HABITAT** May occur over all habitats from fields to forests, and at all elevations.

**WHITE-COLLARED SWIFT** *Streptoprocne zonaris* (Vencejo acollarado) 20–22cm (8–8.5in); 100g. **BAHAVIOR** Aerial, flocks. **DESCRIPTION** Large swift, black with *distinctive white collar*. **VOICE** High-pitched *screee-screee* or rapid *chip-chip-chip-chip*. **FLIGHT** Fast and erratic. Shallow, rapid flapping on stiff, bow-shaped wings. **STATUS AND RANGE** Vagrant to Puerto Rico (2005; 2019—photo), including Vieques (1971). **HABITAT** Primarily over foothills, mountain valleys, and forests, including open areas. Less regular over lowlands.

imm

♀

♀

♂

Violet-green Swallow

Short-tailed Swift

Common Swift

White-collared Swift

**WESTERN KINGBIRD** *Tyrannus verticalis* (Tirano occidental) 21–24cm (8–9.5in); 40g. **BEHAVIOR** Sallies from exposed perch for insects. **DESCRIPTION** Head and hindneck pale, with dark gray line through eye; *pale gray upper breast; yellow belly; conspicuous white edges to outertail feathers.* (Tropical Kingbird is larger, has a darker breast, and lacks white in outertail feathers.) **STATUS AND RANGE** A vagrant to Puerto Rico (2015—photo). Most likely to occur in October and November. **HABITAT** Open country.

**TROPICAL KINGBIRD** *Tyrannus melancholicus* 23cm (9in); 32–46g. **BEHAVIOR** Sallies for insects. **DESCRIPTION** Fairly large, with *primarily yellow underparts,* pale gray crown, greenish back, and *gray facial mask*. Crown patch usually concealed. (Western Kingbird smaller, with paler breast, and white in outertail feathers.) **VOICE** Similar to Gray Kingbird, but softer, less emphatic *pip-pri-pip-pri-pip-pri* … **STATUS AND RANGE** A vagrant in Virgin Islands, including St. Thomas (2017—photo) and St. Croix (2019—photo). **HABITAT** Open, semiarid scrubland.

**HISPANIOLAN PEWEE** *Contopus hispaniolensis* (Pibí de la Española) 15–16cm (5.75–6.25in); 11g. **BEHAVIOR** Sallies from exposed perch for insects; flicks tail upon landing. **DESCRIPTION** A small flycatcher, its underparts gray with olive, yellow, or brown wash; wing bars inconspicuous or absent. Lower mandible pale at base. **VOICE** Strong, mournful *purr, pip-pip-pip-pip.* Dawn song loud, rapid-fire volley with paired syllables rising in pitch. **STATUS AND RANGE** A vagrant in Puerto Rico, where known from only a single Mona Island specimen (1967). Endemic to West Indies. **HABITAT** Pine and broadleaf forests, forest edges, shade coffee, and orchards, at all elevations.

**ACADIAN FLYCATCHER** *Empidonax virescens* (Mosquero verdoso) 12cm (4.75in); 13g. **BEHAVIOR** Sallies for insects. **DESCRIPTION** Very difficult to locate. Note conspicuous yellowish eye-ring; two grayish or whitish wing bars; most of lower mandible yellowish; throat and belly white. (Yellow-bellied Flycatcher is yellower below, particularly on throat. Willow Flycatcher is less yellow below, with less conspicuous eye-ring. Differences minimal. Nearly indistinguishable except by call. Eastern Wood-Pewee has less-green upperparts and less-yellow underparts.) **VOICE** Usually silent in region. Call note a soft *weet*. **STATUS AND RANGE** A vagrant in Puerto Rico (2005—photo; 2006), where most likely to occur September–April. **HABITAT** Open woodlands, forest edges, tree clumps, and gardens.

**WILLOW FLYCATCHER** *Empidonax traillii* (Mosquero saucero) 15cm (5.75in); 15g. **BEHAVIOR** Sallies for insects. **DESCRIPTION** Underparts grayish-white with almost no yellow; chin white. Lacks noticeable eye-ring; has whitish wing bars. (Eastern Wood-Pewee has heavier, whitish wing bars. Acadian Flycatcher slightly yellower below, with more conspicuous eye-ring and greener back. Nearly indistinguishable except by call.) **VOICE** *Fi-bi-o*, cross between whistle and buzz. Also, harsh *fitz*. **STATUS AND RANGE** A vagrant in Puerto Rico (2005—photo; 2012). Most likely to occur mid-September through mid-October. **HABITAT** Wetland edges, woodlands, tree clumps, and gardens.

Western Kingbird

Tropical Kingbird

Hispaniolan Pewee

Acadian Flycatcher

Willow Flycatcher

**AMERICAN ROBIN** *Turdus migratorius* (Zorzal pechirrojo) 23–28cm (9–11in);
60–90g. Identified by *primarily dull red underparts*. **MALE** Blackish head and tail.
**FEMALE** Paler. **STATUS AND RANGE** A vagrant in Puerto Rico (2005, 2006, 2009), including
Mona Island (1971). Most likely to occur October–April. **HABITAT** Open woodlands, gardens,
parks, and open scrub.

**VEERY** *Catharus fuscescens* (Zorzalito rojizo) 16–18cm (6.25–7in); 25–43g. Difficult
to locate. **BEHAVIOR** Primarily terrestrial. **DESCRIPTION** *Upperparts reddish-brown*, rarely
olive-brown. Underparts whitish with *faint spots* on pale tan breast. Inconspicuous grayish
eye-ring. (More reddish-brown above and more lightly spotted below than other migrant
thrushes). **STATUS AND RANGE** A vagrant in Puerto Rico (2005—photo) and St. John (1978).
May occur in numbers. Most likely to occur September–October and April–May.
**HABITAT** Open forests, woodlands with substantial undergrowth, scrub, and gardens.

**WOOD THRUSH** *Hylocichla mustelina* (Zorzalito maculado) 18–21cm (7–8.25in);
40–70g. Difficult to locate. **BEHAVIOR** Highly terrestrial. **DESCRIPTION** Distinguished by
*cinnamon-colored crown, conspicuous white eye-ring, and white underparts with heavy
dark spots*. (Ovenbird smaller, with cinnamon-colored crown bordered by black stripes.)
**VOICE** Short *pit-pit-pit* notes. **STATUS AND RANGE** A vagrant in Puerto Rico (1800s—
drawing/specimen; 2018–19—photo). Likely to occur primarily mid-September to
November and March–April. **HABITAT** Mature semideciduous forests, tree plantations, and
large gardens.

**GRAY-CHEEKED THRUSH** *Catharus minimus* (Zorzalito carigrís) 17–19cm
(6.7–7.5in); 26–50g. Difficult to locate and identify. **BEHAVIOR** Highly terrestrial in dense
thickets. **DESCRIPTION** Grayish-brown above, whitish below; spots on breast and throat.
*Gray cheeks; lacks conspicuous eye-ring; lacks reddish-brown coloration.* (See extremely
similar Bicknell's Thrush. Swainson's Thrush has distinct whitish eye-ring.) **STATUS AND
RANGE** A vagrant in Puerto Rico (2005; 2015—two), and Guana Island (2006) in Virgin
Islands. Most likely to occur September–November and March–May. Status somewhat
unclear because of extreme similarity to Bicknell's Thrush and its stealthy behavior.
**HABITAT** Open forests and woodlands.

American Robin

Veery

Wood Thrush

Gray-cheeked Thrush

**CERULEAN WARBLER** *Setophaga cerulea* (Reinita cerúlea) 10–13cm (4–5in); 9g. Note *blue in plumage and two white wing bars.* **ADULT MALE** *Light blue head and upperparts; dark band across breast.* **ADULT FEMALE AND IMMATURE MALE** *Upperparts grayish-blue,* underparts dull white with yellowish tinge on throat and upper breast and faint streaks on sides. **IMMATURE FEMALE** Olive-green above, yellower below; two white wing bars. **VOICE** A thin *chip.* **STATUS AND RANGE** A vagrant in Puerto Rico (2013—photo), including Mona Island (1987). Most likely to occur in September and October, and perhaps April. **HABITAT** Forest canopy, also low bushes and small trees.

**PINE WARBLER** *Setophaga pinus* (Reinita de pinos) 12.5–14.5cm (5–5.75in); 12g. **ADULT MALE** Greenish-olive upperparts; *unstreaked back; two white wing bars;* faint yellow eyebrow stripe; variable yellow on chin and throat; faint gray to blackish streaks on breast and upper flanks. **ADULT FEMALE** Duller. (Bay-breasted Warbler has streaked back. Yellow-throated Vireo and White-eyed Vireo have yellow spectacles and lack streaking below.) **IMMATURE** Grayish-brown above; grayish-tan below; two white wing bars; whitish eyebrow stripe. **VOICE** Musical trill usually on one pitch. Also, strong *tzip.* **STATUS AND RANGE** A vagrant in Puerto Rico (2019—photo; 2020—photo), including Mona Island (1987) and Vieques (1998, 2005). Most likely to occur October–March. **HABITAT** Mature pine forests or barrens.

**NASHVILLE WARBLER** *Oreothlypis ruficapilla* (Reinita cachetigrís) 11.5–12.5cm (4.5–5in); 7–14g. Conspicuous white eye-ring in all plumages; grayish head contrasts with yellowish-green upperparts. **ADULT** Pale bluish-gray head, yellow underparts except for white belly. **IMMATURE** White eye-ring; brownish-gray head contrasts with yellowish-green upperparts; underparts paler yellow, with whitish throat and tan sides. **STATUS AND RANGE** A vagrant in Puerto Rico (2005, 2011, 2020), including Mona Island (1987), and in Virgin Islands (Tortola and Guana Island—dates unavailable), occurring mid-September through mid-April. **HABITAT** Woodlands.

**WILSON'S WARBLER** *Cardellina pusilla* (Reinita de Wilson) 11–12.5cm (4.25–5in); 8g. **ADULT MALE** Distinct *black cap; bright yellow forehead and eyebrow stripe;* upperparts olive-green, underparts yellow. **ADULT FEMALE AND IMMATURE MALE** Duller; *hint of black cap.* (Yellow Warbler lacks black cap and prominent eyebrow stripe.) **IMMATURE FEMALE** Lacks black on cap. Yellow forehead, eyebrow stripe, lores, and underparts. (Adult female and immature Yellow Warblers have eye-ring rather than prominent eyebrow stripe; less greenish cast to upperparts; and tail spots. Adult female and immature Hooded Warblers are larger; have white tail patches and a yellow face patch rather than an eyebrow stripe.) **VOICE** A husky *chuck.* **STATUS AND RANGE** A vagrant in Puerto Rico (Oct. 2013 banded; 2019–20—photo), including Mona Island (1978—netted). Most likely to occur September–April. **HABITAT** Dense vegetation at all altitudes, but primarily in lowlands.

**TOWNSEND'S WARBLER** *Setophaga townsendi* (Reinita de Townsend) 13cm (5in); 9g. *Dark cheek ringed with yellow.* **ADULT MALE** Black cheek, chin, throat, and side streaks; yellow lower breast and belly; white outertail feathers. **ADULT FEMALE** Slightly duller; yellow chin and throat; white belly. **IMMATURE** Paler; cheeks olive-green; underparts may lack black or have only fine streaks. (Black-throated Green Warbler has paler, yellower cheeks; less yellow on breast. Blackburnian Warbler has striped back.) **STATUS AND RANGE** Vagrant to Puerto Rico (2020—photo). **HABITAT** Forests, primarily conifers.

Cerulean Warbler

imm ♀

adult ♀ &
imm ♂

adult ♂

Pine Warbler

adult ♂

adult ♀

imm

Nashville Warbler

adult

imm

Wilson's Warbler

adult ♂

imm ♀

Townsend's Warbler

adult ♂

imm

PLATE 86    VAGRANTS — Hummingbirds and Small Land Birds

**RUBY-THROATED HUMMINGBIRD** *Archilochus colubris* (Zumbadorcito gorjirrojo) 8–9.5cm (3–3.7in); 3.2g. **MALE** *Red throat*; moderately forked tail. **FEMALE** Grayish sides; dark bill; rounded, white-tipped tail. Often has white spot behind eye. **VOICE** Peculiar twitter, similar to a mouse. **STATUS AND RANGE** A vagrant to Puerto Rico, where known from a drawing (late 1800s), a photo (date unavailable), and a sight record (1950s). **HABITAT** Gardens, wood edges, and clusters of trees.

**PURPLE-THROATED CARIB** *Eulampis jugularis* (Zumbador gorjimorado) 11.5cm (4.5in); 10 g. Large hummer with *purplish-red throat and breast, emerald-green wings*, and down-curved bill. **FEMALE** Longer, more sharply down-curved bill than male. **VOICE** Sharp *chewp*, repeated rapidly when agitated. **STATUS AND RANGE** Vagrant to Puerto Rico (2014, 2015), including Culebra (2004), and to Virgin Islands on St. John (1987, 2001, 2013) and St. Croix (1987, 2002). Genus endemic to West Indies. **HABITAT** Mountain forests, occasionally at sea level.

**WARBLING VIREO** *Vireo gilvus* (Vireo gorjeador) 12.5–15cm (5–5.75in); 11–18g. Note pale gray upperparts; slightly lighter crown and hindneck; *whitish eyebrow stripe*. Throat to belly whitish, often with wash of pale or greenish-yellow. (See Philadelphia Vireo.) **VOICE** A complaining *shway* similar to Black-whiskered, Red-eyed, and Philadelphia Vireos. **STATUS AND RANGE** A vagrant to Puerto Rico (1997; 2014—photo). Most likely to occur September–October and April. **HABITAT** Forests and gardens.

**NORTHERN WHEATEAR** *Oenanthe oenanthe* (Collalba gris) 15cm (6in); 18–33g. **BEHAVIOR** Active, *flicks and fans tail, terrestrial*. **DESCRIPTION** *Distinctive white rump and tail patches*. **FEMALE AND NON-BREEDING MALE** Pale reddish-brown below, grayish-brown above; *white eyebrow stripe*. **BREEDING MALE** Gray upperparts, *black ear-patch*. **STATUS AND RANGE** A vagrant in Puerto Rico (1966; 2011—photo), including Mona Island (2016—photo). **HABITAT** Open ground such as lots, fields, and meadows.

202

**WHITE-THROATED SPARROW** *Zonotrichia albicollis* (Gorrión gorjiblanco) 17cm (6.75in); 26g. **BEHAVIOR** Feeds on ground or in low bushes. **DESCRIPTION** The *white throat patch, yellow lores, and black-and-white striped crown* are distinctive. **IMMATURE** Fainter head markings. **STATUS AND RANGE** A vagrant to Puerto Rico (1971) and St. Thomas (2018—photo). Most likely to occur October–May. **HABITAT** Undergrowth, scrub, and gardens.

Ruby-throated Hummingbird

♂

♀

Purple-throated Carib

♀

Warbling Vireo

imm

adult

Northern Wheatear

♀ & non-br ♂

br ♂

White-throated Sparrow

adult

imm

Plate not to scale

**BLACK-BILLED CUCKOO** *Coccyzus erythropthalmus* (Pájaro bobo piquinegro) 30cm (12in); 50g. Note the white underparts, long tail, *black down-curved bill, reddish eye-ring, and brown wings*. (Yellow-billed Cuckoo has yellow in bill, lacks a truly red eye-ring, has reddish-brown in primaries, and more conspicuous white marking under tail.) **VOICE** *Cu-cu-cu-cu*. **STATUS AND RANGE** Vagrant in Puerto Rico (1800s—drawing/ specimen; 2002, 2006, 2015) and St. Croix (2006). Most likely to occur September– November and April–May. **HABITAT** Scrublands, lowland forests.

**BAHAMA MOCKINGBIRD** *Mimus gundlachii* (Sinsonte de Bahamas) 28cm (11in); 60–85g. Large; with a long, broad tail tipped with white; upperparts brownish-gray with fine streaks; underparts whitish with dark streaks on sides. Two white wing bars not conspicuous. **FLIGHT** Tail almost fan-shaped, tipped with white. (Northern Mockingbird is smaller and shows conspicuous white in wings and sides of tail. Pearly-eyed Thrasher has darker upperparts, pale bill, and white eye.) **VOICE** Series of phrases, each repeated several times. **STATUS AND RANGE** A vagrant to Puerto Rico (2007—photo). Endemic to West Indies. **HABITAT** Semiarid scrub, woodlands. Infrequent around human habitation.

**GREATER ANI** *Crotophaga major* (Garrapatero mayor) 46–49cm (18–19.3in); male 165g, female 140g. Distinguished by its large size, *glossy blue-black plumage, long tail, distinctive parrot-like bill, and whitish eye*. (Similar Smooth-billed Ani is smaller, has dark eye, and lacks bluish sheen.) **STATUS AND RANGE** Vagrant to St. Croix (2010—photo) in Virgin Islands. **HABITAT** Mangroves, open woodlands, thickets, and forest edges, often near water.

**YELLOW-HEADED BLACKBIRD** *Xanthocephalus xanthocephalus* (Tordo cabeciamarillo) Male 26.5cm (10.5in), female 22cm (8.5in); male 100g, female 60g. **ADULT MALE** Black overall with diagnostic *orange-yellow hood and white wing patch*. **ADULT FEMALE** Grayish-brown above; *yellowish-orange eyebrow stripe, throat, breast, and line below cheek*. **STATUS AND RANGE** A vagrant in Puerto Rico (1985; 1997–99; 2006—photo; 2013). Most likely to occur September–March. May occur in numbers and more frequently than previously known. **HABITAT** Swamps, marshes, and sometimes agricultural fields.

**PAINTED BUNTING** *Passerina ciris* (Azulillo sietecolores) 13cm (5in); 13–19g. **ADULT MALE** Blue head, red underparts, and green back. **FEMALE AND IMMATURE MALE** Green above, yellowish-green below. Brighter green than vireos, with much heavier bill. **IMMATURE** Much duller, but with hints of green. **VOICE** Loud *chip*. **STATUS AND RANGE** A vagrant to Puerto Rico (1999 and other, unavailable dates), where most likely to occur November–March. **HABITAT** Thickets, brush, and grassy areas, particularly semiarid areas, often near water.

Black-billed Cuckoo

Bahama Mockingbird

Greater Ani

non-br adult ♂

non-br adult ♀

Yellow-headed Blackbird

♀ & imm ♂

Painted Bunting

adult ♂

# VAGRANTS WITH INSUFFICIENT RECORDS

Northern Fulmar (*Fulmarus glacialis*)—Among Virgin Islands, August 1975

Northern Gannet (*Morus bassanus*)—Puerto Rico (Manati), October 30, 2010

Western Reef-Heron (*Egretta gularis*)—Tortola (Josiah's Bay), 2001

Garganey (*Spatula querquedula*)—Puerto Rico, January–March 1978

Greater Scaup (*Aythya marila*)—St. Croix, December 23, 1984, to February 17, 1985; November 8 and 27, 1985

Virginia Rail (*Rallus limicola*)—Puerto Rico, January 28, 1976

Common Ringed Plover (*Charadrius hiaticula*) Puerto Rico (Toa Baja), September 7, 2011

Common Greenshank (*Tringa nebularia*)—Puerto Rico (Copamarina), December 24, 2009

Spotted Redshank (*Tringa erythropus*)—Puerto Rico (Monte Grande), August 25, 2000

Long-billed Curlew (*Numenius americanus*)—St. Croix, September 20, 1981

Bar-tailed Godwit (*Limosa lapponica*)—St. Croix, May 19–28, 1987

Little Gull (*Hydrocoloeus minutus*)—Puerto Rico (San Juan), March 7, 1992; Río Añasco, September 27, 1999

Mississippi Kite (*Ictinia mississippiensis*)—Puerto Rico (Toa Baja), early November 2005; February 14, 2016

Black Kite (*Milvus migrans*)—British Virgin Islands, mid-October 1999

Bald Eagle (*Haliaeetus leucocephalus*)—Puerto Rico, October 8, 1975; St. John, February 21, 1977

Northern Potoo (*Nyctibius jamaicensis*)—Puerto Rico (Mona Island), December 5, 1974; Desecheo, October 24, 1987

Alpine Swift (*Apus melba*)—Puerto Rico (Desecheo), July 20, 1987

Common House-Martin (*Delichon urbicum*)—Puerto Rico (Cabo Rojo), December 12, 2012

Ringed Kingfisher (*Megaceryle torquata*)—Puerto Rico, 1960

Hairy Woodpecker (*Dryobates villosus*)—Puerto Rico (Mona Island), March 27, 1974

Vermilion Flycatcher (*Pyrocephalus rubinus*)—Puerto Rico (Vieques), February 1–9, 1999

Great Crested Flycatcher (*Myiarchus crinitus*)—Puerto Rico, winter sighting ca. 1960

Eastern Kingbird (*Tyrannus tyrannus*)—Puerto Rico, ca. 1847 and 1960

Scissor-tailed Flycatcher (*Tyrannus forficatus*)—Puerto Rico, December 1960

Brown Trembler (*Cinclocerthia ruficauda*)—St. Thomas, March 4, 1976

Dark-eyed Junco (*Junco hyemalis*)—Puerto Rico, October 16, 1963; St. Thomas, November 11, 1928

# UNESTABLISHED INTRODUCTIONS

Mute Swan (*Cygnus olor*)—Virgin Islands, winters of 1968–1970, one individual.

Black Swan (*Cygnus atratus*)—Puerto Rico (Culebra), May 1988, one individual.

Ring-necked Pheasant (*Phasianus colchicus*)—Puerto Rico, February 6, 1974, and other unidentified pheasants. St. Thomas, intentionally introduced without success. St. Croix, flock released March or April 1988.

Indian Peafowl (*Pavo cristatus*)—St. Croix, semiferal on some estates.

Crested Bobwhite (*Colinus cristatus*)—St. Thomas, intentionally introduced over a century ago. Did well for a time, but now extirpated.

Northern Bobwhite (*Colinus virginianus*)—Puerto Rico, intentionally introduced in 1860 and subsequently; bred but now extirpated. St. Croix, intentionally introduced in 1810 and thrived. Survived until late twentieth century.

California Quail (*Callipepla californica*)—St. Croix, intentionally introduced in 1958 without success.

Spotted Dove (*Streptopelia chinensis*)—St. Croix, intentionally introduced, survived until late twentieth century.

Gray Parrot (*Psittacus erithacus*)—Puerto Rico, February 24, 1973, and March 1973, one individual.

Scaly-headed Parrot (*Pionus maximiliani*)—Puerto Rico, February 17, 1971, and subsequently, one individual.

Lilac-crowned Parrot (*Amazona finschi*)—Puerto Rico, January 1, 1983, and subsequently that year, one individual. Also St. Croix.

Yellow-headed Parrot (*Amazona oratrix*)—Puerto Rico, bred in small numbers in 1970s. Now extirpated.

Nanday Parakeet (*Aratinga nenday*)—Puerto Rico, introduced in 1970s, occurred in small numbers, now rarely seen. St. Croix, one record.

Rainbow Lorikeet (*Trichoglossus moluccanus*)—Puerto Rico, September 8 and 22, 1974, one individual.

Rose-ringed Parakeet (*Psittacula krameria*)—Puerto Rico, flock of 12 in Bajura Aguadilla in 2012, but only a few individuals seen of late.

Mitred Parakeet (*Psittacara mitratus*)—Puerto Rico, May 1956, bred at university in San Germán. St. Croix, four individuals in 1980s.

Parrotlet (*Forpus* sp.)—Puerto Rico, September 6, 1974, one individual.

Red-and-green Macaw (*Ara chloropterus*)—Puerto Rico, very small numbers in recent years. St. Croix, two individuals. Tortola, two individuals 2000–2005.

Chestnut-fronted Macaw (*Ara severus*)—Tortola, several individuals; caged bird at Little Bay escaped and was recaptured at least twice in the early 2000s.

Toucanet (*Aulacorhynchus* sp.)—Puerto Rico, November or December 1973.

Red-billed Blue-Magpie (*Urocissa erythrorhyncha*)—Puerto Rico, 1972, one individual.

Crow (*Corvus* sp.)—Puerto Rico, January 1973, May 29, 1973, one individual.

Brahminy Starling (*Sturnia pagodarum*)—Puerto Rico (Caja de Muertos), May 22, 2005, one captured.

Javan Myna (*Acridotheres javanicus*)—Puerto Rico, introduced around 1980s, centered in Bayamón, but now extirpated.

Great Myna (*Acridotheres grandis*)—Puerto Rico, last recorded December 20, 2004, in Fajardo.

Common Hill Myna (*Gracula religiosa*)—Puerto Rico, introduced in late 1960s, was uncommon and very local, but now extirpated.

Yellow-fronted Canary (*Crithagra mozambica*)—Puerto Rico, introduced around 1960, was rare and local along north coast in 1970s, but now extirpated.

Red Avadavat (*Amandava amandava*)—Puerto Rico, introduced in late 1960s and became locally common in lowlands in 1970s, now extirpated.

Black-rumped Waxbill (*Estrilda troglodytes*)—Puerto Rico, introduced in 1960s, became uncommon but widespread, now extirpated. St. Thomas has reports.

Red-headed Finch (*Amadina erythrocephala*)—Puerto Rico, two records, one very poor photo. First report August 1, 2005, in Utuado. Second in Coamo.

Red-crested Cardinal (*Paroaria coronata*)—Puerto Rico, 1973, 1976, single individuals; a pair at Dorado Beach Hotel was seen constructing nest beginning August 1987. St. Croix, December 15, 1982, one individual.

Eastern Paradise-Whydah (*Vidua paradisaea*)—Puerto Rico, September 8, 1974, January 1975.

# HYPOTHETICAL

Barolo Shearwater (*Puffinus baroli*) / Little Shearwater (*Puffinus assimilis*)—Puerto Rico, January 30, 1977.

Ringed Teal (*Callonetta leucophrys*)—Puerto Rico (Humacao), January or February 2013, specimen, likely escaped from private collection.

Yellow-legged Gull (*Larus michahellis*)—Puerto Rico (west coast, photo), February 27, 2005; (west coast, photos), February 17–24, 2006. Challenged by experts. Require additional analysis.

Ridgway's Hawk (*Buteo ridgwayi*)—Puerto Rico, (Culebra), April 1984 for three days.

Common Black Hawk (*Buteogallus anthracinus*)—Puerto Rico, based on specimen of unknown origin.

Blue-headed Quail-Dove (*Starnoenas cyanocephala*)—Puerto Rico, comments of hunters to Virgilio Biaggi.

White-tailed Nightjar (*Hydropsalis cayennensis*)—Puerto Rico, November 23, 1974.

Eastern Bluebird (*Sialia sialis*)—St. John.

Bachman's Warbler (*Vermivora bachmanii*)—St. Croix, October 21, 1982.

Golden-cheeked Warbler (*Setophaga chrysoparia*)—St. Croix, November 23, 1939.

Red-winged Blackbird (*Agelaius phoeniceus*)—Puerto Rico (Mona Island), September 22, 2018.

# PLACES TO BIRD

A wonderful array of bird species, including nearly all 19 endemics, can be enjoyed by the avid birder in several days with appropriate planning, depending on the season. Larger islands have good paved road systems and access by air or ferry. Smaller inhabited islands can be reached by ferry or charter boat. Once at your destination, the road networks provide easy access to most of the best birding spots, except for seabird colonies. Local guides are an option, as is vehicle rental. Public transportation can be used in Vieques, Culebra, and the Virgin Islands if you plan to visit areas within walking distance of main roads. The following are some excellent sites to consider visiting and the birds you might see there.

## PUERTO RICO

**El Merendero (Guajataca) Cliffs**—A popular stop along Road PR-2, from February through June these cliffs support the largest nesting colony of White-tailed Tropicbirds on Puerto Rico proper. These beautiful birds can be seen over the ocean, sometimes performing aerial courtship displays. A short walk may reveal beauties such as Adelaide's Warblers, Puerto Rican Todies, and Puerto Rican Woodpeckers. Pearly-eyed Thrashers and Greater Antillean Grackles greet visitors year round, while Caribbean Martins and Black-whiskered Vireos join during spring and summer. The vegetation along the trails is representative of native coastal forest and is one of the best sites to encounter the endangered and endemic Harlequin butterfly.

**Camuy Coastline**—Outstanding for waterbirds, this area includes stops along Road PR-485 and near downtown Camuy on Road PR-119. Yeguadas Pond along Road PR-485 is a freshwater pond, part of a dairy cattle farm. It is clearly visible and borders the road. Park near the gated entrance. Waterbirds breed year round and include Least Grebes, White-cheeked Pintails, Ruddy Ducks, and the white-shielded form of American Coot. Hundreds of Glossy Ibises, herons, egrets, and shorebirds feed in the pond's environs. Yellow-breasted Crakes are possible at dawn and dusk. Fall migration brings flocks of waterfowl, shorebirds, and swallows. The fields are home to the Grasshopper Sparrow.

Eastward on PR-485 is Peñón Amador Beach. Close to the beach is Cayo de Afuera (it has a small wooden cross), and across the road is a brackish pond. Waterbirds such as Wilson's Plovers and White-cheeked Pintails are regulars. During late spring and summer the cay is used by Roseate Terns and Brown Noddies. Very rare visitors include American Flamingos and Little Egrets. Puerto Rican Woodpeckers, Caribbean Martins, and Monk Parakeets nest in the coconut palms.

Farther east, near the town of Camuy, is the protected area of Finca Nolla Nature Reserve. Its sand dunes, coastal thickets, and mangroves are associated with the Río Camuy estuary. This site is an important stopover for fall and spring migrant shorebirds and seabirds, and winter habitat for Snowy Plovers and Red Knots. The sandy beaches are breeding grounds for Least Terns and American Oystercatchers.

**Río Abajo Commonwealth Forest**—Near Arecibo and Utuado, this reserve is one of the best examples of the haystack hills characteristic of Puerto Rican karst. The predominant habitats are dense tropical limestone forest and timber plantations. This forest is the last stronghold of the endangered Broad-winged Hawk, an endemic non-migratory subspecies of this widespread raptor. A dawn visit may yield up to 17 island endemics, including the reintroduced, critically endangered Puerto Rican Parrot. Park at the gate on Road PR-621 (campground) and walk the paved road past the gate. Be aware that there may be seasonal restrictions on the use of side trails because of the presence of the parrot. Access to the reserve is via Road PR-10; then take PR-6612 all the way to PR-621 and continue left until you reach the gate.

**Maricao Commonwealth Forest**—A priority for visiting birders, this is the best location to encounter the "gem of the forest," the Elfin-woods Warbler. In addition, Puerto Rican Tanagers and Puerto Rican Pewees lead mixed-species flocks through the forest while Green Mangos and Puerto Rican Emeralds visit flowers that bloom all year. As if finding most island endemics were not enough, this forest is home to the critically endangered resident subspecies of Sharp-shinned Hawk. Maricao Forest is intersected by Road PR-120 (take the exit to the town of Sabana Grande from Highway PR-2). Although birding is excellent once you enter the reserve, look for km 16.2 and walk the many trails by the administration building. Visitors with disabilities can enjoy most Caribbean and island endemics around the parking area.

**Cabo Rojo salt flats and mangroves**—Located at the extreme southwest tip of Puerto Rico along Road PR-301 in the township of Combate, the area contains large tracts of mangroves, salt flats, and dry coastal forest. Most of the area is part of the Cabo Rojo National Wildlife Refuge, and a smaller portion is part of the Boquerón State Forest. The site is recognized as one of the most important stopover sites for migrating shorebirds in the Western Hemisphere. This site also serves as the only breeding area for the Snowy Plover in Puerto Rico. Besides shorebirds, this is the last stronghold of the endangered Yellow-shouldered Blackbird. If exotics are of interest, the Indian Silverbill and Venezuelan Troupial are likely to be found around Combate.

**Laguna Cartagena**—Located between Lajas and Cabo Rojo, this mystical place is one of only a handful of large freshwater lagoons on the islands. It is part of the Caribbean National Wildlife Refuge. This is the premier spot for native and migratory waterfowl as well as other aquatic species. Best periods for bird activity are dawn and dusk, but because it is secluded, we recommend the former. From Road PR-101 take the south exit to PR-306, a dirt road that takes you across hay fields and cattle ranches. Once you pass the farm's main buildings look for the second gate on the left and park there. This is the entrance to a productive dike. Early in the morning visitors are greeted by waterbirds including the West Indian Whistling-Duck and Yellow-breasted Crake. Patience is sometimes rewarded with the Masked Duck. While admiring the beautiful Sierra Bermeja to the south you will notice an observation tower. To get there, drive toward the next gate on the left and walk the trail bordering the lagoon. Grassy fields associated with the lagoon are one of the few remaining spots in Puerto Rico for the exotic Northern Red Bishop and Pin-tailed Whydah.

**Guanica Commonwealth Forest**—This reserve is one of the best examples of tropical dry forest in the Western Hemisphere. Among birders it is the first choice for finding the endangered Puerto Rican Nightjar, as well as 14 other island endemics. Road PR-334 serves as the main access (it passes through a small community; stay left at the fork). Early morning birding is very productive either along the road or on side trails. An alternate route to the forest is Road PR-333. From PR-116 take the east exit. This route takes visitors to popular beaches and a hotel. Dawn walks are best to avoid crowds (and for security reasons). Nightjars call constantly from the hills. Beach access and saline lagoons mean seabirds, waders, and shorebirds along the coast.

**Hacienda La Esperanza Nature Reserve**—Located on the eastern side of the mouth of the Río Manatí, it is known for its beaches and cultural resources. But it is fast becoming popular among local birders. This reserve is managed by the organization Para la Naturaleza and contains many nice loop trails and dirt roads that allow access to a great diversity of habitats. Among its specialties is one of the few accessible breeding colonies of Bridled Terns in Puerto Rico (late spring and summer). Roseate Terns also breed here, while Brown Noddies rest and forage around the cays. Reserve facilities are located at the end of Road PR-616 and offer parking and bathrooms. Nice trails go through open pasturelands and haystack hills that provide habitat for the Grasshopper Sparrow, Yellow-faced Grassquit, Puerto Rican Vireo, Puerto Rican Woodpecker, and Adelaide's Warbler.

**Cambalache Commonwealth Forest**—A must-see site on any birding trip to Puerto Rico, this popular spot is one of the best options to find the most endemics when you have but a few hours to spare. Forest facilities are located off Road PR-682 and offer parking and bathrooms. Caribbean endemics are plentiful, 14 of which occur only in Puerto Rico. Puerto Rican Owls call near the parking area past dawn and are soon joined by Red-legged Thrushes, Puerto Rican Vireos, and Adelaide's Warblers. Look for Ruddy and Key West Quail-Doves strutting on the ground. Come early during weekends, summer, and holidays, as mountain bikers abound after midmorning.

**Jobos Bay National Estuarine Research Reserve**— Second only to the Cabo Rojo salt flats in its importance for migrating shorebirds. The Green-throated Carib and Antillean Crested Hummingbird are regulars here. The reserve also hosts a small population of the endangered Yellow-shouldered Blackbird, and the last flock of the exotic Red-crowned Parrot is in the Aguirre community (PR-705). Reserve areas are connected by Road PR-3. Look for the sign for Jagueyes Forest and Road PR-703 for Las Mareas Community salt flats, the best birding spots.

211

**El Yunque National Forest**—The largest protected area in the region, it is probably the most popular birding spot. It is home to the last original population of Puerto Rican Parrots, though these birds are unlikely to be encountered because of their very low numbers and restricted habitat. Nevertheless, there are 16 other island endemics to look for. Notably, the Elfin-woods Warbler is found on the highest peaks, particularly along the Trade Winds Trail (top of Road PR-191). Consider starting at the top of PR-191 and going down the road, stopping at each recreational area. You should have great views of the Puerto Rican Tanager, Puerto Rican Tody, and Puerto Rican Bullfinch. End at El Portal (pay a small fee) and walk the loop trail and around the parking area, where the Puerto Rican Oriole nests in palm fronds and the Antillean Euphonia sings in the treetops. Road PR-3, with a turnoff into the small community of Palmer, is the principal access to the forest.

**San Juan Botanical Garden**—One of the few "green" areas in San Juan, it is part of the University of Puerto Rico. Road PR-1 divides the property into north and south sections; visit the latter. Garden ponds may produce Least Grebes. Walking along the Río Piedras river offers Caribbean specialties including six island endemics. Morning visits usually include exotic parrots such as the impressive Blue-and-yellow Macaw and Orange-fronted Parakeet. As you walk the trails Pearly-eyed Thrashers are conspicuous while Zenaida Doves strut nearby. Pay attention to flowering heliconias for the Antillean Mango and Green-throated Carib hummingbirds.

**Piñones Commonwealth Forest**—The largest contiguous mangrove forest in our region and just minutes from San Juan, Piñones offers the chance to observe seabirds, shorebirds, and waders. Fall is very productive for migrants. Key areas are around the administration office and the kiosks in front of the reef (La Pocita) accessed by Road PR-187. Both areas have parking and are connected by a boardwalk that passes through mangroves, lagoons, and coastal forest. The Mangrove Cuckoo, Puerto Rican Flycatcher, Puerto Rican Spindalis, and Puerto Rican Woodpecker are common year round along the trail. The Puerto Rican Vireo is also a possibility. Spring and summer bring Caribbean Martins around palm groves and Roseate Terns resting on the reef.

# U.S. VIRGIN ISLANDS

## St. Thomas

*By Renata Platenberg, PhD, Wildlife Biologist*

**Red Hook Pond**—Located along Route 38 by the ferry terminal at the edge of the town of Red Hook, this mangrove-fringed salt pond offers a boardwalk with viewing platforms and informative signs. It's well worth adding an hour to a Red Hook visit to immerse yourself in the mangroves where wetland birds, seabirds, and the occasional shorebird can be easily observed. Common sightings include Brown Pelicans, White-cheeked Pintails and other ducks, and Great Egrets; Cattle Egrets are often abundant. Overwintering migrants, including sandpipers, may be present from late fall to early spring, and the air becomes noisy with Laughing Gulls from late spring to the end of summer. American Kestrels can often be observed on the overhead wires along the main road, especially in the spring when fledglings emerge.

**Magens Bay Nature Trail**—This rugged trail, popular with hikers, offers a unique opportunity to observe a variety of land birds, wetland birds, and even seabirds. The approximately 2.4 km (1.5 mi) trail descends through several distinct ecosystems within the 129 ha (319 ac) Magens Bay Watershed Preserve. The upland dry forest offers sightings of Pearly-eyed Thrashers, Scaly-naped Pigeons, Green-throated Caribs, and the ubiquitous Bananaquit. Smooth-billed Anis and Bridled Quail-Doves are occasionally sighted, while Mangrove Cuckoos are a rare treat. In the winter months migratory land birds, including American Redstarts, are often observed. As the trail levels out and enters the basin of moist woodland and mangrove wetland, flocks of colorful and noisy Brown-throated Parakeets take up residence with Zenaida and Common Ground Doves. Waterbirds such as Green Herons, Great Egrets, sandpipers, and Yellow-crowned Night-Herons are frequently observed in the moist woodland and open areas during the wet months of October and November. A visit to the beach allows excellent viewing of fishing Brown Pelicans, Brown Boobies, and Royal Terns. Laughing Gulls are abundant in summer months. The upper trailhead is located 0.8 km (0.5 mi) from the junction of Routes 35 (Magens Bay Road) and 40 (Skyline Drive) near Drake's Seat. The unmarked drive-through parking area is on the left (north) side of the road. Parking is extremely limited. The lower trailhead can be found by following the forest edge after the bridge to the left of the entrance gate at Magens Bay Beach. It is not always signposted.

**Mangrove Lagoon**—Compass Point Salt Pond and Mangrove Lagoon are part of the St. Thomas East End Reserves, designated in part for their valuable habitat for seabirds. The mangroves and mangrove islands within the Inner Lagoon provide breeding and roosting sites for a variety of seabirds and shorebirds, only accessible by kayak, and the fiddler crab–dotted mudflats at Compass Point offer foraging opportunities for waders. Red-tailed Hawks are often observed soaring overhead or perched on a post. Access to the mudflats is at the entrance to Compass Point Marina; take the only turn to the south between the traffic lights by the National Guard Armory and the grocery store on Route 32. The mudflats are directly across the road from the marina parking lot. The Inner Lagoon reserve is accessible only by kayak, which can be rented at Ecotours along Route 32. There is a public boat ramp next to Ecotours. Motorized vessels are not allowed in the Inner Lagoon.

**Northern Coastal Areas**—While there are no specific viewing areas, St. Thomas's north side can be productive for bird viewing. American Kestrels are often chasing off Red-tailed Hawks over northern forested slopes, with Scaly-naped Pigeons, White-winged Doves, and Smooth-billed Anis watching from treetop or power line perches. Acrobatic Tropicbirds stand out white against the blue ocean background, and a visit to a rocky shoreline usually allows observation of American Oystercatchers and Ospreys. Humpback whales have been observed during March and April from north-side viewpoints.

## St. John

*By Laurel Brannick, Supervisor of Education, Virgin Islands National Park*

**Francis Bay Trail**— This trail (0.7 km; 0.4 mi) is located on the North Shore of St. John and is part of Virgin Islands National Park. The trail starts at a parking lot adjacent to the ruins of a small sugar factory. It then proceeds into the dry tropical forest that borders the Mary's Point salt pond and the coastline of Francis Bay Beach. Not only is the trail one of the best locations to view birds, but other wildlife such as crabs and iguanas can also be found. Along the trail many forest birds can be seen and heard. Year-round in the trees you can find the Yellow Warbler, Bananaquit, Lesser Antillean Bullfinch, Mangrove Cuckoo, Smooth-billed Ani, Scaly-naped Pigeon, Zenaida Dove, and White-winged Dove. The winter and fall migration season brings many neotropical warblers to the trail. In the mangroves that line the salt pond there are opportunities to see the Prothonotary Warbler, Northern Parula, and Northern Waterthrush. Overlooks and two platforms along the trail provide good views into the pond. Depending on the time of year and the amount of water in the pond, you can see a variety of waterfowl, herons, and shorebirds. Common birds in the pond include the White-cheeked Pintail, Black-necked Stilt, and Clapper Rail. As you make your way around the trail, you can stop at the beach to scan the ocean. Soaring above, you may find Magnificent Frigatebirds, Brown Pelicans, and Brown Boobies. From April to September, flocks of summer resident seabirds fishing in the bay may include Sandwich and Roseate Terns. As you scan for the seabirds you are sure to see the resident green sea turtles that frequently surface. Other good birding places close to Francis Bay include Mary's Creek and the Annaberg mangroves. Both can be visited by leaving the Francis Bay parking lot and walking east along Route 20. Check with Virgin Islands National Park to find out about ranger-guided bird walks and to obtain a bird checklist.

**Cinnamon Bay Nature Loop**—This trail (0.8 km; 0.5 mi) is on North Shore Road across from the Cinnamon Bay Campground. It traverses a moist tropical forest. There is a small stream (locally called a gut) that runs through the trail, and in the rainy season it can resemble a streambed. The shaded forest attracts birds like the Bridled Quail-Dove and migratory Yellow-bellied Sapsucker. During fall and winter migration, the trees are full of a variety of colorful warblers. As you hike around the loop you may spot the American Redstart, Hooded Warbler, Northern Waterthrush, Ovenbird, Black-and-white Warbler, and Black-throated Blue Warbler.

**Frank Bay Marine Reserve and Wildlife Sanctuary**—The small pond at Frank Bay is walking distance from the Cruz Bay Ferry Dock. Because of the abundant wildlife the pond supports, it was designated in 2000 as a marine reserve and wildlife sanctuary by the Virgin Islands government. The pond has been adopted by the local Audubon Society, and there is a viewing platform as well as a trail that leads around the small pond. Unlike other salt ponds, this one is not seasonal and does not dry up. Quite a few native birds can be observed in the pond, including the White-cheeked Pintail, Common Gallinule, and Black-necked Stilt. In breeding season, you can find these birds accompanied by their chicks. During fall migration and winter, you will find Spotted Sandpipers and Lesser Yellowlegs. Many perching birds, such as the Lesser Antillean Bullfinch and Zenaida Dove, can be found in the trees surrounding the pond. You may also find night-herons resting in the trees. Only a short stretch of road and beach separates the pond from the ocean. The shoreline is a good spot for pelicans, boobies, herons, oystercatchers, and kingfishers.

## St. Croix

*By Jennifer Valiulis, Executive Director, St. Croix Environmental Association*

**Southgate Pond**—Located within the Southgate Coastal Reserve, 4 km (2.5 mi) east of Christiansted on the north shore, Southgate Pond is a key hotspot for avian diversity on St. Croix. In the rainy winter months (approximately October—March) the salt pond fills, and hundreds of fiddler crabs attract shorebirds and waterbirds, aquatic vegetation attracts resident and migratory ducks, and the thick mangroves surrounding the pond provide shelter for the migratory warblers that join the resident Yellow Warblers. In summer months, the pond dries and Least Terns and Wilson's Plovers nest on the salt flats. In the transition between the two seasons, when water levels are low and food is concentrated, large groups of egrets, herons, stilts, and terns feed at the pond. Southgate Pond is also one of the easiest to access of the significant birding spots on St. Croix. Visitors can follow a short trail (0.6 km; 0.4mi) to a bird blind that is always open to the public. The reserve is also one of the key locations for the restoration of the endemic endangered Eggers's agave. In addition, leatherback, green, and hawksbill sea turtles nest on the beach adjacent to the pond. The reserve is owned and managed by the St. Croix Environmental Association.

## BRITISH VIRGIN ISLANDS

### Tortola

**Josiah's Bay**—On the eastern end of Tortola, Josiah's Bay is the best and most easily accessible pond for birding. The road from the ridge passes through dry forest and scrub before ending in mangroves and the sandy beach. Birding is good along the entire length of the road, especially during migration. Access to the pond varies from open areas along the road to private property. People tend to be friendly and usually do not mind birders walking across their land. Water level and salinity vary according to rainfall, creating different environments for birds. Waterbirds are abundant most of the time. White-cheeked Pintail, Ruddy Duck, Blue-winged Teal, Least Grebe, American Coot, and Common Gallinule are usually common. Mixed in, look for rarities, especially ducks and shorebirds during winter and migration. During summer, the Black-necked Stilt nests in large numbers. A special treat for birders is the frequent presence of the American Flamingo. Flocks sometimes exceed 100 birds. Nesting occurs, so look for gray juveniles. Check out the surrounding mangroves and coastal scrub for Yellow Warbler, Lesser Antillean Bullfinch, Black-faced Grassquit, Antillean Crested Hummingbird, and wintering

Golden-winged Warbler. Clapper Rail and Yellow-crowned Night-Heron are also common. Nearby, the popular surfers' beach is a good spot to see Brown Booby, Magnificent Frigatebird, and the occasional Red-billed Tropicbird. Afterward, a refreshing dip in the sea is worth a try.

**Sage Mountain National Park**—For land birding, Sage Mountain National Park offers wonderful hiking trails through a variety of habitats including moist forests. Native trees and plants are labeled for easy identification. Tree ferns and heliconia indicate moist habitats that attract hummingbirds, wintering warblers, and lots of butterflies and invertebrates. At over 1,750 feet elevation, the breeze is always cool and comfortable. On the shaded trails, look for flowering plants that attract Bananaquit, Green-throated Carib, Antillean Crested Hummingbird, and many species of native butterflies. The Pearly-eyed Thrasher is common, as are the Zenaida Dove, Scaly-naped Pigeon, and Bridled Quail-Dove. During migration and winter, warblers and small passerines are often abundant. Search the tree canopy for Black-throated Blue Warbler, Yellow-billed Cuckoo, and Rose-breasted Grosbeak. Blackpoll Warbler is often present in large numbers. In the undergrowth, look for Ovenbird and Black-faced Grassquit. Down the mountain slopes search the streams (locally called guts) for Northern Waterthrush, Spotted Sandpiper, and Mangrove Cuckoo.

**Cane Garden Bay**—A popular tourist destination, Cane Garden Bay is developed on the beach and inland. The developments contain gardens planted with a variety of flowering plants, most exotic. However, they attract hummingbirds, Bananaquit, Black-faced Grassquit, Pearly-eyed Thrasher, Zenaida Dove, and wintering land birds. The gardens are a good place to spot escaped parrots. Budgerigar, Cockatiel, and even large macaw are occasionally seen. Several parrot species have also been reported over the years. On the eastern end of the bay is a small pond surrounded by mangroves. Most easily accessible on foot from the main road, the pond is visible through breaks in the mangrove barrier. Since there is little disturbance, it is a good place to view Least Grebe, Clapper Rail, Common Gallinule, and ducks. Yellow-crowned Night-Heron and Mangrove Cuckoo can be sighted in the mangroves. The ever-present Gray Kingbird may be found hawking for insects in all types of vegetation. Near the middle of the bay is the famed Callwood Rum Distillery. The entrance road crosses a small bridge over a mangrove channel that is the remnant of a salt pond. It is a good place for Common Gallinule, Spotted Sandpiper, Mangrove Cuckoo, Caribbean Elaenia, and warblers, especially the resident Yellow Warbler. The bay itself usually contains lots of Brown Pelican, Brown Booby, and Laughing Gull in summer. Roseate Tern, Royal Tern, and occasional rarities are possible. In winter, Ospreys are often seen foraging along the shore.

**Ridge Road**—The main central road on Tortola runs along the ridge crest at elevations often exceeding 300 m (1,000 ft). It is windswept and breezy, offering spectacular views of all the islands. Habitats vary from small patches of moist forest to dry scrub, open grasslands, occasional ponds, and residential sites. The best birding is done from the car. A spotting scope is helpful. The winds and strong updrafts attract birds of prey and swallows. The Red-tailed Hawk and American Kestrel are permanent residents. In winter look for Merlin and Peregrine. During fall migration, swallows pass through in the thousands. Most common are the Barn Swallow, Northern Rough-winged Swallow, and Bank Swallow. Both the Cave Swallow and Cliff Swallow may show up briefly. Along the telephone wires look for Gray Kingbird, Zenaida Dove, White-winged Dove, and Caribbean Martin in the summer. The brushy fields are a good place to find Smooth-billed Ani and Black-faced Grassquit. Search the same open fields at dusk for the resident Short-eared Owl.

## Anegada

Anegada is a birders' paradise: remote, lightly populated, and home to Ramsar-designated wetlands. The most popular bird is the American Flamingo. It was extirpated by the early 1900s, but a reintroduction project was launched in the 1990s, and the population has increased steadily. Current numbers approximate 300 birds, with most sighted in the western salt ponds. Driving from the ferry dock to the settlement, you cross a small bridge. Next to it you will see a wildlife viewing tower constructed by the National Parks Trust, which will give you a panoramic view of the western salt ponds. A viewing scope is available to get a better view of the pink birds across the pond. If you are lucky, pink flocks will circle overhead. Also, look for Willet, Yellow-crowned Night-Heron, Black-whiskered Vireo, and Osprey. During winter, Peregrine and Merlin are common. Along the roads in the brush look for Antillean Crested Hummingbird, White-winged Dove, Gray Kingbird, and the occasional Puerto Rican Flycatcher. If you are lucky you might spot a rare Antillean Mango. Do not miss The Settlement and fisherman's dock. The Settlement is the best place to find introduced Eurasian Collared-Dove and House Sparrow. Surrounding wetlands teem with shorebirds during migration. Rarities are often found. Whimbrels are common on mudflats. During summer, Antillean Nighthawks nest and can be seen and heard overhead. While birding in the underbrush, keep alert for the Anegada rock iguana, an endangered lizard that is the largest endemic land animal in the British Virgin Islands.

## Jost Van Dyke

Jost Van Dyke offers a variety of birding spots. At the eastern end of the island near the Taboo restaurant, take the hike to the Bubbly Pool. You will pass a salt pond that may contain White-cheeked Pintail, Common Gallinule, Blue-winged Teal, Black-necked Stilt, and Wilson's Plover. The surrounding mangroves and coastal scrub are a good place to spot Yellow Warbler, White-winged Dove, Pearly-eyed Thrasher, and Black-faced Grassquit. At White Bay, the salt pond has been degraded by pollution and dumping but still may have Least Grebe, White-cheeked Pintail, Black-necked Stilt, and Spotted Sandpiper. A short boat ride to the island of Great Tobago will reward you with hundreds of Magnificent Frigatebirds—the only Virgin Islands breeding colony. Satellite tracking has revealed that frigatebirds fly hundreds of miles from the colony, some as far as the north coast of South America. While on the boat, look for Roseate Tern, Bridled Tern, Brown Noddy, Brown Booby, and the ever-present Brown Pelican.

## Sandy Cay National Park

Just east of Jost Van Dyke, Sandy Cay is accessible only by boat. A former Rockefeller property, the island is uninhabited. Previous efforts were made to eradicate rats and restore native vegetation. A marked trail circles the cay and passes through several interesting habitats. The Red-billed Tropicbird nests on the eastern cliffs. At times, flocks of Scaly-naped Pigeons can be found foraging in the dry forest. Bananaquit and Green-throated Carib are common throughout all habitats. During summer, Roseate Tern and Laughing Gull are common on the beach and surrounding waters. Fall migration is the best time to see land birds, though Yellow Warbler, Caribbean Elaenia, and Gray Kingbird are always present. After birding, take a plunge into some of the clearest water imaginable. The beach is spectacular, and you may have it all to yourself.

# INDEX

217

219

# INDEX OF LOCAL NAMES

This list contains the first Spanish and English local names in the species accounts.

223

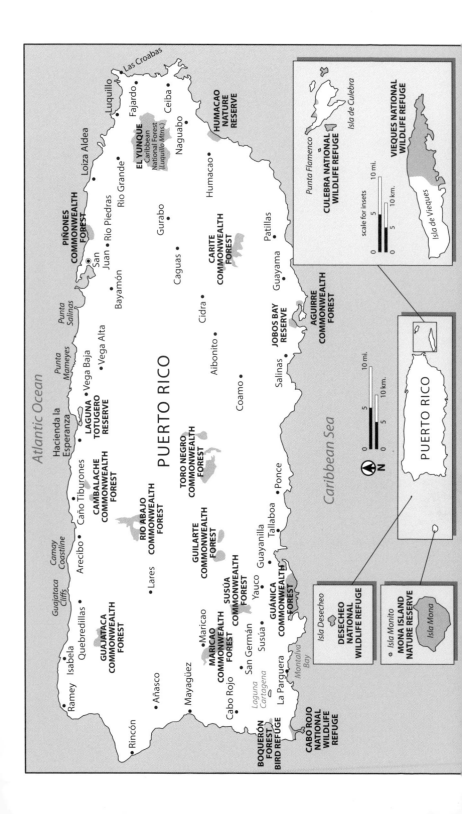